SLAVERY AND THE AMERICAN SOUTH

Slavery and the American South

Essays and Commentaries by
ANNETTE GORDON-REED
PETER S. ONUF
JAMES OAKES
WALTER JOHNSON
ARIELA GROSS
LAURA F. EDWARDS
NORRECE T. JONES, JR.
JAN LEWIS
ROBERT OLWELL
WILLIAM DUSINBERRE
STERLING STUCKEY
ROGER D. ABRAHAMS

Edited by
WINTHROP D. JORDAN

UNIVERSITY PRESS OF MISSISSIPPI
Jackson

www.upress.state.ms.us

The University Press of Mississippi is a member
of the Association of American University Presses.

Copyright © 2003 by University Press of Mississippi
All rights reserved
Manufactured in the United States of America

Print-on-Demand Edition

Library of Congress Cataloging-in-Publication Data
Porter L. Fortune, Jr. History Symposium (25th: 2000: University of Mississipi)
    Slavery and the American South : essays and commentaries / by
Annette Gordon-Reed . . . [et. al.] ; edited by Winthrop D. Jordan.
       p. cm — (Chancellor's symposium series ; 2000)
Includes bibliographical references and index.
   ISBN 1-57806-581-X (cloth : alk. paper)
    1. Slavery—Southern States—History—Congresses. 2. African
Americans—Southern States—History—Congresses. 3. Southern States—
History—Congresses. I. Gordon-Reed, Annette. II. Jordan, Winthrop D.
III. Title. IV. Series.
   E441.P68 2003
     306.3'62'0975—dc21   2003002100

British Library Cataloging-in-Publication Data available

Contents

Acknowledgments   vii

Introduction   ix

ANNETTE GORDON-REED
Logic and Experience: Thomas Jefferson's Life in the Law   3
   Commentary: Peter S. Onuf

JAMES OAKES
The Peculiar Fate of the Bourgeois Critique of Slavery   29
   Commentary: Walter Johnson

ARIELA GROSS
Reflections on Law, Culture, and Slavery   57
   Commentary: Laura F. Edwards

NORRECE T. JONES, JR
Rape in Black and White: Sexual Violence in the Testimony of Enslaved and Free Americans   93
   Commentary: Jan Lewis

ROBERT OLWELL
The Long History of a Low Place: Slavery on the South Carolina Coast, 1670–1870   117
   Commentary: William Dusinberre

STERLING STUCKEY
Paul Robeson and Richard Wright on the Arts and Slave Culture   147
   Commentary: Roger D. Abrahams

Notes 177

Contributors 213

Index 215

Acknowledgments

The Porter L. Fortune, Jr. Symposium in History at the University of Mississippi is sponsored by the Department of History, with the assistance of the Center for the Study of Southern Culture. The Symposium is supported by the generosity of Elizabeth Fortune and other members of the family of the former Chancellor, Porter L. Fortune, Jr. His and their interest in history has meant a very great deal to its ongoing success.

The History Department at the University has long been a remarkably collegial group of people. For this occasion, special thanks go to Nancy Bercaw, Ellen Wright Douglas, Betty Harness, Robert Haws, Bryn McDougall, John Neff, Harry Owens, Michelle Palmertree, Charles Ross, David Sansing, and Douglass Sullivan-Gonzalez.

Most of all, gratitude and appreciation go to Kevin D. McCarthy, who is embarking on such a promising career in history. He took over much of the work on the Symposium when illness rather suddenly prevented my doing it. He also greatly forwarded completion of this collection of essays. The enterprise would have collapsed had it not been for his great energy, efficiency, skill, and grace. I am very grateful to him as a friend for all he has done. His accomplishments deserve much more than mere pro forma words of appreciation and thanks.

Introduction

The essays in this book derive from the twenty-fifth annual Porter L. Fortune, Jr. Symposium on History, held at the University of Mississippi in the fall of 2000. This particular symposium celebrated the first one, which was held in 1975. In that earlier year the History Department at the University of Mississippi offered its first national symposium, successfully gathering a small group of distinguished scholars from across the country. The Department decided to plunge directly into a topic which carried a special import at the University—slavery in the United States. It had been only a dozen years since the "Meredith riot" at Ole Miss, the crisis over admission of the first black student, which resulted in two deaths and massive federal intervention. The little town of Oxford then had a population of about five thousand, with the university having a similar number of students. Edgy federal authorities sent thirty thousand troops to back up the court-ordered integration. These dramatic events received massive coverage in the nation's news media and confirmed in the minds of many outsiders (even in such bastions as Virginia) that Mississippi remained hopelessly mired in a brutal system of race relations that was becoming increasingly out of step with the nation as a whole. During the next few years, as is well known, the reactions of white officials to civil rights marches, as well as the murders of civil rights workers, further solidified the state's notoriety.

A dozen years later the ghost of that crisis still lingered at the University. Though the Oxford public schools had finally been racially integrated two years before, a great deal had not changed. Outsiders at the Symposium in 1975 were warmly greeted, but some of them sensed that many University administrators thought the topic of slavery egregiously unsuitable and likely to lead, if anywhere, to a race riot. Busloads of students from Mississippi Valley State College, a "Negro" institution, were rumored to be coming—and actually came and listened and debated and left peacefully. Today, the enrollment of African Americans at the

University is large enough to permit a far more relaxed atmosphere, though of course not entirely free from interracial tensions and incidents. A telling symptom of the numerical change is that African-American students at Ole Miss no longer all know each other personally.

For the Symposium of 2000, the History Department decided to tackle a twenty-five-year retrospective of the historical field of slavery in the U.S. South. Participants were chosen with the deliberate intention of excluding certain important developments that have taken place during the fissiparous enlargement of knowledge and definition of the field. Thus this Symposium deliberately ruled out important arenas of closely related historical developments, including slavery in the northern states, the abolitionist movement (both U.S. and trans-Atlantic), and the development of slavery in the entire Atlantic world. This latter field, including the Atlantic slave trade, has since the 1990s shown many signs of being the cutting edge of present and future scholarship, and it will soon be connected with a burst of studies of slavery and the slave trade in eastern Africa and the lands bordering the Indian ocean. Recognizing the limitations of a short symposium, and out of mercy for its participants and readers of this book, we have parochially retained the focus of the original Symposium held in 1975, for even within that field there have been profound changes in both accumulated knowledge and historical perspectives. The essays in this book reflect only some of the developments that have occurred in a field that even in 1975 historians sensed was downright exploding, a field that was at the time (as one European historian put it) "the hottest field in historical scholarship."[1]

One reason why the field erupted is that for so many years it had been neglected or marginalized by most people in the community of professional historians. Not only was Africa still a "dark continent" but, according to prevailing assumptions, Negroes had no worthwhile history of their own in the United States or, indeed, anywhere. Many readers will recall that the first person to tackle this problem was George Washington Williams, a "Negro" himself, who published his two-volume *History of the Negro Race in America* in 1882–83. Williams had served in the Union army; later he became a Baptist minister, a lawyer, and eventually the first colored member of the Ohio legislature.[2] He wrote in a

Introduction

mode similar to the earlier George Bancroft and to the then popular John Fiske, and publication of his book roughly coincided with the beginnings of the professionalization of historical study in the United States. His work appeared at a time when the bookshelves of thousands of middle class parlors displayed multivolume paeans to the triumphal progress of American history, and his two volumes sold more copies than the press runs of most historical monographs today.

Williams's work appeared at a time when a community was beginning to develop among historians, with the beginnings of formal graduate study at American universities and the founding of the American Historical Association in 1884. The new graduate schools required apprenticeship in seminars, and several universities published the results of the required dissertations in their own separate series. Beginning in the late 1880s, several such studies dealt with some aspect of slavery, particularly in an individual colony/state.[3] These published dissertations were, by today's standards, rigidly institutional, often relying heavily for source material on colonial and state statutes. They now seem woefully dated. Yet they did offer one dimension that the historical profession managed to ignore (largely) until about 1970—the fact that slavery existed in all thirteen original colonies for a full century prior to the American Revolution and, indeed, for a century and a half before the "classic" era of the institution in the antebellum period, from 1830 to Emancipation. Williams's own volumes had covered all of American history, starting not with Jamestown or slavery but the magnificent achievements of African civilization in Egypt. Ironically the most enduring of these published dissertations was by an African-American scholar who today is not commonly associated with the professionalization of history in the United States: W. E. B. DuBois's *The Suppression of the African Slave Trade* was the first volume published in the new history series at Harvard, in 1896.[4]

Even as African-American historians themselves struggled and sometimes managed to acquire professional training, they remained confined within a separate tributary to the main stream of historical scholarship. It was not DuBois but Carter G. Woodson who led the campaign to put "Negro history" on a professional footing. Woodson, the son of a former slave, was the second African American to obtain a Ph.D. (from Harvard in 1912), after working in coal mines to support his earlier education. He founded The Association for the Study of Negro Life and History and *The Journal of Negro History* in 1915; later he established Negro History Week, which was to be held in February in honor of the birthdays of Abraham Lincoln and Frederick Douglass. Woodson himself edited the new journal single handedly. Its second issue offered primary sources which themselves suggested a mood of protest: "Eighteenth Century Slaves as Advertised by Their Masters."[5] Though it is one of the oldest of the specialized historical journals, *The Journal of Negro History* was marginalized by much of the historical establishment, despite its editor's insistently integrationist openness to scholarship by whites.

Despite Woodson's efforts, the study of slaves and slavery soon fell under the sway of a genteel white man from Georgia who became a professor at the University of Michigan and the virtual pope of the field. Ulrich Bonnell Phillips's *American Negro Slavery* (1918) offered a subtitle of nearly eighteenth-century dimensions which made clear the stance of the author: *A Survey of the Supply, Employment and Control of Negro Labor as Determined by the Plantation Regime*. In his preface, the author cheerily summarized the friendly race relations prevailing at a U.S. army camp: "The men of the two races are of course quartered separately; but it is a daily occurrence for white Georgian troops to go to the negro companies to seek out their accustomed friends and compare home news and experiences. The negroes themselves show the same easy-going, amiable, serio-comic obedience and the same personal attachments to white men, as well as the same sturdy light-heartedness and the same love of laughter and of rhythm, which distinguished their forbears."[6]

For some thirty-five years Phillips's view of the history of slavery dominated U.S. history textbooks. It took about fifteen years for his information and views to be absorbed by these rather new entrants in the field of history. Close to all of them were authored by northerners. The earliest college texts of the 1920s did not deal with slaves or masters as such; rather, they discussed slavery solely as a political and sectional issue, beginning usually with the Missouri Compromise. From Boston and Harvard in the 1930s, however, when Samuel Eliot

Introduction   xiii

Morison's text came to deal with slave life it famously began with the now-astounding pronouncement: "As for Sambo, . . . there is some reason to believe that he suffered less than any other class in the South from its 'peculiar institution.'"⁷

Countering such views was an uphill battle. For most of the twentieth century two college texts successively carried on the lonely fight for inclusion of Negroes in American history. Woodson published the first one, *The Negro in Our History*, in 1922. Its eventual nine editions dominated the small market until it was rapidly superseded by John Hope Franklin's *From Slavery to Freedom* (1947), which achieved similar dominance in the growing (sub)field for nearly the rest of the century, as the topic moved from the periphery to near the center of the study of American history. Franklin was partly responsible for this shift, especially in 1956 with his *The Militant South*, a work that achieved a wide audience. It benefitted not only from the paperback revolution in publishing but also from the name of the book and its subject matter. Franklin's choice of title did not announce explicitly that the book had to do with the enslavement of Negroes, but his treatment of unrestrained militancy made clear that such magnolia-scented traditions as dueling, military schools, and secession politics all rested squarely on the presence of the peculiar institution.⁸

Franklin wrote at a time when the intellectual ground under the predominant scholars already showed signs of shifting. A number of white professionals began to examine, with skepticism and even outrage, the century-old figure of the contented ol' darky. This early line of attack frequently involved looking both for and at evidence of slave resistance, that is, for any concerted efforts in the form of revolts and conspiracies. The first such person was Harvey Wish, a white professor who had written critically about the proslavery argument. Born in Chicago and a professor at Western Reserve, in 1937 Wish took the then somewhat bold step, for a white scholar, of publishing an important article in the *Journal of Negro History*. It was entitled simply, "American Slave Insurrections before 1861."⁹

A broader assault came from a white American Marxist scholar whose *American Negro Slave Revolts* was published during World War II.

Herbert Aptheker suffered in his own way from partial marginalization by historians, at first because there was a war on and then because of the Cold War, as well as the concomitant reign of "consensus history" in the 1950s. Later, Aptheker's work became widely acknowledged, but usually at a heavy discount. Most historians who cared at all decided that he had greatly overestimated the number of slave conspiracies and indeed had mistakenly treated frightened rumors among whites as evidence of actual slave plotting.

The same doubt, hesitancy, and disagreement among historians has been remarkably persistent, largely because they have allowed themselves to be guided by prevailing fashions and their own ideological prejudices. Even today, the profession is still scratching a Manichaean itch to decide whether even purportedly major conspiracies were either instances of genuine and admirable plotting among slaves or (as if it were the only alternative) merely fearful and vengeful panic among white men. Even the Vesey Conspiracy, which included the hanging of dozens of blacks in Charleston in 1822, has again become a matter of controversy, recently aired in a forum in the *William & Mary Quarterly* which was picked up in the *New York Times*, as most such materials in that journal customarily are not.[10]

The scholarly attack on white society's vision of the contented, inferior Negro was thus aimed at what appeared to be its most vulnerable contention. For if slaves actually plotted to gain their freedom it would appear absurd to describe them as contented. But, as the modern controversy over the Vesey Plot suggests, the assault had been vitiated from the beginning by attitudinal concerns that were and are capable of overriding the rudiments of logic and of "fact." Some participants in the *William & Mary Quarterly* forum remained convinced that a heroic Denmark Vesey must have headed a massive slave conspiracy; others thought the conspiracy was led by a frightened court. The durability of this disagreement may be confirmed by reference back in time to the debates in the Virginia state legislature that took place almost immediately after the Nat Turner revolt. Following a slave rebellion that resulted in the deaths of some sixty whites and many more blacks, a prominent Virginia legislator announced to his colleagues and the reading public (and to himself) that "our slave population is not only a happy one, but it is a contented, peaceful and harmless one."[11] This, in the wake of the bloodiest slave rebellion in North American history.

Partly because it was mired in a mode of duality, the question of outright resistance by groups of slaves proved a fragile weapon for American scholars who were becoming interested in revising the antebellum stereotypes that had captured the nation as a whole during and after Reconstruction. When Wish and Aptheker were writing, the intellectual and attitudinal ground was, as we can see now, already undergoing a subtle but major shift. Such shifts often take on nearly geological dimensions: like continental drifts, they are marked by sudden incidents that can range greatly in their apparent importance and impact. The twentieth-century alterations in prevailing white orthodoxies about African Americans have been truly revolutionary and have rightly been the subject of book-length studies. For present purposes it will serve, by way of shorthand, to point to the Great Depression, the Second World War, the collapse of European overseas empires, belated cognizance of the Nazi Holocaust, the rise of modern social science, the Civil Rights Movement, and, of course, TV.

To be sure, there were countercurrents, since human societies commonly fail to act exactly like continents. Mainstream social scientists began to write about white "attitudes" toward Negroes in the 1930s, the same decade in which the pooh-bahs of professional football banned Negro players from their teams.[12] In 1935, the Carnegie Corporation invited a Swedish economist to study "the Negro problem" in the United States. Gunnar Myrdal eventually produced an influential study which in effect treated the problem as a white and national one. His *An American Dilemma* (1944) was broad in scope, widely read, and seriously discussed. The study was written with the assistance of both white and Negro scholars. It was reviewed, favorably, in the *New York Times* by a white female novelist from Mississippi.[13]

In the changed atmosphere after World War II, a white American historian from Wisconsin turned the Phillips consensus upside down. On few occasions in the course of American historiography has such a radically new consensus been reached so quickly on the basis of a single book. Kenneth M. Stampp's *The Peculiar Institution: Slavery in the Ante-Bellum South* included a chapter entitled "To Make Them Stand in Fear" which reintroduced the whip to the history of American slavery.[14] Published in 1956, Stampp had begun work on his project several years before the 1954 Brown Decision, or Black Monday as it was still called by some white Mississippians when Stampp came to the first Porter Fortune Symposium nearly twenty years later.

The sheer timing of these developments underlines the crudity and sheer erroneousness of assigning the new stance among professional historians solely to the modern Civil Rights movement. When Mrs. Rosa Parks got "uppity" on that bus in December 1955, Prof. Stampp's book was already in press. For his basic assumptions Stampp had relied on a new reading of original historical sources and on recent studies in the social sciences.[15] But as with all historians, his general stance was of long standing. Publication dates are always outmoded as keys to the several years of development of most respectable history books and the much more prolonged formation of individual approaches toward human beings and institutions of the past.

Stampp's book altered the curriculum in many graduate schools and caused a major bustle in college textbook houses. As usual, there was a delay of more than several years, but there were also signs of reluctance. The pattern of reaction to the new scholarship confirmed that regional background was not always a governing factor in such matters. One prominent Bostonian scholar at Harvard remained determined at heart not to abandon his old ship, no matter how devastating the storm. His textbook treatment in 1962 offered students a choice. Having asked, "What did the Negro himself think of this system [of slavery]?", the text responded that "Here we have inferences that are poles apart," and then went on to quote Jefferson Davis's comments about "'human beings of an inferior race'" who were "'peaceful and contented laborers in their sphere.'" Tacked on at the end of that paragraph was a less than eager nod to the new scholarship: "On the other hand, Negro slavery in the South has been called the most oppressed and exploited system of labor in history, maintained only by fear and force." With such language, it was the poor old system of slavery itself that was oppressed and

Introduction   xvii

exploited. Unable to call slavery oppressive and exploitive, the discussion eventually lapsed into use of the first person singular. The same author managed to straighten out this linguistic difficulty three years later in a general history of the American people, but at the cost of claiming that the new negative view of slavery was not only wrong but derived from "the fashion" of "Negro intellectuals."[16] By this time, however, it was clear to most historians who was out of step.

Most other college textbooks of the 1960s embraced the new reversal. Rather than considering slaves themselves, however, they tended to focus on the sheer brutality of the peculiar institution. In 1967 the discussion in the second edition of one such text, for example, attempted some balance, but the gravamen was a catalog of facts rather resembling Theodore Dwight Weld's old abolitionist attack, first published in 1839. Students were informed: "The custom of flogging recalcitrant Negroes was widespread. Some planters set their dogs on runaway slaves, and hundreds of authentic records testify to the brutal punishment of Negroes who struck white men or who committed misdemeanors. Some were burned alive; others were starved, shot, or hanged."[17] Readers were left pretty much on their own as to what slaves thought about such treatment, but the appropriate conclusions were presumptively clear.

In the years about 1970, professional historians began spelling out in monographs what slaves long ago had thought about. In doing so, they focused especially on the "culture" and even the "community" of slaves themselves. At the same time, some historians rediscovered the fact that slavery had been in existence for nearly two centuries prior to its classic period after about 1830, with virtually no expressed recognition that both Phillips and many black historians had dealt at length (though very differently) with that period.

While studies of slave culture would surely have been written eventually, they were hastened by the appearance of Stanley Elkins's *Slavery* in 1959. Without resort to direct empirical evidence, Elkins took "for granted" the actual existence of "Sambo," who as "the typical plantation slave was docile but irresponsible, loyal but lazy, humble but chronically given to lying and stealing." This plantation personality, Elkins wrote, "come[s] principally from Southern lore."[18] What he did not say—and many reviewers did not notice—was that "Sambo" was a *male*, that "Southern lore" was *white*, and that the appearance of this character on the American stage occurred quite suddenly, about 1830. Nonetheless, rarely if ever has the assertion of an unproven and inaccurate major premise stimulated so much profitable research by other historians.

Several of these authors presented papers at the Symposium on slavery in 1975. Most continued to focus on slavery as it existed during its final thirty-five years, but other historians were already dealing explicitly with the colonial period—and usually with changes through time. Several of the papers emphasized the agency, and indeed the "community," of slaves themselves. This emphasis was to continue in the expanding field, though within a decade other historians began to object that the rush to include slaves as agents in their own right was slighting the sheer brutalities and personal costs of the institution. Whatever the emphases, the proliferation of studies from the 1970s has resulted in a corpus that has a huge number of components—scores, even hundreds, rather than mere dozens. In 2000, none of the participants in the Fortune Symposium were asked to provide an historiographical summary; no such gathering could possibly summarize all the changes of those twenty-five years.

Rather, each participant was invited to formulate thoughts arising from their own special interests and experience. Thus the first of these essays is by an attorney who had been devastatingly critical of the historical profession's treatment of the relationship between Thomas Jefferson and Sally Hemings even before DNA evidence caught widespread public attention. That relationship underlined the existence of the North American one-drop racial rule and the ongoing gradual deraciation of American society. But Annette Gordon-Reed reminds us here that Jefferson was, among other things, a lawyer, and that his attachment to his profession did much to shape his life and thinking, including his views on slavery and on Negroes in general.

Using a different lens, James Oakes's essay deals with more than a century of intellectual wrestling with the paradoxes of bound labor in a larger free society. He traces the vicissitudes of classical political economy on the matter, from Benjamin Franklin and Adam Smith through and beyond the famous and tortuous debates in the Virginia legislature that took place after the Nat Turner rebellion. In doing so he shows, as Gordon-Reed does, how closely political theory could become entangled with assumptions about racial superiority.

The next essay, by an historian who is also an attorney, takes more direct aim at the culture of slaves and arrives at a sophisticated and balanced assessment. Ariela Gross utilizes lower court records as a means of getting at important aspects of slave culture, despite the fact that slaves were barred from testifying directly against whites. She does this so profitably as to make us wonder why such sources have been so long neglected by historians. Such neglect is reminiscent of the far more scandalous disregard of the interviews conducted with elderly former slaves especially in the 1930s, interviews that of course have their difficulties as historical sources but were largely ignored by historians (though skimmed by folklorists for their own purposes)[19] for more than thirty years after they became readily available.

The essay by Norrece Jones deals with a tragic red thread that ran through relationships between the races. That white men sexually exploited slave women is of course not a novel discovery; antebellum abolitionists were aware of the fact but were under powerful Victorian restraints in writing about such matters. What Jones's essay presents is a powerful, unremitting litany of the abuse of power—of rape after rape after rape. As such, it resonates with the recent tendency of other historians to emphasize once again the violence and brutality which the slave "community" commonly had to deal with.

In recent years, also, historians have taken particular interest in slavery as it existed in and molded a single state, South Carolina, especially in its Low Country and the extension of that region into Georgia. Indeed during the past some dozen years, more books have been written about slavery in South Carolina than any other such location in the United States. Robert Olwell seizes upon another present tendency and offers a periodization of change through time, an emphasis which white historians of slavery neglected so conspicuously for so long.

The Symposium's final essay also deals, from a different angle, with slave culture. Sterling Stuckey provides striking evidence of the persistence of earlier African-American experiences into the twentieth century. He focuses on two men, Paul Robeson and Richard Wright, who might well have been surprised to find themselves linked together but who in Stuckey's treatment join to reflect the great power of cultural persistence.

Since each of the essays has its own commentary, readers are thus provided with learned, specific, and penetrating reactions to them. These commentaries inherently contain their own introductions. On balance, reflecting about the whole can convey a further sense of the condition of this field of scholarship at the very end of the last century, which was surely an improvement over what prevailed at the beginning. But of course present historical views always look best in the present, and the field shows no signs of permanent stasis.

SLAVERY AND THE AMERICAN SOUTH

Logic and Experience:
Thomas Jefferson's Life in the Law

ANNETTE GORDON-REED

One could say that Thomas Jefferson lived a life in the law. He saw the workings of the American legal system from nearly every vantage point: as a student, a practicing attorney, a legislator, as an executive who had to enforce the law, and in later years, as a quasi-professor to young men who came to Monticello to read law in his extensive library. Jefferson's outlook on life was greatly influenced by his understanding of the role law plays in the operation of any ordered society. He understood it, admired it, and lived with it.

But like so many other areas of his life, there was a paradox at the heart of Jefferson's relationship to law. In the time of the American revolution, Jefferson was a revolutionary, achieving lasting fame while acting in that capacity. The events leading up to and immediately after 1776 shaped his view of himself and shaped others' view of him. To the end of his days, Jefferson styled himself a revolutionary, forever fighting against the forces of (what he viewed as) reaction that could come in any guise—Federalists, crypto-Monarchists, bankers, priests—anyone whom he thought threatened the march of progress toward social and scientific Enlightenment. For many of his contemporaries, friend and foe alike, the image of Jefferson as having the heart of a revolutionary was an article of faith. Some feared him for this, while others admired him.

Jefferson's hyperbolic musings about "tree [s]" of liberty needing "blood" for fertilizer, extolling the virtues of periodic rebellion within society, his views against the inter-generational transfer of debt, and his liberal conception of private property as a creature of government power instead of a natural right places him, on paper at least, toward the radical end of the spectrum of political thought. Jefferson evidently found personal satisfaction in being thought of in this way, or he would not have written the things he wrote. The famous passage in his letter to William Short about the French Revolution stating that "rather than it should have failed, I would have seen half the earth desolated. Were there but an Adam and Eve left in every country, and left free, it would be better than as it now is" showed the force of Jefferson's feelings (at least at that moment) about revolutionary action. But even in the letter to Short, one sees Jefferson's attention to the system of law. In an earlier passage he made plain that those who had been killed in the Revolution should be considered as having fallen in "battle." In battle, all restraints on murder and mayhem are removed as the parties are operating outside of society's law. There were no murderers among the French revolutionaries (as defined by law), only soldiers fighting a just war.[1]

While Jefferson's writings show his attraction to the romantic aura of revolution, he was trained as a lawyer and spent much of his life grappling with problems that had their origins and, he believed, their solutions in the legal system. Can one be a revolutionary and a lawyer at the same time? Lawyers, and those who have a stake in a given legal system and choose to operate within it, may make changes and offer solutions to problems that over a period of time—years, decades—eventually work a revolution in a given society. But changes that take place over time are more properly described as evolutionary rather than revolutionary. The law, and the system that supports it, tends toward conservatism, depending as it does upon precedent, procedure, and perhaps most of all, due concern for the settled expectations among members of the community.

Jefferson's career can be described as an effort to mediate between his idealistic hopes for the future and his very practical attachments to the familiar structure of the world into which he was born, a world that nurtured its own brand of settled expectations. Slavery and white supremacy were salient features of the legal world in which Jefferson operated, and it is well-known that he lived on the fruits of the former and adhered to the tenets of the latter. While one should be reluctant to say that a particular outcome in history would have been impossible, it is safe to say that it was highly improbable that the end of chattel slavery in the United States could have been achieved through the reformist operations of the law. It was the total breakdown of law—a breakdown that resulted in a civil war—that ended American slavery. As to white supremacy, efforts during Reconstruction to use law to mount a challenge to racism were unsuccessful. Even the twentieth-century's model of anti-racist legislation, which ended *de jure* white supremacy and ameliorated racism in society at large, has not dealt a death blow to racial prejudice. Whatever is the answer to that particular problem, it is clear that the law can at most set the proper atmosphere, but cannot be the primary solution.

This paper will examine how Jefferson applied and thought about the law in relationship to slavery and race. I do not mean to present this as an exhaustive look at the subject. That is an undertaking for another time. Instead I want to focus on several key Jeffersonian encounters with the law as it related to black people and slavery during his time. These encounters were as follows: Jefferson as a practicing lawyer handling a suit for freedom by a mixed race man, Samuel Howell; second, Jefferson as a legislator in Virginia flirting with various anti-slavery provisions; and finally, Jefferson as a slaveholder and father of mixed race children whom he had to maneuver out of slavery.

JEFFERSON THE LAWYER

One scholar has commented that it was "lawyers thinking about law, not societal conditions . . . that determined the shape of legal change" during the time of American slavery.[2] When faced with the problems of the day, lawyers looked for solutions that could be obtained within the legal system as they knew it. For the most part, Jefferson's dealings with the laws regarding slavery and black people adhered to this formula. This, in part, is one reason that many present day observers find Jefferson so frustrating and, ultimately, disappointing. The high flying rhetoric of his natural law formulations in the Declaration was simply no match for a mind trained to value, apply, and rely heavily upon the positive laws that served as the practical engine and protector of the society in which Jefferson lived.

From our present perspective, the tenet of natural law that all men are born free and equal in terms of their basic humanity was the most powerful argument for the dissolution of the institution of slavery. It also remains a powerful statement against the concept of white supremacy. Yet Jefferson was never moved to act decisively (either in his private capacity as a slaveholder or as a public official) on the basis of his rhetoric about the natural equality of mankind. The weapon that could have been used to combat the evil of slavery (Jefferson's own reputation) was deployed mainly in his private letters and then, always with great ambiguity. Even when Jefferson speaks with seeming passion about the wrongs of slavery and the necessity for ending it, one senses restraint. Something is holding him back from taking the steps that could have at least pointed the country in the direction that he claimed to want it to go on the question. In the end, Jefferson retreats into process, emphasizing what is practicable within the system (legal and social) as it existed, virtually guaranteeing the continuance of the status quo.

Even his plans for the colonization of blacks were grounded in his understanding and acceptance of the rules of private property. The expatriation of emancipated blacks required attention to the loss of property rights in the whites who owned them, despite the fact that it was whites who had broken the laws of nature when they held blacks in bondage. The thought that the wrongful expropriation of black labor mandated some sort of payment to the former slaves apparently never entered Jefferson's mind. The injury to blacks, though severe, was not enough to ignore the system of private ownership embedded in Anglo-American law which had helped build the world as Jefferson knew it. The settled expectations of the majority white culture took precedence over whatever hopes blacks and their supporters had for the future.

There was a time, when he was a young man, that Jefferson did attempt to move beyond the law as it was written and commonly understood to argue forcefully in favor of the natural right to freedom of all people. In 1771, two years after he began practicing law, Jefferson took the case of a young mixed-race man named Samuel Howell. Howell's grandmother was the daughter of a white woman and a black man. A statute put in place to deter such unions mandated that the children born to such couples would be put into the custody of church wardens, and be bound to service for thirty-one years.³

The question naturally arose, as it did in other gradual emancipation statutes that held young women in servitude for significant periods of their childbearing years: what was to be done with children who were born to these women during the time of their service? The general rule, *partus sequitur ventrem*, suggested that the children were born into the same condition as their mother, which would mean that they were bound to service for thirty-one years. This circumstance could give rise to almost perpetual servitude down the generations of a given family. This was exactly the circumstance that Jefferson was hired to prevent.

Howell's grandmother gave birth to a child who was also bound for thirty-one years. This child, Howell's mother, gave birth to Howell during the time of her servitude. The church wardens who had claim to Howell's mother and to Howell sold him to a third party. Howell, through Jefferson, brought suit claiming his freedom.

Howell v. Netherland provides a rare look into the mind of Jefferson the lawyer. As Dumas Malone suggested, Jefferson's effort on Howell's behalf was "doomed from the outset." The court did not even wait to hear what the opposing counsel, who was Jefferson's law teacher and mentor, George Wythe, had to say in opposition to Howell's claim. The court summarily rejected Howell's application for freedom.⁴ By most accounts Jefferson was considered a good lawyer. Even though he lost this particular case, his work for Howell shows him to have been diligent and creative on behalf of his client. Quite simply, he did the very best that could be done with a very weak case.

Howell is typically highlighted for Jefferson's reliance on natural law to argue that Howell should be free. The case was not really about slavery because Howell was bound to service only until age thirty-one. It is, nevertheless, noteworthy because it was the first public expression of Jefferson's views about natural law and what can be taken as his first statement on the morality of slavery. He wrote: "Under the law of nature, all men are born free, [and] everyone comes into the world with a right to his own person which includes the liberty of moving and using it at his own will. This is what is called personal liberty, and is given him by the author of nature, because necessary for his own sustenance." Jefferson went on to state unequivocally that "reducing the mother to servitude was a violation of the law of nature. He then honed in on the central flaw of the statute, " . . . surely then the same law cannot prescribe a continuance of the violation of her issue and that too without end, for if it extends to any, it must extend to every degree of descendants."[5]

But there was more to Jefferson's case than simply an ineffectual flight of fancy into natural law thinking that, if accepted by the court, would have mandated the end of slavery itself. That does not do justice to the actual time and thought that Jefferson put into this matter. It is clear that he took his duties as Howell's lawyer quite seriously. In addition to the natural rights argument, Jefferson offered several other avenues of attack. The first centered on the differences in how the individual came to lose his or her freedom. Jefferson noted that there were people who became slaves because they were captured in war. Drawing on the works of ancient legal commentators Jefferson argued that these individuals were in a state of "perfect slavery." Their children belonged to the master, who fed and clothed all of them. He said that it was as if these "infants" had contracted a "debt" that ran from them to the master. Then there were individuals who became slaves by contract. These people were not in a state of perfect slavery. Jefferson argued, somewhat confusingly, that their children should not of "necessity" be slaves. Their maintenance and care was owed them by the master as a "just debt" since they were part of the contract that gave over their freedom.[6]

In Jefferson's view, Howell and his ancestors who had been bound to servitude were more akin to the children of people who had become slaves by contract. The statute bound the child of the union of black and white over to a specific entity; the "church wardens." Thus, Howell's great-grandmother was best described as a "temporary" servant to the wardens. This should not have made her offspring subject to a servitude that followed her own. Jefferson argued: "Temporary service of a while does not take away from the appellation of a free woman, in the sense of the act and her children under this clause are free, as being the children of a free woman." Jefferson then noted that the statute of 1705 under which

Howell was claimed as a servant had been followed by a 1723 statute which explicitly stated that children of woman like Howell's grandmother followed the status of their mother. Why, Jefferson asked, was the 1723 law needed if it was clear that the 1705 law mandated the same result?

Jefferson continued his attack on the interpretation of the statute by suggesting that Howell's present master could have no rights over him because the church wardens should never have been able to "alienate" Howell in the first place. The statute put the mixed race child in the care of the wardens. It could not have been in the contemplation of the drafters of the law that the wardens could then freely sell the children that the legislature had place in their custody.[7]

Jefferson's argument was not all bad. It did not win the day, but it was good strategy designed as it was to force the judge to think about the true reason for the statute's existence. It was an invitation to consider whether the results obtained by having Howell remain in bondage after several generations served any legislative purpose. What duties did the church wardens have to the individual placed in their care? Were they to be mere brokers for the trade of servants? Why did the legislature enact the law at all? Jefferson's answer to the last question was clear. "The purpose of the act was to punish and deter women from that confusion of species, which the legislature seems to have considered an evil, and not to oppress the offspring."[8]

One commentator has noted the tinge of sarcasm in Jefferson's characterization of the "confusion of species" as something that "the legislature seems to have considered evil". Why not just say, "the purpose of the act was to punish and deter women from the evil of the confusion of the species?" Didn't Jefferson think the confusion of species was evil? His subsequent writings on the topic certainly suggest that he did. His subsequent actions in his private life, however, suggest that his real view on the matter was encapsulated by this quip, which he made when he was twenty-eight years old, before he carried the weight of a public reputation on his shoulders.

In the end, Jefferson's legal maneuvering did not persuade the judge. The statute was unfair, but in the judge's view, the matter was clear. Howell was to remain a servant until he reached thirty-one.

What can be made of Jefferson's involvement in this case? This is a difficult matter because the Jefferson we see in *Howell* is acting in his capacity as a lawyer. There is always a great danger in assuming that arguments made during the course of a representation reflect the views of the lawyer. Lawyers make the arguments that they think will win the case. Jefferson had a bad case and, therefore, had to be especially creative as he tried to do the best he could for his client.

Still, it is worth noting that Howell was Jefferson's client. He did not have to take the case. Acting the role of hired gun for paying clients is one thing: Money is the motivation. But pro bono cases, those taken for the good of the public, are another matter. It will require further investigation to know with certainty just what role the acceptance of pro bono work played in the legal culture in which Jefferson practiced. Nonetheless, it is safe to venture that then, as now, lawyers choose particular pro bono cases because they involve an issue (or person) near to their hearts in some way. If there is no money to be made up front, or indirectly from association with a fashionable cause, it is likely the substance of the issue at hand that motivates the pro bono attorney.

Jefferson was essentially a land patent lawyer, who spent a good amount of his practice helping members of his class and those who wanted to become part of his class in their various attempts to get a hold of, maintain control of, large tracts of land. Exactly why Jefferson chose to concern himself with the problems of a mixed-raced man trapped in servitude will always remain a mystery, especially given that he had mixed-raced individuals under his ownership who, undoubtedly, would have wished that he had used some of his natural rights arguments on their behalf.

What we see most of all in *Howell* is Jefferson's deep seriousness about the role he played in the legal system. He tried to win the case by using the completely conventional techniques that lawyers employ: arguing on the basis of the legislative purpose, suggesting that there had been a breach of an agreement that led to something akin to a forfeiture—the kinds of tactics that any good lawyer would employ under the circumstances. As an extra measure, he was willing to go outside that boundaries of positive law to talk about natural law in order to obtain the result wanted by his client. When acting as a lawyer, even on behalf of a man of mixed race, Jefferson fell in line and played the role he felt that the system demanded. He made arguments that if taken to their logical conclusion would have meant that he could not have lived the life of a slaveholder. He knew, however, that even if he had won the case, it was extremely unlikely that his sentiments would be taken to their logical conclusion. Thus, from the safety of a private law action, Jefferson could espouse views that would never be applied to society at large.

JEFFERSON THE LEGISLATOR

At some point in his life, Jefferson decided that he wanted to be a public man. His early service in the legislatures of Virginia was in furtherance of this goal. Although he could not have known when he entered that arena just how far he would rise, because he could not have foreseen the changes that would take place in his "country," there is no reason to think he doubted his ability succeed to its highest ranks.

What is sometimes lost in the dissection of Jefferson's career and personality is that he was an extremely effective individual. By any measure his was a successful public life. This did not happen by chance. No one could have been in the places and positions that he held without having an instinct for just the right move at just the right time. Wherever he was, either in success or failure, Jefferson was always left standing, ready and able to go to the next level, should he choose to do so. What does it take to be able to do this?

It is useful when considering Jefferson's early life as a legislator to think of him as a young man embarking upon a career at which he hoped to be successful and effective, in much the same way that he approached his career as a lawyer. It is also worth noting the difference between the requirements of lawyering and those of legislating. As a lawyer Jefferson's primary focus was on his duty to his client. Signing on as an attorney signals a unity of purpose between the lawyer and client. Jefferson could, according to his own preferences, make arguments that he believed (or did not really believe) while ensconced in the role of advocate. Except in the most extreme cases, no one could fault him for this.

Legislators occupy a different, more precarious position in the legal system of a republic. They are supposed to use a combination of their judgement and intellect to draft laws for the benefit of society. In one sense they are considered free actors. At the same time, legislators must pay attention to the will of the people who elected them, or risk losing public support and with it, their positions. They can be held specifically accountable for the choices they make and the goals they choose to pursue. Legislators are, in the first instance, politicians. They have to be very good politicians if they want to make their name in the world of politics.

Whatever assessment can be made of his other talents, there is little doubt that Jefferson was the master politician of his era. His genius at politics, helped along by his great ambition, co-existed with a thin skin and a desire to be seen as a man of steadfast principle. This was an extremely difficult mixture of traits to manage. Politicians of steadfast principle do not last long if the principles they support cannot take root in the political environment in which they live. Thus, knowing a futile effort when one sees it is the mark of a good politician. Exertions on behalf of futile efforts waste time and political capital. Sometimes, of course, it can be worth it to take a risk. Politicians who are personally averse to open rough and tumble cannot be counted on to take the risk involved when one attempts to lead the public away from cherished and comfortable notions. When the politician cares deeply about his or her image, as Jefferson certainly did, there is often a strong tendency to hide or ignore the compromises that are inherent in the rise through the political ranks. In Jefferson's case this conflict seems to have been resolved by simply acting as if no compromises had ever been made. Playing the role of philosopher-king shielded him from the down-and-dirty aspects of his ascent through the ranks of politics.

We can consider Jefferson's career as a legislator in this light. If there was ever a time for Jefferson to have exerted himself on behalf of whatever anti-slavery views he held it was during the period he served in the Virginia House of Burgesses and the House of Delegates. While in those bodies, he developed a reputation as an opponent of slavery. During his first term in the Burgesses, in 1769, he supported a law that would have allowed the private manumission of slaves. The measure did not pass until 1782. Jefferson's *Summary View of the Rights of British America*, written in 1774, was the first of his attacks on the slave trade. In later life he claimed that he was responsible for bringing the bill in the Virginia House of Delegates that banned the importation of slaves into Virginia. Although he had long supported halting the trade even before the Revolution, he did not sponsor the bill that actually ended importing slaves.[9]

As numerous scholars have pointed out, opposition to the slave trade did not automatically signal one's opposition to slavery because the institution could, and did, survive and thrive after the slave trade was outlawed. But certainly all who truly wanted to end slavery totally would also have wanted an end to the slave trade. It would have been seen as a necessary first step. Whatever mixed motives may have existed, ending the trade in slaves can be counted as a legitimate anti-slavery objective.

During his time as legislator Jefferson was involved in other measures that called for emancipation. In his *Notes on the State of Virginia* Jefferson indicated that he had helped prepare an amendment to a bill pertaining to slaves which would have provided for the education, emancipation, and then expatriation of all slaves born after 1800. The amendment was not sent along with the bill because in Jefferson's view, "the public mind would not yet bear the proposition." In his draft of a revision of the Virginia state constitution Jefferson wrote a clause providing that: "The General Assembly shall not . . . permit the introduction of any more slaves to reside in this state, or the continuance of slavery beyond the generation which shall be living on the 31st day of December 1800; all persons born after that day being hereby declared free." Jefferson shared this draft with James Madison, and indicated that he felt that Madison should take the lead in pressing for adoption of the measure. The provision was never considered because the anticipated constitutional convention where it would have been discussed was never called.

Jefferson's last public action on behalf of ending slavery was his draft of the Ordinance of 1784 which would have prohibited the spread of slavery into the Western territories. Like his other draft proposals against slavery, Jefferson delayed the application of the laws. The prohibitions in the Ordinance would not take effect for sixteen years. Again, 1800 was set as the magic date. Congress ultimately rejected the anti-slavery provision that Jefferson had written into the document.[10]

When recounting Jefferson's actions or inaction against the institution of slavery it is almost impossible for modern observers to resist judgement. With the advantage of hindsight we know the price that was paid, and is still being paid, for the failure to come to grips with the problem of slavery during Jefferson's time. As we consider the matter, what appear to be missed opportunities on his part carry the weight of later developments. Today, it is easy to lay blame because Jefferson's anti-slavery activities were cast in too bright a light for a very long time.

But when we look at Jefferson not as "the-revolutionary-who-failed-us" but as the astute politician/lawyer that he was, perhaps we can view his actions with less of a sense of personal shock or hurt. As much as we may regret his unwillingness to work to change the public mind, as much as we may wish that he had spent more of his political capital on efforts to end slavery, there is every reason to believe that his political judgement on the likely futility of such efforts in Virginia was sound. When another prominent Virginian, St. George Tucker, championed a gradual emancipation plan, sending out pamphlets criticizing the institution, working very hard to garner support, his efforts went no where. George Wythe, who did what he could during his time on the bench, was similarly ineffectual. These men have our admiration today, but their exertions completely failed in their time.[11]

Certainly Jefferson's view that blacks and whites could not live in society together as equal citizens contributed to his ambivalence about emancipation during the years he seemed most interested in the question of freedom for blacks. The law as a mechanism for the social control of black people seemed uppermost in his mind when he served on a committee to revise the laws of Virginia. While he argued for more humane provisions for the treatment of white criminals, he took no similar measures with respect to blacks. He proposed a more draconian provision for the punishment of white women who had children by black men. Apparently as a member of the legislature, he had come to believe that it was important for that body, as it had done in the time of *Howell v. Netherland*, to make a public statement that sex between the races was evil.[12]

Jefferson's view of slavery and emancipation was heavily bound up with his view of both the right to private property (and the expectations among members of white society that had grown up around that right) and the need to control the alien and potentially hostile group of people who were held in bondage. As Philip Schwarz observed, "Jefferson publicly displayed some ambivalence about the existence of that 'species of property', but he rarely wavered about its legal status."[13] His membership in the planter class and his credentials as a property lawyer would have solidified this determination. Despite his championing of liberalized property rules, ending primogeniture and entail, despite his substitution of the phrase "pursuit of happiness" for the right to property in the Declaration of Independence, Jefferson knew that the wealth of his fellow Virginians was founded on their property rights in slaves. It would take a revolution, or something akin to it, to make individuals give this up.

Even as Jefferson knew slavery was wrong, or at the very least, that it was a problem for his society, he also knew that despite his own intuitions on the subject, he was not personally prepared to give up living on slavery. He would not be the first or the last person to have a set of intellectual beliefs (sometimes deeply felt) that he or she was not able to act upon. Still, his half-hearted efforts on behalf of the anti-slavery cause appear more than just hypocrisy. Given the astuteness of his political judgements about the likelihood of reforming Virginia out of slavery, when looking at his spotty record, one has to ask why did Jefferson bother to take the modest steps against the institution that he took? Why did he want posterity to believe that he was a solid opponent of slavery, so much so that in later life he seems to have embellished his credentials? Why did he believe that he could be thought of in that manner without doing the one thing that would have established his bona fides, which would have been to have freed his slaves?

There was, of course, Jefferson's image as the apostle of freedom to protect. This would not entirely account for his early involvement. Even more, his association with the Declaration of Independence virtually assured that people would think of him in that way without much more effort on his part. It is safe to venture that most people who think, or ever thought of, Jefferson as an apostle of liberty have little acquaintance with his legislative activities. Had Jefferson never participated in the legislative efforts described above he would have, in all likelihood, continued his rise to the highest levels of government.

On the other hand, it is also likely that Jefferson would never have gotten to be the man he became had he pressed the anti-slavery cause as strenuously as he could have, or as much as we would like him to have. Which brings us back to the question of just what it was that Jefferson set out to do when he decided to become a public man. The answer seems to be that he wanted to go as far as he could in the best way he knew how. We can see the pragmatic and effective politician knowing well the terrain in which he was traveling and also having a good knowledge of how to get where he was going. There is no question that Jefferson would appear a more admirable figure today had he worked harder on behalf of the ideals he claimed to have supported. Still, admirable politicians, then and now, are rare creatures. In the end, we must conclude that while Jefferson understood that slavery was a problem that should be solved, the issue was never very high on his list of things to be accomplished as he set his course for life as a mover and shaker within the new American society.

JEFFERSON THE SLAVEHOLDER AND THE FATHER OF MIXED RACE CHILDREN

The issue of slavery was as close to Jefferson as family. Through the memoirs of his son, Madison Hemings, we see Jefferson confront the law as a citizen bound by its terms in the most intimate ways. Between the years of 1790 and 1808, Jefferson fathered seven children with his slave Sally Hemings. As Virginia followed the rule *partus sequitur ventrem* these children were slaves by law. The only thing that could save them from their fate was emancipation by their father or his successor in interest.

As one scholar has noted, Jefferson "believed that conformity to the law of slavery constituted a civic duty, protected him from some of the dangers inherent in slavery, preserved his liberty to hold human beings in bondage, and even, secondarily gave some personal security to the enslaved." Jefferson was also bound by the social conventions of the day with regard to interracial mixing. Joshua Rothman, who has studied interracial relationships in Jefferson's home area of Charlottesville, has determined that couples involved in interracial relationships were generally left alone by their neighbors unless they began to act as if they had the legal status of man and wife.[14]

We can never know what Jefferson thought about his children with Sally Hemings. He certainly knew that by law they were slaves. Madison Hemings' memoir refers to a "treaty" between his mother and father to the effect that any children born of their union would be freed when they reached majority at age twenty-one. This extra-legal contract, which bound Jefferson only by the terms of his own conscience, assured that the period of childhood and slavery would be coterminous for the Hemings-Jefferson children.

The Hemings children, along with Sally Hemings, were listed in Jefferson's Farm Book with his other slaves. This suggests that he viewed them in the same manner. However, he knew that they were different in the most important way. Slavery for them, like servitude for Samuel Howell, would not be perpetual. If he fulfilled the terms of his agreement, they would be free.

These children were not, however, to be treated as legal heirs or to be acknowledged in any legal fashion. I have suggested on another occasion that the naming of the Hemings children was a form of private acknowledgment of their connection to the Jefferson-Randolph family. All were named for relatives or friends who were close to him. However, this could in no way bring them into the fold of Jefferson's legal family from which they and their progeny would forever, it seems, be outcast.

The Hemings children were, of course, of mixed blood. In fact, according to the laws of Virginia they would be considered white people.

There is no specific statement from Jefferson about how he viewed this aspect of his children's predicament or of the many other mixed race individuals who were in the same condition. In 1815, a man named Francis Gray visited Jefferson at Monticello. Gray asked Jefferson about the law regarding mulattos in Virginia. What degree of the blood did it take for a mulatto to be considered a white person?

Jefferson later wrote to Gray to elaborate on his answer. Jefferson explained that "four crossings" with a white person cleared "the issue of the negro blood," and went on to document this assertion with a complex algebraic formula to explain what he meant. He was careful to say that even if the person was considered white, that did not entitle the individual to become free. The status of that individual was determined by "the condition of the mother." Only the positive act of emancipation could make the "white" slave free. When that happened, the white slave "becomes a free *white* man, and a citizen of the United States to all intents and purposes."[15]

There is a great deal to consider in Jefferson's exchange with Gray. In an epistolary legacy consisting of thousands of pages, there are comparatively few references by Jefferson to the subject of mixed race individuals. There is very little discussion of miscegenation beyond the several well-known condemnations that form the core of our thinking about his attitudes on the subject. Those references occur literally over decades with many years in between each pronouncement. Given his tendency to return endlessly to subjects that were of true interest to him, this suggests that Jefferson was not, without the prompting of others' queries, deeply preoccupied with the status of people with a mixed race heritage—even when some of them were white and were being held in bondage. Jefferson pontificated about many things, how to bake macaroons, the nature of government, the sizes of the "organs of generation" of the various races. But there simply is very little evidence of any great interest in mixed race individuals.

Jefferson had to have known that there were people on his plantation who would be considered white under the law as he cited it. Yet, there was no great urgency on his part to get those white people out of slavery. As Lucia Stanton put it, "thus future citizens of the United

States were being held in bondage at Monticello." Law and property rights, in this instance, trumped race.[16]

Under whatever formulation Jefferson used, he knew that Beverley, Harriet, Madison, and Eston Hemings were white people under Virginia law. He knew that by emancipating them, they would not only get their freedom, they would become citizens of the United States. The stain of slavery would be removed from their generation and generations to come as long as they married white people or, if the males among them married free women of either color.

The children's whiteness gave Jefferson a choice of how to go about getting them out of slavery. The oldest children, Beverley and Harriet left Monticello in 1822 to live as white people. Beverley was twenty-three at the time and Harriet was twenty-one. There was no formal emancipation of either. Thus, they were not, in the law according to Jefferson, free citizens of the United States. Jefferson simply let them go, placing a misleading notation in the Farm Book that they both had simply run away. These children married into white families and disappeared from view as they left slavery, blackness, and their family behind them. This was an instance when Jefferson was willing to forgo the formality of law and let the power of the physical presentation of whiteness do what formal emancipation would have done: turn his children into free white citizens of the United States.

The two youngest children, Madison and Eston, were freed in 1826 by the terms of Jefferson's will. He provided that they were to be freed as of their twenty-first birthdays. Madison was already a few months past twenty-one when Jefferson wrote his will. Eston was eighteen. This situation was fraught with danger, however, because Jefferson was bankrupt when he died and his creditors would have had the right to take his property, including slaves, in satisfaction of his debt. There must have been some arrangement with creditors to allow for the freedom of a small number of Jefferson's "favored" slaves so that his will with respect to them could be followed.

In addition Jefferson wanted the slaves he freed to be able to remain in Virginia. The law at the time provided that emancipated slaves had to leave the state within one year—a result, ironically, that Jefferson had always favored. He petitioned the legislature to allow the Hemings men to remain in the state, a request that was granted after Jefferson died.

Because the condition precedent to Madison's freedom had been fulfilled (he was already twenty-one when Jefferson died) Madison Hemings was free upon Jefferson's death. Eston Hemings was not yet twenty-one. But he was "given the remainder of his time" shortly after Jefferson died.[17] Their mother was never formally freed. She left Monticello with her sons and lived on Main Street in Charlottesville until her death in 1835.

The continuing thread of expedience, political maneuvering and sensitivity to public opinion runs throughout Jefferson's treatment of his slave family. The aim seems to have been to accomplish the goal of emancipation with the least amount of attention and discomfort to his white family. Thus Beverley and Harriet simply disappear without a trace, Harriet on a stagecoach with a nominal sum of money from her father. In his will Jefferson used creative language to infer that he had freed Madison and Eston solely as a favor to John Hemings, their uncle to whom they had been apprenticed and who also received freedom in Jefferson's will. Sally Hemings's "freedom" was left to Jefferson's family members who must have known who she was and what was expected of them. The name "Sally" appears in no public document under Jefferson's, or any other of his relative's, hand. But in the end, Jefferson, as effective and stealthy as ever, had accomplished what he set out to do.

* * *

Commentary

PETER S. ONUF

Annette Gordon-Reed offers an intriguing prospectus for a new biography of Thomas Jefferson that takes into account his long-term relationship with his slave, Sally Hemings. Biographers have long sought to solve the riddle of this sphinx-like figure, looking for clues to his "character" in the twists and turns of a long, not always distinguished public career and of a private life complicated and obscured by his slave-ownership. Most other Jefferson scholars do not aspire to biography. They are content instead to trace one dimension of his life or career in their "Jefferson and . . . " studies, leaving in place their subject's split personality, and its continuing mystery.[1] Gordon-Reed's superb study of *Thomas Jefferson and Sally Hemings* makes a new look at this old subject more compelling than ever. Nobody is better equipped to undertake such a project, and her essay in this volume provides the framework for a larger study I hope she will undertake soon.[2]

Gordon-Reed sketches Jefferson's related careers as a lawyer, revolutionary politician, and as the slave-owning father of an unrecognized, "shadow" family at his Monticello plantation. These portraits multiply our perspectives on the great Virginian and, with them, our standards of judgement. She thus bucks the now prevalent tendency to judge Jefferson as a hypocritical racist who failed to live up to revolutionary ideals he so eloquently articulated. If such judgements satisfy us about our own righteousness, they also make Jefferson more of a "sphinx" than he really was. The past may be a "foreign country," but Annette Gordon-Reed's map of Jefferson's world will guide us to and through its most important sites.

The conclusion of all of her biographical sketches is that Jefferson was at the least effective, and often masterful, in all the roles he assumed. As lawyer for Samuel Howell he was "diligent and creative," deploying "completely conventional techniques" as would any good lawyer who understood the way courts worked: he was not arguing for posterity (that is, for us), but rather for his client. As a politician, Jefferson was also "extremely effective," perhaps even "the master politician of his era." Given his disappointing performances as Virginia governor (1779–81) and as president (particularly his second term, 1805–09), Gordon-Reed's assessment may seem overly generous. Yet again, however, we have to distinguish the judgements we make—in this case, based on information that was *not* available at the time—from the adulation of his supporters (and condemnation of his foes). Whatever setbacks he experienced, Jefferson "was always left standing," eligible for still higher office.

Finally, perhaps most surprisingly, Gordon-Reed argues that Jefferson was successful in his private life, protecting his "white," recognized family from the scandal and shame that so easily could have marked his relationship with Sally Hemings while at the same time guaranteeing that his unrecognized, mixed-race children with Hemings would ultimately gain their freedom. The measure of his success is the image that has been passed down to us by his white descendants of the widowed Jefferson as a devoted father and grandfather—and the obliteration of virtually any trace of his other family, with the white Jeffersons extraordinarily persistent across the generations in denying its very existence.[3] In his private life, Jefferson was "as effective and stealthy as ever," Gordon-Reed concludes: he "accomplished what he set out to do."

Gordon-Reed knows that Jefferson's life was not one unbroken string of triumphs. If we introduced a fourth role or persona, that of the self-professed "farmer," the plantation manager and slave owner, a much less effective Jefferson would emerge. The liquidation of his debt-ridden estate and the dispersal and break-up of his slave families was shameful and pathetic, testimony to his ultimate failure as plantation "patriarch."[4] But such failures—and they could be multiplied—are beside Gordon-Reed's point. She asks us instead to see Jefferson's world from his perspective, or rather from the perspective of the roles he embraced. Jefferson, for instance, would have attributed his financial problems to long periods of absence on public business; they were the measure of sacrifices *he* made for his country, not the price his people—and his own families—paid for his incompetence and profligacy. Gordon-Reed is not defending Jefferson. She does not ask us to choose between these conflicting verdicts. But she does force us to ask the right questions, to explore the implications of the choices Jefferson made. What did Jefferson hope to accomplish? As he looked back on his life, what did he think he had accomplished? And how was his self-understanding shaped by performing the roles that defined his career?

The result of Gordon-Reed's preliminary survey is a balanced—even generous—view of Jefferson, though I sense a slightly rising note of skepticism and disapproval as we move toward the conjunction of "effective and stealthy" in her assessment of his private life. Of course, the regime of slavery and white supremacy forced Jefferson to be "stealthy." Paradoxically, it was in the privacy of his home that the "master of Monticello" was most rigorously subjected to the mores and customs of slave society. We might wish for another Jefferson, one who could stand in judgment on that society (and on himself), a Jefferson courageous enough to bring Sally Hemings and their children out of the shadows. But this is anachronistic nonsense, a projection of our romantic conceptions of authentic selfhood onto Jefferson—and a denial that our own selves are, in fact, drearily banal and utterly conventional expressions of our time and place ("social constructions," we might say). I would suggest that it is a mistake to privilege one of Jefferson's personas over the others, as we in this therapeutic age are so prone to do. Perhaps, instead, we might reconsider the opportunities for "self"-expression in Jefferson's performance of his other, more public roles.

We are familiar with the constraints on lawyerly performance. Lawyers are conservative, bound by process, apparently oblivious to the moral and ethical dimensions of practice: as creatures of their clients, or "hired guns," they sink to a sub-human level. Is there such a thing, we might ask, as a genuine "life" *in* the law? As a lawyer, Gordon-Reed is well qualified to respond to this tendentious question. She reminds us, in her assessment of Jefferson's legal career, that lawyers are in fact free to voice their own most fundamental values under cover of advocacy, as they give effective voice to their clients. They are also free to take on clients, such as Samuel Howell, with whom they identify or whose cause they endorse, particularly when they take on work in a *pro bono* capacity. But even here they are, as advocates, playing a role that leaves their own position—the degree of their identification with any particular client—ambiguous, or rather, moot. If lawyers jeopardize their social standing by virtue of the courtroom company they keep, they would have no social standing at all. Everyone, even a poor, mixed-race indentured servant such as Samuel Howell, deserves good representation.

Gordon-Reed speculates interestingly on what Jefferson *might* have meant in his arguments in *Howell v. Netherland* about race-mixing in view of his own "subsequent actions." Perhaps "his real view on the matter was encapsulated by this quip": "The legislature *seems* to have considered the confusion of species . . . an evil." Jefferson planted a doubt here about what the legislature did in fact "consider" on the subject of race-mixing, a doubt that squinted obliquely at the discrepancy between legal norm and social practice. Perhaps Jefferson exploited this opportunity to explore the local implications of natural rights philosophy; or he might simply have been doing what any good advocate would do, probing ambiguities and contradictions in Virginia's racial regime that could be worked to his client's advantage. In any case, Gordon-Reed suggests, the advocate's role-playing was potentially liberating, or at least carnivalesque. Did Jefferson thus leave us some traces of his own most fundamental beliefs as he performed various roles on behalf of his clients?

However much the law offered Jefferson an arena for self-fashioning, or at least for playing with personas, it was a career that he happily abandoned when he turned toward his next major role, as revolutionary politician. Though technically able, Jefferson was never comfortable as a courtroom performer: the gifted orator Patrick Henry cut a much more brilliant figure.[5] But the revolution offered extraordinary opportunities for someone with the bookish Jefferson's estimable skills as thinker and writer. In his new role as revolutionary statesman, as law-giver and founder for Virginia and the nation, Jefferson became exquisitely conscious of his own role in world history. Instead of performing multiple roles in the courtroom (though mostly, in fact, on behalf of the gentry's real property interests), Jefferson would now perform a more exalted role both for the "living generation" and for generations to come. He would now step forward, presumably as his "own" man, and no longer as the voice of his clients. But would Jefferson's identification with the "people" and his consciousness of posterity mean also that he would no longer be able to voice his own "real" feelings?

The self that Jefferson fashioned in politics and in view of posterity was much more sharply defined than that of the provincial planter and lawyer. This political persona dominates our own thinking about Jefferson, underscoring the ambiguity of his earlier, pre-political life. Jefferson's peculiar gift, or burden, was to see everything and everyone in starkly defined black and white terms. Identifying totally with the world-changing and, for him, life-changing American Revolution, Jefferson cast himself as the living embodiment of republican righteousness. He understood that his beloved "country," Virginia, was not perfect, but the revolutionary reformer could help make it so. In his lifelong (and largely abortive) efforts to give the commonwealth a proper constitution, in his mixed success as revisor of its laws, and, most revealingly, in the vision of a glorious future in *The Notes on the State of Virginia*, Jefferson sought to obliterate a less than perfect, often sordid, provincial past. His republican faith was predicated on the capacity for improvement over time and through history. Republican Virginians could fulfill their collective potential only if their republic was truly independent and constituted on proper foundations.

Jefferson was certainly well aware of Virginia's imperfections, and therefore of the need for republican reform. But these flaws were a legacy of the monarchical old regime, not of the true character of Virginians. Most famously, Jefferson attributed the very existence of slavery to the "infamous practice" of a "few African corsairs" who, with the sanction of the King, egregiously assaulted "the rights of human nature."[6] Jefferson was hyper-sensitive about outside interference, which would necessarily compromise Virginian independence and therefore its status as a republic, for he was convinced that republican self-government was the great engine of political and moral improvement. The ultimate solution for the slavery problem was colonization, the emancipation and expatriation of the captive nation of enslaved Africans. Through colonization, Virginia would demonstrate its capacity for improvement, thus vindicating the commonwealth's character.[7] Virginians were never evil, *conscious* perpetrators of injustice. Before the Revolution, Jefferson recalled in 1814, few Virginians doubted that slaves were as "legitimate subjects of property as their horses and cattle. The quiet and monotonous course of colonial life has been disturbed by no alarm, and little reflection on the value of liberty."[8] But Virginians now knew better, and they ultimately would succeed in purging the land of the "blot" of an African presence.[9]

The paradox of Jefferson's revolutionary republicanism is that it combined a truly radical vision of progressive improvement toward perfection with the apotheosis of the "people" as they are, in light of what they one day will be. His republicanism thus was both visionary and conservative. When Jefferson looked confidently to the future, he was a trenchant critic of the imperfections and injustices of his own day. But when he found himself on the defensive, doing battle against counter-revolutionaries of all sorts—whether Tories, Federalists, or Restrictionists who sought to stop the spread of slavery into the new state of Missouri—Jefferson's conception of republican self-government obliterated any sense of those flaws, for any interference with Virginia's domestic affairs portended its own enslavement. Precisely because he drew such a sharp distinction between the freedom he cherished and the "slavery" he feared, Jefferson could draw a sacredly inviolable line around Virginia that justified the perpetuation of the peculiar institution.[10]

This is the Jefferson whose record on race and slavery we find so frustrating and disappointing, who is so anxious not to offend his neighbors or to give any countenance to Virginia's critics that he does nothing. Leave us alone, this Jefferson tells the world, we will deal with our own problems. As Gordon-Reed suggests, war alone could destroy an institution that pervaded and defined this slave society. Jefferson's meditation on race-war in the *Notes on Virginia* glimpses this awful possibility, and that is why colonization is so desperately imperative: "Deep rooted prejudices entertained by the whites; ten thousand recollections, by the blacks, of the injuries they have sustained; new provocations; the real distinctions which nature has made; and many other circumstances, will divide us into parties, and produce convulsions which will probably never end but in the extermination of the one or the other race."[11] This would be a war in defense of slavery, as the Civil War in fact would be, a great struggle in behalf of Virginia's sole jurisdiction over this peculiar, "domestic" institution.

In the meantime, in the absence of such a war, the masters of Virginia were unlikely to take any steps to end slavery, despite the pleas of Jefferson and other colonizationists. The diffusion of authority under antebellum federalism provided slaveholders several lines of defense against outside interference. Jefferson was, of course, the great theorist of federalism: "divide the counties into wards of such size as that every citizen can attend, when called on, and act in person," Jefferson urged a Virginian constitutional reformer in 1816, and "ascribe to them the government of their wards in all things relating to themselves exclusively." Jefferson's wards are most famously associated with his scheme for public education, but the first "things" he proceeded to list were all critical to the maintenance of slavery: "a justice, chosen by themselves, in each, a constable, a military company, a [slave] patrol. . . . "[12] The subdivision of authority would proceed still further, beyond the ward, "until it ends in the administration of every man's farm by himself; by placing under everyone what his own eye may superintend, that all will be done for the best."[13] If every "farmer" thus governs himself, it is also chillingly true that every slave-holding planter governs his slaves, without outside interference, absolutely. In the end, it is impossible to extricate Jefferson's democratic vision from a fantasy of patriarchal omnipotence and slaveholder sovereignty.

Jefferson eloquently evoked the image of a more perfect Virginia, freed from incubus of slavery while at the same time justifying the perpetuation of the institution which was the foundation of Virginia's "republican" social order. Was Jefferson conscious of this contradiction or paradox? We will never know, though we might like to think he was. Annette Gordon-Reed prompts us to speculate that as a lawyer Jefferson would have been better equipped to take the small steps that the system permitted to ameliorate the condition of the people he owned—including members of his own family. At the very least, he could have imagined himself in the place of clients such as Samuel Howell and given voice to their aspirations for freedom. But when Jefferson embarked on his career as a revolutionary politician—the career that makes his life worth remembering—he chose to identify with "Virginia," not with its slaves. Gordon-Reed's careful reconstruction of the roles Jefferson played and the personas he assumed helps us make more sense of this choice, and perhaps as well of the choices that shaped the divergent histories of his two families. If anyone can explicate the "and" that connects "Sally Hemings *and* Thomas Jefferson," if anyone can bring these two families back together again, it is Annette Gordon-Reed.

The Peculiar Fate of the Bourgeois Critique of Slavery

JAMES OAKES

In 1835 a young William Seward, traveling through the Shenandoah valley, was struck by the dilapidated state of the southern slave economy. "An exhausted soil and decaying towns, wretchedly-neglected roads, and, in every respect, an absence of enterprise and improvement, distinguish the region," Seward wrote. "Such has been the effect of slavery."[1] By the 1850s Seward's long-held belief in the economic inefficiency of slavery became a central theme in the ideology of the Republican Party in the North. Slavery, Republicans argued, undermined the incentive to work by depriving all slaves of the fruits of their labor, including the prospect of upward mobility. "Enslave a man and you destroy his ambition, his enterprise, his capacity," the Republican editor Horace Greeley wrote in the 1850s.[2] From this stone tossed into the pond a widening circle of consequences rippled outward. Critics charged that independent slaveless farmers and tradesmen would not live or could not flourish where slavery prevailed. The absence of a thriving middle class meant that slavery had eliminated opportunities for upward mobility among free whites as well as black slaves. Thus slavery degraded the value of *all* labor. The cumulative effect was to drag the southern economy down, condemning the entire region to poverty, stagnation, and finally, decay.

It was a long, harsh indictment. But it rested, in all of its various manifestations, on a simple but powerful assumption: that slave labor was intrinsically inferior to free labor. For at least a generation American historians have recognized this assumption as a staple of Republican Party ideology in the 1850s. It is less widely recognized that by the 1850s the assumption of slavery's economic irrationality was already a hundred years old. It had been articulated in the middle of the eighteenth century, elaborated as theory in the classical political economy that emanated

29

from the Scottish Enlightenment. The leading lights of the American Revolution believed in the superiority of free labor, and that belief profoundly shaped their ambiguous legacy with regard to slavery. In the early nineteenth century, even defenders of the South took slavery's intrinsic inefficiency for granted. And when pro-slavery ideologues took up their cause in earnest beginning in the 1830s they, too, accepted what was by then the common sense of the matter: that slave labor was less productive than free labor.

But there was a problem. If slave labor was so inefficient, why did the slave economy grow so dramatically over the course of the eighteenth century? How did a system that almost everyone agreed was economically irrational manage to survive the serious challenges of the American Revolution, especially in the upper South where the slave economy was relatively moribund in the late eighteenth century? And why, having survived those challenges, did the slave economy expand dramatically over half a continent in the space of one or two generations? Finally, how did it happen that, even as the free labor system of the North was racing into the modern world, the slave economy of the antebellum South grew richer and richer along the way? By the time the Republican Party hoisted the banner of free labor, Americans had believed for generations that a slave economy should not, indeed *could* not, do what southern slavery had been doing for more than 150 years: expand, grow, and even flourish. Slavery's prosperity belied the pessimistic predictions of classical political economy. Instead, slavery generated tremendous wealth and expanded at a pace many Northerners found alarming. Yet in the face of a century and a half of dramatic evidence that the assumptions of classical political economy were incorrect, the conviction persisted that slavery's profitability was an exception to the general rule of free labor's superior efficiency.

Benjamin Franklin asserted the superiority of wage labor over slavery as early as 1751 in his famous essay, *Observations concerning the Increase of Mankind, Peopling of Countries, &c.* . . . Franklin claimed that as a general rule free labor was so cheap that slavery could never truly compete with it. He computed the costs associated with the use of a slave, beginning with the interest lost on the original purchase price. To this

Franklin added the costs of insuring slaves and providing for their food and clothing as well as caring for them in "Sickness and Loss of Time." Finally, there were the losses associated with the slave's "Neglect of Business," for as Franklin put it—in an emblematic formulation of the problem—"Neglect is natural to the Man who is not to be benefited by his own Care or Diligence." For these and other reasons, Franklin wrote, the labor of English workers would always be cheaper than the labor of slaves in America.[3]

Franklin's indictment did not end there. Besides being more expensive than free labor, slavery had baneful social consequences for all those who came into contact with it. So pervasive were these consequences that Franklin listed "The Introduction of Slaves" as one of the things which "must diminish a Nation." To begin with, slaveless farmers cannot thrive, and they therefore abandon, those regions where slavery is introduced. In place of a middling class of thrifty farmers, slavery creates a "few Families" with "vast Estates" who purchase only luxuries. A slave economy thereby lacks a thriving middle class and the bustle of merchants that goes with it. Finally, Franklin argued, slavery distorted the families of the whites who indulged in it. The "white Children become proud, disgusted with Labor," he wrote, "and being educated to Idleness, are rendered unfit to get a Living by Industry." A hundred years later, William Seward was still saying the same thing.[4]

Adam Smith had two copies of Franklin's essay in his library, and it is quite possible that it influenced the way Smith formulated his classic rendition of the bourgeois critique of slavery. As early as 1759, in his *Theory of Moral Sentiments*, Smith spoke of domestic slavery as the "vilest of all states," denouncing its barbaric tendency "to sell them, man, woman, and child, like so many head of cattle, to the highest bidder in the market." A decade later Smith fleshed out the critique in his famed *Inquiry into the Nature and Causes of the Wealth of Nations*. "The experience of all ages," Smith declared, "demonstrates that the work done by slaves, though it appears to cost only their maintenance, is in the end the dearest of any." Why? Because "a person who can acquire no property, can have no other interest but to eat as much, and to labour as little as possible. Whatever work he does beyond what is sufficient to purchase his own maintenance, can be squeezed out of him by violence only, and not by any interest of his own." Here was the core precept in the bourgeois critique of slavery: slaves lacked the self-interest that motivated free laborers and as such any economy grounded on slavery was bound to lack the efficiency of a free labor system.[5]

Right from the start, however, both Franklin and Smith recognized the flaw in their critique of slavery. Franklin's own catalogue of slavery's hidden costs prompted him to raise the obvious question: If free labor was intrinsically superior to slave labor, he asked, "why then will Americans purchase slaves?" His answer foreshadowed one of the themes that would continually reappear in the debate over slavery. Economic opportunity was so great in the New World, Franklin argued, that employers who needed the labor of others were forced to rely on the otherwise inefficient labor of slaves. Whereas a slaveholder could keep his slaves for as long as he pleased, hired men in the American colonies "are continually leaving their Master . . . and setting up for themselves." The exceptional economic conditions in the American colonies artificially inflated the value of slave labor. Back in England, where those conditions did not exist, wage labor easily prevailed over slavery.[6]

Franklin's answer only raised another question: at what point did the conditions that artificially sustained the viability of slave labor cease to be artificial? How long could the slave economy remain profitable and competitive before the general rule of slave labor's intrinsic inferiority ceased to be credible? This was the problem that bedeviled everyone who followed in Franklin's footsteps, and in most cases they responded in the same way Franklin did. Having asserted the general rule that free labor was more productive than slave labor, they declared that there were exceptional conditions that sustained slavery, at least for the time being.

Not even Adam Smith escaped the dilemma. If slavery was so irrational and slave labor was *always and by definition* less productive than free labor, as Smith argued in *The Wealth of Nations*—what could possibly explain the efflorescence of slavery in the New World? Faced with the highly profitable sugar and tobacco plantations in the Americas, Smith posited yet another general rule, this one holding that human beings will dominate others whenever possible. The "pride of man," Smith wrote, "makes him love to domineer." Accordingly, Smith explained, "Wherever the law allows it, and *the nature of the work can afford it . . .*, he will generally prefer the service of slaves to that of freemen."[7] But what did it mean to say that slave labor was generally less efficient than free labor except "when the nature of the work can afford it?" Smith appeared to be saying that slavery was unprofitable, except when it was profitable.

What saved Smith, presumably, was his implicit claim that certain crops, at certain times, produced profits so prodigiously that prideful men could indulge their love of domination by employing inefficient slave labor, and still survive in the marketplace. "The profits of a sugar-plantation in any of our West Indian colonies are generally much greater than those of any other cultivation that is known either in Europe or America," Smith explained. "And the profits of a tobacco plantation, though inferior to those of sugar, are superior to those of corn."[8] But wasn't this too clever by half? The southern slave economy thrived for more than one-hundred and fifty years, and at the moment of its demise it was positively flourishing. Are we to conclude that this rather lengthy episode in modern history constituted an exception to the general rule, or was there something wrong with the rule?

Arthur Lee, one of the leading planters of colonial Virginia, might have been expected to dispute the bourgeois critique of slavery, for he was genuinely offended by Adam Smith's characterization of slavery's barbarism in *The Theory of Moral Sentiments*. Yet even Lee accepted the political-economic indictment of slavery. It was in the nature of slavery, Lee wrote in 1764, that the slaves themselves could never be stirred to industry or imagination. As a result, an entire society based on the labor of slaves was forever "unfavorable to trade and manufactures, which have flourished in free states." In the absence of such improvements, Lee argued, no slave society could achieve happiness and power in the world. How, then, did Lee explain the growth of slavery in the colonies? For Franklin it was the exceptional economic opportunities for free labor in America. For Smith it was the unusual profitability of certain crops. Lee blamed the Atlantic slave trade, and in so doing he spoke for a large part of the revolutionary generation. For Lee the slave trade functioned like an artificial life support system for an otherwise sickly social order. Cut off from the infusions of the trade, Lee believed, slavery would inevitably die out on its own.[9]

By the time they declared their independence from Great Britain many Americans were already well-versed in the economic critique of slavery. Like Lee, they focused their animus on the African slave trade for artificially keeping alive an institution that undermined the general prosperity. In the words of one petition from the citizens of Prince George County, Virginia, the African slave trade "is injurious to this Colony, obstructs the population of it by freemen, prevents manufacturers and other useful emigrants from Europe from settling amongst us, and occasions an annual increase in the balance of trade against the Colony." Thomas Jefferson said nothing out of the ordinary when he complained that slavery undermined the work ethic among white men. Seventy-five years before northern Republicans savagely indicted the political economy of slavery, Virginia slaveholders were already doing the same thing.[10]

By the late eighteenth century the bourgeois critique of slavery had become something like the consensus among leading Americans. That consensus helps explain the remarkable spread of antislavery sentiment during the American Revolution. Not everyone agreed that all men were created equal and were therefore universally entitled to their liberty. And not all Americans were inspired by evangelical Protestantism's growing conviction that slavery was a sin against God. But a significant body of public sentiment was able to rally around the bourgeois critique of slavery as intrinsically inferior to free labor.

The principles of classical political economy persuaded many otherwise skeptical Americans that slavery was a curse upon the land. Armed with that conviction the Revolutionary generation began ending slavery in the northern states and restricted its geographic expansion, thereby sectionalizing the institution; put in place a mechanism for the nation's withdrawal from the Atlantic slave trade; and by the processes of manumission in the upper South and emancipation in the North created the basis for the development of free black communities up and down much of the eastern seaboard. But the same generation produced a Constitution that recognized and protected the institution of slavery in a variety of different ways, and then justified its action by asserting that *somehow*, and in *some way*, the intrinsic superiority of free labor would lead eventually to slavery's demise.[11]

The widespread assumption among the Founders that slavery would ultimately fail in the global competition between free and unfree labor helps explain the great paradox of the Revolutionary legacy: the reluctance of otherwise bold men, men who went on record opposing slavery, to do much to bring about its complete abolition. Precisely because the classical economic critique of slavery foresaw the labor system's eventual demise, bourgeois antislavery had politically quietistic implications. At several points, for example, Thomas Jefferson expressed the hope that future generations would rid the nation of the curse of slavery. If he and his contemporaries genuinely believed that slavery was doomed by the inexorable laws of political economy, their impulse to leave the problem to succeeding generations seems depressingly logical.

John Taylor's famous essays on southern agriculture, *Arator*, extended the passivity of the revolutionary generation almost to the point of a proslavery defense. First published in 1803, Taylor's essays took direct aim at one of then-President Jefferson's most powerful claims against slave society: that it threatened republicanism by training its children to "loose their passions" in the intemperate overlordship of the slaves. Yet having forcefully repudiated one of the harshest political arguments against slavery, Taylor freely acknowledged its economic weaknesses. "Negro slavery," he declared without qualification, is "a misfortune to agriculture." Like Jefferson, Taylor called for the establishment of a colony of free blacks "in some fertile part of Africa."[12]

But Taylor never explained precisely why slavery was "a misfortune" to agriculture or why colonization was necessary at all. His overriding interest in reforming Virginia farming practices to make them more productive suggests that he believed slave labor was somehow inefficient. He proposed that overseers be paid in wages rather than crop shares, betraying some faith in the superior efficiency of the market mechanism. But to the extent that Taylor could explain why slavery continued to exist despite the fact that it was always a "misfortune to agriculture," he followed Adam Smith's lead by proposing a natural human impulse to domineer. Even the best constituted societies, Taylor wrote, could not cure human nature "of a disposition to command, and to live by the labor of others." For Taylor this meant that rash attempts by anti-slavery philanthropists to "suddenly change human nature" would not solve the problem of slavery.[13] Still, Taylor's support for voluntary emancipation and colonization suggested that the bourgeois critique of slavery still had adherents in the South in the early nineteenth century.

Certainly James Madison never abandoned it. In 1825 he wrote a letter to Frances Wright arguing that because slave labor was compulsory plantations could never produce impressive surpluses. Even if a slave managed to overcome his "habitual repugnance to labour" he was unlikely to be motivated if he worked in a gang with other slaves, "where each individual would feel that the fruit of his exertions would be shared by others whether equally or unequally making them; and that the exertions of others would equally avail him, notwithstanding a deficiency of his own."[14]

But the startling growth of the slave economy in the first decades of the nineteenth century placed a tremendous burden on those who, like Madison, continued to believe in the intrinsic superiority of free labor. It is hardly surprising that some southerners began to suggest that slave labor might be profitable after all. John Taylor's faith in the efficient reform of slave plantations may be read as a tentative step in that direction. Nevertheless, long after slavery's vitality might have caused more significant doubts to arise, many Southerners held fast to the conviction that slave labor was more expensive than free labor. Not until the famous Virginia slavery debate of 1832 did Southerners openly argue among themselves over whether a slave labor system was economically viable. And even then, most Virginians held fast to the tenets of the bourgeois critique.

Indeed, the debate in the Virginia legislature provides a useful measure of how widespread the principles of classical political economy were, and how the economic success of slavery was straining those principles. The debate was provoked by Nat Turner's brutal but unsuccessful slave rebellion in Southampton, Virginia. The immediate issue up for discussion among the legislators was a non-binding resolution proposed by John

Randolph that would put Virginia on record in favor of a program of gradual emancipation and colonization of all *post nati* slaves, those "born after" a specified date. Opinions on slavery ranged widely, even among those who opposed it. Eastern planters were most likely to defend slavery while western farmers attacked slavery most vociferously, although there were a number of important exceptions to the rule. But regardless of the class or regional origins of the various legislators, the assumptions of classical political economy ran like a red line throughout the entire debate. Over and over again the legislators declared slavery inferior to free labor. It encouraged wasteful agriculture. It destroyed the slave's incentive to work while degrading useful labor in the eyes of whites as well. It discouraged the growth of industry while encouraging the flight of white yeomen.[15]

Despite the plethora of themes developed by the various participants in the Virginia slavery debates, no one argument recurred with such regularity as the classical critique of the political economy of slavery. "The slave perceives that he can never attain to the least distinction in society," Samuel Moore argued. Because slaves were generally occupied in agricultural labor, he added, "it is very generally regarded as a mark of servitude, and consequently as degrading and disreputable."[16] Philip Bolling claimed that slavery "drives from us the laboring man," adding that slavery exhausted Virginia's soil, depressed its markets and left the masters so deep in debt that they could scarcely feed and clothe their slaves properly. "Why," Bolling asked, "is slave-labor more expensive, and consequently less profitable than the labor of the white man?" The answer was simple: "They have no *immediate self-interest* to act upon them. . . . This great, this all-powerful motive of action is wanting to stimulate the slave to labor. It fails to operate upon him for good, because he knows his master is bound to provide for him, whether he labors much or little, and whether his master makes little or much. Therefore he is idle and wasteful. . . ."[17]

Thomas Marshall argued that slavery was "ruinous to whites—retards improvement—roots out an industrious population. . . . Labor of every species is disreputable," he claimed, "because performed mostly by slaves."[18] For a relatively young society, Samuel Garland argued,

Virginia showed "evidence of premature decay . . . And to what known cause can this be assigned but to the existence of slavery?"[19] Similarly, Henry Berry held that slavery was "a grinding curse upon this state." After all, Berry asked, "What stimulus has the slave to work, other than the lash?"[20]

If Berry represented the dominant opinion in the Virginia legislature, he was not without his opponents. At crucial points in the debate several members rose to suggest something that struck their colleagues as shear heresy: that the slave economy was doing just fine, that Virginia was not in the deplorable shape its critics imagined it to be, that the bourgeois critique of slavery was quite simply wrong. James Gholson, for example, positively swore that the "gentlemen who draw these gloomy pictures of Eastern wealth and agriculture, are—my life upon it!—better poets than planters." Gholson readily admitted that the prosperity of slavery in Virginia rested on the sale of its surplus slaves to the new plantation regions further west and south. But this only proved that slavery in Virginia was profitable after all.[21]

The most articulate of slavery's defenders in the Virginia debate effectively turned Adam Smith's principles against Smith's critique of slavery. But first they tried to bury the factual claims of their opponents. Like James Gholson, Charles Faulkner insisted that "the sombre pictures which have been drawn of the deplorable condition of the commonwealth, are in a great measure, imaginary—and so far as they are true, the causes have been mistaken." If Virginia was poor and indebted, Faulkner argued, it was not because slavery was unprofitable but because the profits of slavery were siphoned off to the northern merchants who monopolized the commerce in slave-produced goods. To the claim the slavery retarded the growth of the white population by spurring the emigration of independent farmers to the West, Faulkner answered with statistics showing that an even larger portion of the independent farmers of Massachusetts migrated west. John Shell agreed. Migrants were not leaving Virginia "to escape the evil and curse of slavery," he declared. On the contrary, most of them settled in slave states further west, where they "can enjoy greater facilities to market, and reap the full harvest of more abundant agricultural production."[22]

William Goode offered one of the most coherent economic defenses of southern slavery by developing a line of reasoning that today would be called "comparative advantage." Among small farmers and graziers in the western and northern states, Goode explained, the demand for labor was "but occasional." For such enterprises, it made no sense to employ slave labor. By contrast, on the tobacco, cotton, and other plantations of the South, there was "a constant, and unremitted demand for a regular force, the whole year round." Thus the planter's operations "must not depend on any precarious supply of labor; it must be certain, and always at command." For this reason the southern planter "has a greater demand for the labor of a slave" than does the northern farmer or the western herdsman. For Goode the market itself would determine where slave labor was efficient and where it was not. "The labor of the slave like every thing else, will go where it is most useful—will meet the most effectual demand." It was precisely this market mechanism, however, that persuaded Goode that slavery in the Upper South would eventually disappear on its own. As Virginia planters, responding to market forces, transformed their tobacco plantations into wheat farms, they would steadily sell off their slaves to the cotton plantations of the lower South. Goode's point, however, was that politicians should not meddle with the invincible forces of the free market. If slavery was slated to die a natural death, let it do so on its own.[23]

These were not fully developed claims for the profitability of slavery, but they rubbed sufficiently against the grain of the longstanding consensus to provoke the ire of several legislators. "That slavery is a grinding curse upon this state," Henry Berry declared, "I had supposed would have been admitted by all." Instead he was compelled to rehearse yet again the classical indictment of slave labor. For James M'Dowell no proposition could be "more easily or conclusively established . . . than *this*, that the labor of a free white man, in the temperate latitude of Virginia, is more productive than that of a slave—yielding a larger aggregate for public and private wealth."[24] Here again the terms of the debate remained strictly within the standards established by classical political economy—which system was more profitable, slavery or free labor?

This was the backdrop for Thomas Roderick Dew's influential analysis of the Virginia slavery debate. Most scholars still recognize Dew's essay as a turning point of some sort, but with the notable exception of Laurence Shore few historians have recognized the centrality of political economy to the southern discussion of slavery. T. R. Dew was a professor of political economy at William and Mary, and his commentary on the Virginia slavery debate was clearly inspired by the classical tradition of Adam Smith and his nineteenth-century followers, John Stuart Mill and especially Thomas Malthus.[25]

Dew found Malthus congenial for several reasons. The English theorist had applied the principles of classical political economy to the study of human population, arguing for a self-regulating mechanism that held population growth in check only when it reached the limits of the earth's productive capacity. As population grew, wages declined until desperate laborers worked harder and harder to maintain a bare subsistence. Advocates of slavery's "diffusion" invoked the prospect of a Malthusian crisis in the South if the growing population of slaves were squeezed into the current limits of the slave economy. For others Malthus's claim that wages tended to decline to subsistence level proved that free laborers were doomed by the laws of political economy to be more miserable—but more efficient—than the slaves. Thus the widespread acceptance of Malthusian theory fastened Dew and other proslavery writers more firmly to classical economics and with it to the belief that slaves were less efficient than free laborers. This only heightened the intellectual problem presented by slavery's profitability and expansion.[26]

Dew recognized from the opening sentences of his *Review* that the prosperity of slavery explained the steady rise in the slave population—"growing with our growth and strengthening with our strength"—and that this flatly contradicted the premises of classical political economy. Indeed, the speedy growth of the slave population rendered *"totally impracticable"* all of the colonization schemes proposed by slavery's opponents in the Virginia legislature. But aside from its formidable statistical calculations, the novelty of Dew's argument against colonization was his Malthusian analysis of the problem.[27]

The more interesting feature of Dew's essay was his attempt to reconcile his commitment to classical political economy with his recognition that southern slavery was both profitable and productive. His initial impulse was to claim that the market itself was the only real test of slavery's viability. To the contention "that free labour is infinitely superior to slave labour," Dew answered that the high price of slaves "is an evidence of his value with every one acquainted with the elements of political economy." Later, in a longer and more considered response, Dew came close to turning the bourgeois critique of slavery into a proslavery argument. One of the central points of the classical argument against slavery was that it deprived the slaves of the "self-interest" that motivated free laborers to develop habits of discipline, diligence, sobriety, and thrift. Slave labor was unproductive, critics charged, because the slaves had every incentive to be careless at work. Dew picked up this argument, combined it with a Burkean reverence for the force of habit and tradition, and pronounced the slaves irredeemably incapable of meeting the challenges of freedom. Centuries of African tyranny, combined with generations of enslavement in America, had inculcated in African Americans habits of idleness and dissipation that could never be undone. "The blacks have now all the habits and feelings of slaves, the whites have those of masters;" Dew explained, "the prejudices are formed, and mere legislation cannot improve them."[28] Why not? Why couldn't the slaves, exposed to the powerful force of self-interest, raise themselves up the same way the illiterate barbarians of western Europe had done? Dew's answer to this question edged him toward proslavery's final trump of the bourgeois critique: racial ideology.

Where the uncivilized masses of Europe were slowly absorbed into the rising middle classes, Dew explained, "difference of colour" would forever preclude a similar absorption of black slaves into free white civilization. Conversely, because of the similarity of color among the educated slaves of antiquity, "the *body* of freemen could readily and without difficulty or danger absorb them." Dew went on to cite racial theorists who claimed that the average black possessed "the form and strength" of an adult man, "but the intellect only of a child." This defect was not the product of recent history. On the contrary, the difference between whites and blacks "is the growth of centuries; which is almost coeval with the deluge." The reference to the deluge was a giveaway. By quoting it approvingly, Dew came within an intellectual millimeter of declaring blacks inherently inferior and as such forever unfit for freedom.[29]

But if Dew dipped his toes into racial ideology, he never really dived in. The most overt racism in his essay was contained in citations of others, and he hedged his claims of black inferiority in Burkean terms of habits so deeply ingrained as to be *virtually* immutable. Nevertheless, his dalliance with racial ideology had significant consequences for the way he and those who followed him confronted the challenge of classical political economy. When he returned to the issue at the end of his essay, Dew declared that he was "in the main" persuaded by Adam Smith's general theorem that free laborers, "actuated by a desire to accumulate" were "much more efficient" workers than slaves. But for Dew the desire to accumulate had to overcome a countervailing "desire to indulge in idleness and inactivity." Among civilized white men, the desire to accumulate prevailed. Among Native American "savages" and Africans in the old and new world, however, "the principle of idleness triumphed over the desire for accumulation." Everyone who espoused the principle of free labor's superiority was forced to devise some "exception" to explain slavery's profitability. For Dew the exception to the general rule was the economic efficiency of slave labor *when performed by blacks in southern climates*.[30]

The tremendous prosperity of the slave economy in the 1830s had made it all but impossible to sustain the illusion that the South was smothering beneath the weight of slavery's inefficiency. In a final burst of intellectual creativity, proslavery writers constructed a new synthesis that posited both the profitability of slavery *and* the superior efficiency of free labor. These seemingly incompatible elements were fused together by a racial ideology that declared otherwise unproductive African blacks uniquely suited to the coercion of slavery in warm climates. This proslavery synthesis allowed southern writers to openly embrace the profitability of slavery. They boldly declared that the great cultural and intellectual achievements of the West rested on the wealth and leisure afforded to the master class by the labor of slaves. More boldly still, they warned that if slavery in the South were destroyed by abolitionist interference the economic basis of western civilization in the mid-nineteenth century would crumble.

Classical orthodoxy held that slave labor was not merely more expensive than free labor, but that the inferiority of slave labor dragged down the entire economy and inhibited both economic and social progress. There were hints of a break from this orthodoxy in John Taylor's claim, *contra* Jefferson, that slavery elevated rather than subverted the character of the master class. But Taylor was still ambivalent about whether slave-based agriculture could ever be profitable. William Harper's 1838 *Memoir on Slavery* went much further. Slavery might not be as profitable as wage labor, Harper conceded, but the profits of slavery were very real indeed. Without slavery, he claimed, "there can be no accumulation of property, no providence for the future, no taste for comforts or elegancies, which are the characteristics and essentials of civilization." This was especially true in "tropical" climates, Harper added, where slavery alone could sustain civilized society. So it was that in the southern states, "where good government and ... domestic slavery are found, there are prosperity and greatness."

Freed from the gloomy premises of classical political economy, proslavery writers jumped to the opposite extreme and began to make preposterous claims for the indispensability of modern slavery. Some went so far as to reject the labor theory of value, a staple of classical theory. Smith and his followers defined economies—and therefore economic efficiency—by the way labor was organized, since labor was the ultimate source of all value. But as slavery's prosperity defied classical assumptions some of the South's more exhuberant champions abandoned this labor theory of value in favor of a simpler "market" mechanism. The optimists at the Virginia slavery debate had moved in this direction: the market, they argued, would decide whether slavery was or was not profitable. This line of reasoning peaked on the eve of the Civil War and was enshrined in the title of a major 1860 anthology of proslavery writings called *Cotton is King*. The anthology in turn borrowed its title from the lead essay by David Christie. That Christie referred at all to a "cotton" economy rather than a "slave" economy is one indication of his move away from the production paradigm of classical political economy toward the "market" model whose star rose in the second half of the nineteenth century. "Cotton is King" claimed to take no position on the morality or efficiency of slavery itself. Instead, Christie ostentatiously deferred to what he believed was the irresistible force of the cotton market, or King Cotton, for it was the market's decree that slave labor was the most efficient mechanism for cotton production.[31]

Christie's phrase was made famous by James Henry Hammond, the wickedly articulate South Carolinian who in 1845 splashed into the front ranks of proslavery ideologues with a couple of forceful public letters responding the English abolitionists. "The system of slavery is not in 'decay' with us," Hammond announced. "It flourishes in full and growing vigor."[32] A decade later Hammond was declaring, on the floor of the U.S. Senate, that King Cotton's strength was such that no power on earth would dare make war upon it. By invoking the abstract force of the market, Christie and Hammond moved away from classical orthodoxy. But in so doing they became not anti-capitalists but neo-classical economists *avant la lettre*.

Yet the retreat from classical political economy was more apparent than real. Even as proslavery writers discarded the ideological illusion that slavery was unprofitable, they continued to assert that slave labor was, as a general rule, less efficient than free labor. Harper acknowledged that the slave had "no opportunity of raising himself to a higher rank in society." Lacking this critical "inducement to meritorious exertion," he noted, the slave was prone to "indolence and carelessness." Hence the less productive quality of his labor. Harper flatly declared that "free labor is cheaper than the labor of slaves."[33] Even James Henry Hammond agreed. "In an economical point of view slavery presents some difficulties," he wrote. "As a general rule, I agree it must be admitted, that free labor is cheaper than slave labor."[34]

This inevitably raised the same question that haunted classical political economy from the outset: if slave labor was more expensive why didn't the slaveholders switch to free labor? Proslavery's reply began with a recapitulation and extension of the same answers given by

Benjamin Franklin and Adam Smith. Hammond, for example, leavened Franklin with Malthus. The vast American frontier had forestalled the development of a Malthusian crisis of overpopulation in the northern states, Hammond argued, making it impossible for southern masters to find free laborers to replace their slaves. Adding an element of geographical determinism to Adam Smith, Dew, Harper, and others claimed that the crops produced on slave plantations were unusually profitable and could only be produced in southern climates.

But as we have already seen, the reference to "warm climates" opened the door to a potent exception to the general rule of classical political economy. Because warm weather indisposed men and women to labor, Harper argued. "Nothing but the coercion of slavery can overcome the repugnance to labor in these circumstances." A few pages later Harper nearly repeated himself, but with a crucial difference. What he previously attributed to climate, he now attributed to the racial character of African blacks: "We know that nothing but the coercion of Slavery can overcome *their* propensity to indolence."[35] In the combination of climatic and racial determinism, slavery's defenders constructed the definitive exception to the general laws of classical political economy.

From this perspective it is easier to see how much of nineteenth-century racial theory was driven by the assumptions of bourgeois ideology. Samuel Cartwright, one of the antebellum South's most prominent "ethnologists," was famed for his research allegedly showing that Africans absorbed less oxygen than whites. For Cartwright, this putative physiological difference explained why blacks were both mentally and physically slower than whites. "Negroes are naturally slower in their motions than white people," Cartwright explained. To some extent this was merely a restatement of the familiar claims of classical political economy, except that the terms "free" and "slave" were replaced with "white" and "black." As Cartwright explained, "every attempt to drive negroes to the performance of tasks equal to what the white laborer would voluntarily impose upon himself, is an actual loss to the master; who, instead of getting more service out of them, actually gets less, and soon none." Racial theory thereby operated within the terms of classical political economy, reinforcing the conviction that free white labor was more efficient than enslaved black labor.[36]

And yet, by naturalizing the difference between free and slave labor, racial theory completely altered the implications of classical political economy. Africans naturally lacked the ambitious instincts of whites, Harper declared, so what difference did it make if slavery stifled opportunities for upward mobility? Black Africans were an "inferior variety of the human race, of less elevated character, and more limited intellect," Harper asserted, and "is it not desirable that the inferior laboring class should be made up of such, who will conform to their condition without painful aspirations, and vain struggles?"[37]

Similarly, Edmund Ruffin accepted the bourgeois ideal of the self-interested laborer, but claimed that blacks simply lacked the capacity to be self-interested.[38] Like Franklin, Smith, and so many others, Ruffin was prepared to argue that certain historically exceptional conditions made slave labor profitable in the South. In a series of influential essays published in the 1850s he repeated the now-familiar claim that black Africans alone were physically suited to labor productively in the semitropical climate of the South. In western Europe, as in the northern states, free labor was more productive than slave labor. But in the South, and with the Negro, slavery "will yield more toward the general increase of production and public wealth" than will free labor.[39]

Here was a theory of political economy that simultaneously preserved and evaded the implications of the bourgeois critique of slavery. In northern climates where white people worked, the general laws of classical economics applied. But in tropical climates, nobody would work except by compulsion. And black people would *never* work hard, in any climate, except by compulsion. Hence the reason southern slavery was profitable: it generated wealth from an otherwise unproductive people in an otherwise unproductive climate.

Having thus explained why slavery was profitable even though the general rule of classical political economy was still valid, proslavery theorists turned the bourgeois critique into a badge of honor. Harper defended the inferiority of slave labor by suggesting that it was compensated by a degree of personal security for the slave that was lacking among free laborers. The price paid for the slave's inferior labor was worth the cost in social benefits to the slaves. Hammond agreed, arguing that the higher costs of maintaining slaves meant only that southern slaves were better off than free laborers. Thus was the bourgeois critique of slavery definitively inverted to become a centerpiece of reactionary proslavery ideology.

It retrospect it is not easy to fathom why nineteenth-century Americans struggled so hard to explain slavery's profitability. We live on the other side of two intellectual transformations that have distanced us from the mindset of antebellum America. The first was the theoretical development of "neoclassical" economics, led by Alfred Marshall and others in the late nineteenth century. Economists ever since then have turned away from the labor theory of value and have focused their attention instead on the operation of markets. This has long since become the standard framework within which Americans discuss the economy. Some of this shift was breaking through in the antebellum debate over slavery's efficiency, but for the most part the participants made their points within the terms of classical rather than neo-classical economic theory. More recently, neo-classical economics gave rise to a "cliometric revolution" that has definitively established slavery's economic profitability. In neo-classical terms if slavery was profitable it was by definition viable. Thus not only have the terms of the debate shifted, but the question of slavery's profitability is no longer in play for most of us.

Nowadays the bourgeois critique of slavery is kept alive primarily by Marxist historians. This is not as odd as it may first seem. Marx was, after all, the last of the great classical economists, those who concerned themselves with how wealth was produced and therefore, how labor was organized. We do not think that way anymore, especially not after the revival of market ideology in the 1980s. Hence our retrospective bemusement at the intellectual struggles of the nineteenth century.

Nevertheless, those intelligent and often articulate gentlemen in the Virginia legislature understood some things better than we do now, precisely because they were guided by classical political economy. Stripped of its teleology, of its deterministic faith in the inevitable triumph of free labor and the intrinsic inferiority of slave labor, classical theory still points us to some of the defining elements that distinguished slavery from free labor. The incentive structure *was* fundamentally different. Direct domination profoundly shaped the way slaves worked, the way they related to those for whom they worked, and even the way slaves interacted with one another. To be sure, classical political economy could not see that a careful balance of economic rationalization and physical coercion could make slavery profitable, even for centuries. But it did see that the social relations of slave society could not be understood from the simple observation that the masters made a lot of money.

This was the conclusion that Abraham Lincoln finally came to. He had very little to say about slavery before the 1850s. The available fragments of his early thinking suggest that he accepted the classical theory of slavery's economic inferiority. But after the Kansas-Nebraska crisis, when he began to speak of slavery at length, Lincoln never claimed that free labor was *economically* superior, nor did he evince any faith in its inevitable demise. In this he parted company with his fellow Republican, William H. Seward. To be sure, Lincoln understood the profound difference between slavery and free labor, and he could articulate those differences with piercing clarity. But for Lincoln, the political economy of slavery was immoral not because it wrecked the southern economy, but because it took from the mouths of enslaved men and women the bread they had earned. For this reason above all others, slavery was simply wrong. Absent the power of classical political economy, Lincoln's argument would have carried no weight.

* * *

Commentary

WALTER JOHNSON

James Oakes's extraordinary paper takes up two of the most important questions in the historiography of slavery: first, the relationship between slavery and what the paper terms "bourgeois" economic thought, and second, the relationship between slavery, economy, and nineteenth-century ideas about race. Indeed, what are perhaps the key terms in defining our understanding of the intellectual history of American slavery—market, race, and region—are here taken up, reworked, and redefined in ways that seem to me to be quite illuminating. Through the critique of slavery, Oakes argues, the exegetes of capitalist social relations were able to make "free" labor (at least in the North and at least for whites) seem like a fact of life. Everywhere the critique of slavery went, the celebration of "free" labor was sure to follow.

The paper begins with a particular strain of Adam Smith's economic thought: the idea that because slaves derived no direct benefit from their own work they were less productive than (self-interested) free laborers and could be governed only by violence. Oakes traces that idea through a series of appropriations, repetitions, and reformulations, which gradually elevated the idea of the superior efficiency of free labor to a theory of history: the idea that free labor would inevitably replace slavery. This strand of "bourgeois" political economy, Oakes notes, served the founding generation as a sort of anti-political politics: if the everyday workings of the market could be counted upon to accomplish the historical task of overthrowing American slavery, then there was no reason to try to accomplish through politics what would eventually be accomplished through economics.

The ideology which converted some premises about the superior motive and creative power of free-labor liberalism into an axiom of historical development had an important racial corollary which made it possible for proponents of slavery to take it on board. This was the idea that African Americans were incapable of participating in the economic revolution that was transforming the world around them.[1] And in the thought of these pro-slavery converts to the bourgeois critique of slavery (and the moderate antislavery thought of many others) this exclusion was itself framed as being beyond politics—as a matter of history. That history could be ancient (as it was in the case of Thomas Dew who, in Oakes's words, argued "centuries of African tyranny combined with generations of enslavement in America had inculcated in African

Americans habits of idleness and dissipation that could never be undone"). Or it could be natural (as it was in the case of Samuel Cartwright who argued that the "Negro or Prognathous race" processed oxygen less efficiently than did whites and thus had to be forced into labor in order to attain physical equilibrium). Indeed, it could be metaphysical (as it was in the case of countless pro-slavery divines who found justification for slavery in the word of God). All such arguments culminated in making black slaves unfit for freedom: the epochal transformations of the world in the image of free-labor liberalism theorized by "bourgeois" economists came to a screeching halt at the color line.

And yet, as Oakes points out, it was the phenomenal, new-world-making power of black labor which provided what was perhaps the strongest argument against the "bourgeois" critique of slavery: if slavery was so much less efficient than free labor, and black workers so inferior to white ones, why was it that so many slaveholders seemed to be making so much money? Here, at least, the exegetes of free-labor-liberalism-and-black-inferiority-as-history had to admit the importance of local variation and temporal circumstance. Some followed Adam Smith to the fitful recognition that there was a human capacity beyond self-interest—"pride" he called it—which led slaveholders to keep employing slaves because they enjoyed the domination of those who were less-powerful than themselves. Others, like Smith again, emphasized the peculiar natural capacity of some crops—notably sugar and tobacco—to provide profits so great that they were able to sustain the slave mode of production beyond its natural life. Still another group, like William Harper, noted that, whatever the many virtues of free labor elsewhere in the world, in "warm climates" like that of the American South slavery alone could sustain economic growth and civilization; they noted that the cultural and economic life of American slavery provided an exception to the laws of history—the exception, in a sense, that proved the rule.

Oakes's paper, then, suggests the ways that, through the terms of "bourgeois" political economy, much of the analysis of American slavery was transposed into a set of terms which placed the institution beyond the pale of political action. These terms could be quite various. They could translate into the quiescent diffusionism of members of the founding generation whose faith in the world-historical power of free-labor led them to regard the early years of the interstate slave trade in a particular way. They viewed that trade not as the essence of an obscene synthesis of economic expropriation and human domination but as a hopeful step on the way to a better future in which blacks would be diffused so widely across the map that it would be possible to emancipate them. They used a set of racial terms of reference which excluded African Americans from what many of the leading thinkers of both North and South regarded as the front-edge of historical progress—liberation through "free" labor. Finally, they used a vocabulary which naturalized both the industrial capitalist development of the North and the slave economy of the South as regional phenomena. Or, put another way, Oakes has here traced the historical process through which historical development of the North came to be characterized in terms of the market while that of the South was characterized in the terms of culture.[2] Oakes's paper, that is, outlines the process by which the discussion of an institution that was by its nature historical, political, and economic was euphemized into a set of terms that were ahistorical, racial, and regional.

As I see it, the paper makes at least three significant contributions to our understanding of American slavery. First, it excavates a rich and forgotten vein of writings about slavery and economy and sustains its argument that the "bourgeois" critique of slavery provided framing premises not only for many of slavery's critics but for some of its defenders. In so doing it sharpens our understanding of the meaning and mutual interaction of the key terms in the intellectual history of American slavery: race, region, slavery, and capitalism.

Second, it provides a way of thinking through the relationship of slavery and race—of economy and ideology—in a set of terms that make sense at the level of everyday life. Within the historical architectonics of the entanglement of American slavery and American freedom, of democratic revolution and racial domination, of liberalism and racism, Oakes's piece helps us to see the way to a smaller set of building blocks. He provides a detailed and sequential account of how various thinkers drew on existing ideas about race in order to resolve specific intellectual problems posed by the bourgeois critique of slavery.³ He has, that is, provided us with an outline of the everyday history of how the categories that shaped and defined slavery were articulated and promulgated, of how intellectuals involved in debates used, redefined, and spread a wider set of ideas about slavery, race, and the market.

Third, in describing how the idea of southern regional and geographical distinctiveness was ultimately used to blunt the force of "the bourgeois critique" by insulating southern slavery from the supposedly inexorable transformative force of "free labor," Oakes has provided a nuanced account of the history of the idea of "the market" in American history generally. In the United States the central premise of Smithian economics, the idea that "the market" was itself an historical force that stood outside of and had a motive force apart from "culture," was mapped onto the division between North and South. Thus northern industrialists could claim that their version of the proper relation between capitalist, worker, time, and wage was in fact an immutable fact of nature rather than a culturally specific argument. Thus they could broadly gesture at the slavery practiced by their southern neighbors and in the same gesture gloss over the distinction between "free" labor (i.e. the freedom to work for a wage) and "freedom" itself. And thus southern defenders of slavery could contend that the system of domination and exploitation over which they presided was, in essence, cultural rather than economic.

What I missed in this extraordinary paper was a better sense of the setting from which these ideas emerged. I sometimes had the feeling that I was reading a transcript of one of the greatest—at least from the perspective of an intellectual historian of slavery—dinner parties ever thrown: Benjamin Franklin, Adam Smith, and Thomas Jefferson on one side of the table, James Henry Hammond, Thomas Roderick Dew (and also George Fitzhugh) on the other. Oakes is at the head of the table as a good-humored host, insistently posing the question that guides the discussion—"but what about the evidence of slavery's productivity, how do you account for that?" I must admit to a sense of pique at not having been invited to the party, but once I realized that Laurence Shore was the only other historian invited to the gathering

I didn't feel so bad. Nevertheless, if part of the paper's promise is the vision of a much more rigorous account of the way that ideas about capitalism, slavery, race, and region were spread over time and space, it seems to me important to be as specific about the historical setting of that process of transmission.

I have in mind three groups of settings. First of all, I think that the paper might profit from more attention to the historical conjunctures which shaped the uses (and abuses) of ideas about capitalism, slavery, and race. For instance, the urgency of William Harper's 1838 claim that western civilization would end with slavery—"Can any sane mind contemplate such a result without terror?" he wrote—would both resonate with and refine Oakes's argument if it was placed in the context of West Indian Emancipation in 1834 and the end of the period of "apprenticeship" in 1838. Indeed, it would be interesting to try to trace the place of the West Indian example, which was widely reported in North American newspapers at the time, in all subsequent United States discussions of what would happen if slavery ever ended.[4]

Secondly, I have in mind the rhetorical or forensic context of these arguments: who, specifically, were these writers arguing with and what, specifically and concretely, were they trying to achieve when they mobilized the "bourgeois" critique. If one of the very great promises of the paper is to point the way to the everyday processes by which ideas about capitalism, slavery, and race were reformulated and reproduced, it seems important to me to replace the polite but insistent voice of James Oakes with a more detailed account of what questions those who made the arguments were trying to answer when they made them and who was asking.

Thirdly, I have in mind the physical setting. For example, many of these arguments seem to reflect at the level of abstract argument the sort of juxtaposition of themes—gross domestic product, historical growth, agricultural practice, management strategy, biological racism—that characterized the table of contents of slaveholding periodicals like *DeBow's Review* or the *Southern Agriculturalist*. Given the importance assigned to the unlikely juxtapositions that characterize "print capitalism" in recent work on how people who have never met one another imagine themselves into national and regional solidarities, it seems worth thinking about the physical setting of these arguments (i.e. in a journal, in a state house, etc.) as being itself an element of the hold an argument might have upon its audience.[5] There is one great exception to everything I have just said about the silences in the paper, of course, and that is Oakes's discussion of the Virginia slavery debate of 1832: it occurred in the immediate aftermath of Nat Turner's Rebellion, it pitted a largely slaveholding group of easterners against a largely nonslaveholding group of westerners, and it occurred in the physical premises of the Virginia State House. The sudden disruptive appearance of Nat Turner at the dinner party, I think, brings the rest of the paper into sharper focus.

With Nat Turner in mind, let's return for a moment to Adam Smith. The version of "the market" that the "bourgeois" critique of slavery elevated to a revealed principle of historical progress was a very specific one. There appears to have been little of Smith's idea that "man" was possessed by an innate capacity to truck, barter, and sell. Nor is there much explicit about the "invisible hand" of macroeconomic distribution in these writings. Now it may be said that these ideas are immanent in the historical teleology of the "bourgeois" critics. But it must be equally acknowledged that the element of "bourgeois" political economy from which their arguments explicitly embarked was the question of labor discipline—of how workers could, on the scale of incentives that ran between the threat of starvation and the promise of shareholding, be convinced that working for someone else was the right thing to do (or as the "bourgeois" critics themselves would have it, in their own best interest).[6] The "bourgeois" critique of slavery, that is, emphasized the producer over the consumer and the internal dynamics of the character of human motivation rather than the external questions about the nature of macroeconomic distribution. To put it another way: the "bourgeois" critique of slavery brought the question of slave agency (and thus, in our terms, of slave resistance) to the center of history.

If we are to accept the notion, outlined above, of the importance of the specific historical context in which the arguments that made up the "bourgeois" critique of slavery were deployed, reworked, and reproduced, then we can begin to see the way to a history in which enslaved people's resistance to slavery—slowing down, acting out, running off, rising up—was, in fact, a central element of the formation American modernity. Indeed, once we see enslaved people's agency as the central problematic of the "bourgeois" critique of slavery, we can begin to see the extent to which the categories that emerged from that debate (as well as from other debates held in other settings) were born of a colossal erasure—the erasure of African-Americans ideas, desires, and politics as a motive force of history. In the formulation of Michel-Rolphe Truillot, the idea that slaves had a fully theorized and occasionally articulated version of events which led them to behave the way they did was, for both slaveholders and their bourgeois critics, an "unimaginable" history.[7] It was within the comfortable confines of this hole in their own imaginations that they developed their ideas about the motive power the market, the waged character of freedom, the biological character of race, and the social and cultural salience of geographical space that have shaped our nation to this very day.

Reflections on Law, Culture, and Slavery

ARIELA GROSS

INTRODUCTION

When I was a graduate student trying to pursue studies in both U.S. history and law, I was keenly aware of the institutional and intellectual divide that prevailed between social and legal history. Time after time, professors asked me to choose whether I would be "using legal records to study society" or "studying the history of law" (which could have no possible interest to students of society). As I became interested in slavery, I found that while there was a rich legal history of slavery, it was primarily an intellectual and economic history; the cultural history of slavery, on the other hand, had been written as though law was largely irrelevant.

Slavery studies were unlike many areas of U.S. history, especially colonial and women's history, which have depended heavily on legal records to give a window onto ordinary people's lives. Since the 1960s, there has been a long tradition in early American history of using county court records to talk about marriage and family, crime, patterns of property ownership, and class relations, to name a few topics.[1] Slavery, however, has been one subject that for many years was thought not to require the use of legal records. To understand the southern white world, one could read the voluminous papers of slaveholders: their plantation books, their diaries, letters, the newspapers they read and the writings they published, their agricultural journals, and so on. To understand the world the slaves made, one could read the narratives of slaves and ex-slaves, the novels, the newspapers, listen to the songs and other folklore, and even interviews made decades later of people who had once been enslaved. Furthermore, cultural historians of the South tended to assume that rituals of honor, for whites, and plantation discipline, for blacks, replaced law as mechanisms to resolve conflicts.[2] So for many years, archival legal records went untouched.

I do not mean to suggest that historians showed no interest in law, but only that the realms of law and culture remained quite distinct. Twenty-five years ago, at the time of the first Fortune Symposium, historians were reading the published reports of opinions by Southern high courts, as well as the laws enacted by Southern legislatures, for evidence of Southern whites' ideology—their beliefs and fears about the women and men they held in bondage. Charles Sydnor, Kenneth Stampp, Eugene Genovese, and James Oakes are prominent examples of historians of slavery who discussed Southern statutes and appellate reports of criminal and constitutional cases.[3]

These scholars came to the law for historically specific reasons. In a reminiscence delivered about six years ago at a symposium entitled "Bondage, Freedom, and the Constitution," historian Stanley Katz described the North Carolina case *State v. Mann* as the "central text" of Southern slavery law.[4] His disquisition on this case perfectly captured a generation's groundbreaking study of slavery and law. Many scholars are no doubt familiar with the case—the slave Lydia ran away from her master John Mann, who shot her in the back as she fled. Judge Thomas Ruffin of the North Carolina Supreme Court held that "the power of the master must be absolute, to render the submission of the slave perfect."[5] This extreme conclusion, sanctioning Mann's actions against Lydia, he argued, was logically compelled by the institution of slavery. *State v. Mann* has triggered many pages of commentary by legal philosophers such as Robert Cover along with southern historians.[6] James Oakes compared *Mann* to the decision five years later by Judge Gaston in *State v. Will*, asserting the power of the community and the state to limit the absolute dominion of the master.[7] As Katz explained, historians and moral philosophers alike were captivated by the *Mann* case because it posed so starkly the ethical question of how a "good" system, the common law, could do evil. In the wake of the Vietnam war, there was an intense interest in the moral responsibility of people within the "system" to defy norms that had gone wrong. These historians took the perspective of the judge in analyzing a case like *Mann*, viewing legal doctrine primarily as ideology. Some suggested that Thomas Ruffin was an "antislavery" judge who pushed the logic of slavery to its limit to expose its horror. They debated whether Ruffin was constrained by the legal system, or whether he could (like Judge Gaston) have decided the other way. And they used the *Mann* case to draw conclusions about the essential nature of Southern law as an instrument of slaveholders' power, or as in constant tension between the slaveholder's power over the slave and the state's power over the slaveholder.

Today there is no single case, no "central text," that has attracted as much scholarly attention as *Mann* or the Dred Scott case did two decades ago. Cultural historians with an interest in law, and legal historians with an interest in culture (all of whom I will call cultural-legal historians), have begun to look at bodies of trial-level records in order to view the law from other perspectives. In a decade in which successive "trials of the century" (Rodney King, O. J. Simpson) have both laid bare racial divisions and shaped the way we talk about race in our daily lives, historians have become interested in the cultural power of trial stories. Trial records seem to shed light on the consciousness of ordinary people, opening a window onto the ways law was understood not only by judges but by litigants, the spectators in the courtroom, and the slaves themselves. Increasingly, historians are turning to trial records rather than appellate opinions, and looking at a broad range of everyday disputes that were decided by legal forums—disputes over contracts, torts, property and inheritance; petty criminal cases; and the regulation of race, gender and sexuality, with particular attention to the role of gender and sexuality in the legal "construction" of race. These works draw on a variety of methods from other disciplines, but particularly on ethnography and performance studies.

Thus, the barriers between "legal history" on the one hand, and "social history using legal records" on the other (which were presented to me as a graduate student searching for a dissertation topic as two hermetically sealed realms), are breaking down. By uncovering new archival sources of law, and asking new questions of legal records, cultural historians have re-oriented older historical debates about whether slave culture was characterized by agency and resistance or should best be described in terms of terrible hegemony; which came first, slavery or racism; and whether American slavery was compatible with capitalism or whether it thrived only in a pre-bourgeois socioeconomic system of "paternalism." They have also contributed to debates about the nature of legal change, and the relationship between law and extralegal norms.

I will start with some of the new approaches to the problem of agency and hegemony in the law; I will then discuss a number of debates about slavery to which cultural-legal history has contributed, and end with what I take to be the chief dangers and possibilities of the new field.

New Approaches to Agency and Hegemony

The most influential interpretations of the role of law in American society have emphasized its function as an instrument of cultural hegemony.[8] Law gave to outright force the stamp of legitimacy. Thus, the first histories of women and the law, slaves and the law, and immigrants and the law tended to portray white women, slaves, and immigrants as people "acted upon" by legal institutions, mostly unjustly, occasionally with surprising fairness.[9] Debate centered on the extent of injustice in their "treatment" by the law. Absent from these discussions was a sense of interaction, or back and forth, between the "subjects" of law (judges and legislators) and the "objects" of law (usually white women and African-Americans).

At the same time, a rich literature in African-American history, working-class history, and women's history portrayed women, workers and people of color as agents in making their own history.[10] Histories of slavery, for example, uncovered the day-to-day resistance of work slowdowns, tool-breaking, and running away; the defiance of slavery in slaves' songs, preaching, and secret writings; slaves' elaborate efforts to maintain family and community ties through naming practices, marrying "abroad," "shouts," and other customs.[11] No less important was evidence of slaves' successes in carving out areas of control—owning chickens, guns, and liquor; hiring out their own time for wages; participating in a vibrant underground economy; taking off holidays and Sundays; and so on.¹² All of these "extralegal norms," as legal scholars would call them, have been described as evidence of an alternative world outside of the law in which slaves exercised agency and maintained African culture. In the 1980s and 1990s, some scholars modified what they saw as too rosy a picture of slave community and culture, emphasizing the limits of slaves' control of their own lives, especially by comparison to other slave and serf societies.¹³ But hegemony and resistance have remained important parameters for the study of slave society.

Yet slaves did not cease to be agents when they entered the courtroom or became subjects of legal dispute. Rather than portraying slave agency as something that could exist only outside the legal system, and the legal system as hegemonic within its sphere, newer histories show that "law" and "social life" were not necessarily "separate spheres." Re-conceptualizing law as an element of culture, a source of cultural narratives and rituals, has allowed legal history to catch up with social history in recognizing slaves and white women as agents; in turn, this work challenges the idea that day-to-day resistance took place only on a private or unconscious level with no public or political dimensions. Resistance in the legal arena had political implications well before the Civil War. Ten years ago, James Oakes demonstrated the impact of slaves who escaped to the North on sectional conflict by chronicling the significance of the battle over fugitive slave laws; runaway slaves also tipped the balance in the War itself as "contraband" soldiers went to fight for the Union.¹⁴ But day-to-day running away, even "petit marronage" as it was known in Louisiana—running away for a few days and returning—also took on public significance when it called into question the mastery and honor of white men who were held responsible for slaves' character in suits for breach of warranty.

White Women's Gossip Networks and Community Resources for Resistance

Here I just want to briefly call attention to some of the excellent work on the agency of outsiders to the law that has been written about southern women. Kathleen Brown's study of race, gender, and law in colonial Virginia, for example, shows the ways that colonial women helped to shape trial and pre-trial procedure when judges called on "good wives" to examine women in cases of miscarriage, abuse, and rape.[15] Midwives, for example, brought official testimony to county courts about the age, physical health or appearance, and paternity of children they delivered. Women's networks of gossip and sexual and reproductive experiences also influenced the conduct and outcome of trials. Gossip was a powerful weapon in battles over social and political position, and the courts' reliance on women's gossip networks may have lent women more power as litigants in the disproportionate number of slander suits women brought in the seventeenth century.[16] The women's world of gossip on which some jurists relied was not exclusively white. Indeed, in one 1714 infanticide case, the chief witnesses for the prosecution were Mary, an African slave and an Indian servant who, although they did not testify directly, transmitted stories about a child in a chamber pot to several male neighbors who testified in court.[17]

Laura Edwards' work on the nineteenth-century South reveals that women brought another kind of lawsuit in surprising numbers—they took their husbands before magistrates and local courts for domestic violence, and were sometimes able, at the lowest level of the court system, to win legal intervention. In both these histories, what appeared from appellate opinions to be law as a hegemonic force controlled by household heads and judges, at the local level, appears much more contested. The point of this work has been not so much to paint a picture of glorious resistance and triumphant agency, but to show that even hegemony takes *work*; as Edwards shows, "[t]he law had to assert *continually* the power of white male household heads precisely because, in practice, that power was neither complete nor stable."[18]

Slave Agency

Unlike white women, slaves could bring only one form of litigation to court, a manumission suit. Thus it is more difficult to find the traces of slaves' own consciousness in legal records. By turning to other sources of African American consciousness, however, it is possible to piece together evidence of slaves' attitudes to law and to commerce, and to speculate about how they might have understood or tried to influence legal transactions. Slaves were certainly keenly aware of the power of law in their lives. African Americans who fled slavery and went on to write or narrate their stories of bondage and escape often commented on the injustice of the white man's law— "*their* judges, *their* courts of law, *their* representatives and legislators."[19] Many, if not most, fugitive slave narratives listed the variety of ways that law made blacks into property and deprived them of rights, sometimes quoting statute books by section number and page.[20] Jon-Christian Suggs's wonderful study of law and African American narrative, *Whispered Consolations*, highlights the centrality of law in African American consciousness.[21]

Slaves were also acutely aware of their own status as objects of property relations and commercial transactions; they could be mortgaged, put up as collateral in credit transactions, split between life estates and remaindermen, or just plain sold down the river. As James Lucas, an ex-slave from Adams County who once belonged to Jefferson Davis, explained to a WPA interviewer, "When Marse Davis got nominated fur something, he either had to sell or mortgage us. Anyhow us went back down de country. . . . I bleeves a bank sold us next to Marse L. G. Chambers."[22] Richard Mack noted that when he was ten years old he was "not really sold, but sold on a paper that said if he didn't take care of me, I would come back—a paper on me—a kind of mortgage."[23] In one dramatic incident, ex-slave Solomon Northup told a tale of his divisible status saving his life. When his cruel master, Tibeats, was about to hang him in a rage, Northup was saved by the overseer, Chapin. Chapin gave two explanations for his action on Northup's behalf: first and foremost, he explained that his "duty [was] to protect [William Ford's] interests . . . Ford holds a mortgage on [Northup] of four hundred dollars. If you hang him he loses his debt. Until that is canceled you have no right to take his life." Only as an afterthought did Chapin add that "You have no right to take it anyway. There is a law for the slave as well as for the white man." Solomon Northup owed his life to the overseer protecting the mortgage interest against the owner of the slave.[24]

Slaves did their best to exert control over transactions in the marketplace involving commerce in their own bodies. As Walter Johnson has persuasively demonstrated, slaves did what they could to shape commercial transactions in which they themselves were the object of the transaction.[25] Slaves tried to undermine sales by making known their feelings about the sale, or communicating things they thought would be considered failings, from physical defects to character flaws, to the buyer. Many ex-slaves wrote of their attempts to influence market transactions—combined with the fear of the utter futility of such efforts. Charles Ball, for example, recounted his mother's attempts to keep from being sold separately from her child, but also about the danger of a slave "speak[ing] the truth and divulg[ing] all he feels."[26] When Ball himself was questioned by a prospective purchaser of whom he had "formed [an] abhorrent . . . opinion," he answered as neutrally as possible, that "if he was a good master, as every gentleman ought to be, I should be willing to live with him."[27] Ball hoped on the one hand to dissuade this "wretch" from buying him, and on the other hand to save himself from "the violence of his temper" should he "fall into [the buyer's] hands."[28] Another former slave recounted the danger of being tricked by an owner: "The mistress asked her which she loved the best her mammy or her daddy and she thought it would please her daddy to say that she loved him the best so she said 'my daddy' but she regretted it very much when she found that this caused her to be sold [along with her father] the next day."[29]

Given slaves' awareness of their own legal status, and the many recorded instances of slaves running away to former owners to keep their families together, or engineering sales to be closer to a spouse or relative, it would not be surprising if some slaves realized in some instances that running away or illness could result in a legal suit whose outcome might be the rescission of their sale.[30]

There are a number of ways to talk about slave agency and the law: several have already been discussed—the likelihood that slaves consciously sought to manipulate litigation involving them; the reflection in court cases of slaves' extralegal efforts to control their own fate or to resist the institution of slavery by, for example, running away, defying orders, trying to shape their own or family members' sales, trying to control their own medical treatment, and so forth. But what is equally, if not more important, to emphasize, is the evidence of the fear and anxiety white southerners felt and expressed about slaves' resistance and moral agency, and their capacity to control their own fate, and the way this *fear* of slaves' agency shaped litigation. That is, trials demonstrate not so much slaves' direct ability to influence the law, but their indirect influence through the efforts of judges as well as masters to *control* slaves' agency. Slaves acting as moral agents were able to throw into question the honor and character of white men in the courtroom, and in response, southern lawyers and judges (unlike southern witnesses and litigants) told stories about slaves' character that minimized or denied slaves' agency.

One South Carolina case in 1838 illustrates this point. In *Johnson v. Wideman*, there is evidence of a great deal of behavior by the slave Charles that contravened formal law but at least some of which accorded with extralegal social norms: visiting a wife "abroad"; owning a dog; drinking and gambling with white men; but also verbally and physically assaulting white men; defending his wife's honor against a white man; and declaring he wished he *were* a white man.[31] He may or may not have done all of these things. It seems likely he did some of them, because there is evidence given by both sides of some of them. So, on one level, legal records give us some evidence of actual resistant behavior that may be surprising to some students of slavery. It is also possible, although we have no direct evidence of it, that Charles himself hoped to be returned to his former owner through this lawsuit, and that he misbehaved in order to be returned. Charles did not speak in court because of the ban on slave testimony; all our evidence is indirect.

We do see the development in the courtroom of several stories about slaves' character, and masters' character, and we see the way Charles' actions threw open for courtroom discussion the character of several white men—their mastery and implicitly their honor. Charles' buyer,

Wideman, portrayed Charles as an insubordinate and vicious drunkard and runaway, while the seller, Johnson, claimed that Charles behaved badly only under bad government by a bad master, "a drinking, horse-racing man."[32] This is the case in which Chief Justice of the South Carolina Supreme Court, who also sat as trial judge, articulated the theory of "like master, like man," in holding Charles' buyer responsible for his character.[33] In doing so, he accepted the theory of slave character most likely to deny Charles agency: Charles himself was only a reflection of his master.

This effort to deny agency was constantly under stress and contest as slaves continually demonstrated otherwise. Just as slaveholders were anxious about slaves' ability to deceive and manipulate them by feigning illness or passing for white, judges were anxious about allowing matters of slave character to be discussed in the courtroom, where they could throw a white man's mastery into question. Fifteen years before the *Johnson* case, the South Carolina Supreme Court had tried to foreclose litigation of slaves' character by ruling that contracts for the sale of a slave for a good price did not imply a warranty of "moral qualities." Judge Abraham Nott held that warranting slaves' good character would be like "opening Pandora's Box upon the community"; opening courtroom contests over slaves' character could give slaves the opportunity to indirectly influence the law.[34]

Performances of Identity

Another way that historians have begun to discuss the agency of slaves and other outsiders in the law is to draw on the notion of racial and gender "performance," both from Judith Butler's theory of the performativity of gender, and from the field of performance studies, in theater and in anthropology.[35] Approaching trials as a place where people perform identities, an arena for the representation of self, tends to lead historians to emphasize individual agency in creating one's own identity. In a recent article, Walter Johnson discusses Alexina Morrison's performance of "slave-market whiteness," in which an enslaved woman suing for her freedom claimed to be white but performed her whiteness through degrading rituals of bodily display that mirrored the slave market more than anything an "authentic" white woman would ever have to withstand.[36]

How should we interpret these performances of whiteness by enslaved women suing for their freedom? For example, in the freedom suit of Sally Miller, who claimed to be a German redemptioner kidnaped into slavery, her lawyer, in his closing statement, dramatically called the attention of the jury to Sally's demure presence. He asked them to look at her, not only at her color, which could be the same as that of a "Quartronne" (a woman with one-fourth "African blood") but at her "moral features"—her simplicity, sexual purity, industry, prudence.[37] Sally Miller's attempt to prove whiteness on the basis of moral character and sexual virtue no doubt confirmed to a wide audience the ideological connections between degradation and blackness on the one hand and among morality, virtue, civic ability, and whiteness on the other. And Sally Miller's successful suit for freedom by no means suggests that the nineteenth-century South was a free-wheeling world in which people could "try on" racial identities as they pleased. It is certainly possible to read their trials as merely reinforcing hegemony. As Eve Sedgwick has written about academic attempts to decide whether performances like passing for white reinforced the status quo: "The bottom line is generally the same: kinda subversive, kinda hegemonic."[38]

Sedgwick's words remind us of the circularity of the hegemony vs. resistance debates that have sometimes dominated slavery studies. Recent historical work has emphasized the subversive aspect, partly in reaction to earlier work that came down so definitively on the side of hegemony, and it will not be surprising if the next revisionist historians emphasize hegemony. Yet it is valuable to recognize that the unpredictability of courtroom battles over "race" allowed *some* enslaved women and their lawyers to fashion performances—and narratives about performance—that they used to win their freedom. White abolitionists also used these weapons in their battle to bring freedom to all southern slaves.

A Household Approach to Slavery and Law

Another important trend in the new cultural legal history has been to look at the regulation of slavery within the context of regulation of the household. Historians such as Stephanie McCurry, Elizabeth Fox-Genovese, and Nancy Bercaw have already reshaped our understanding of Southern politics and class relations by disrupting old ideas of "public" and "private," and revealing the political content of "private" matters such as intra-household relations.[39] Legal historians Peter Bardaglio and Laura Edwards have pointed out that not only were white women and slaves part of the same households and the same web of social relations, but the relations of husband-wife, parent-child, master-servant, and master-slave were legally conceptualized as part of the same category of domestic relations.[40] These writers are careful not to equate the social and legal position of white women and slaves uncritically (in other words, they are not merely echoing nineteenth-century feminists who claimed that they were slaves), but they seek to put the study of law and slavery back into its contemporary context in which all domestic relations were perceived in terms of one's relation to the master of the household.

Some treatments of the household, primarily relying on statutes and appellate opinions, have tended to assume a static patriarchy with little room for legal contestation. Stephanie McCurry argues that households were made inviolable by law in South Carolina—household heads were "masters of small worlds" with power over every aspect of domestic relations, including incest, rape, child custody, and family property. Peter Bardaglio, looking at appellate legal doctrine across the South, argues for a shift from patriarchy of the sort McCurry describes before the Civil War, to what he calls "state paternalism" and legal historian Michael Grossberg has termed "judicial patriarchy," in which courts were more likely to intervene on behalf of individual family members at the expense of the head of household after the Civil War. Victoria Bynum portrays courts upholding the will of the master of households against married women and slaves, and taking the position of the patriarch against "unruly" single women when there was no head of household to discipline them.⁴¹ All of these works tell an important part of the story of the law of domestic relations, but not the whole story.

Laura Edwards, whose recent work on domestic violence uses trial records from North Carolina, sees a more complicated and contested picture of southern law. Edwards emphasizes the power available to domestic dependents, both white women and enslaved men and women, because they were part of a larger community. She places violence against domestic dependents in the context of violence against white men, and locates change at an earlier moment, the political moment of the Revolution, arguing that "[a]fter the Revolution, when the body politic became the white male citizenry—and was no longer the King—a whole range of 'private' injuries theoretically became 'public' wrongs."⁴² While domestic dependents, including slaves, wives, and children, remained subjects, violence against whom was a private injury, white men became citizens against whom violence was a public wrong. Thus, perhaps the southern patriarchal household was a relatively new thing—which may explain its contestability.

Historians working with trial records have also begun to examine more closely cases of rape or sexual coercion of women in the antebellum era—thinking about enslaved and free women, African and white, together so as to discern both commonalities and contrasts. Recent research suggests not only that the roots of the myths that supported sexualization of politics and lynching in the post-Civil War era reach back to the antebellum period, but also that white servant women and enslaved African-American women had certain things in common.⁴³ Sharon Block compares the experience with the law of a white servant woman who was raped, Rachel Davis, and that of Harriet Jacobs, the fugitive slave whose story of sexual coercion is well known to students of southern history as the narrative of Linda Brent. While the servant woman Block describes was able to have her father use legal apparatus for retribution against the rapist, which Harriet Jacobs could never do, Block found a number of parallels in the two cases.⁴⁴ The experience of sexual coercion itself was not dissimilar for the white servant and the enslaved African American: both struggled to avoid their masters' overtures; both were beaten or otherwise abused by their mistresses when they tried to have them intervene; both hid the truth even from people close to them for a long time. Block suggests that although white and black women had very different legal resources available to them to resist their masters' domination, much can be learned from comparative study of their experiences.

All of these works tie legal history much more closely into the historiography of women's history, slavery, and the American South. Just as the new work emphasizing the agency of individuals in making law and contesting legal processes has challenged the assumptions of much southern history that the courtroom was one place where elites exercised hegemony, the new work on households calls into question the idea that law uniformly bolstered the authority of patriarchal household heads. This work also challenges us think about "race relations" and "gender relations" together in the social locations where power is exercised, in particular the "private realm" of the household.

Historical Reinterpretations: Regulation of Sexuality and Race

Seeing the "law" differently suggests new ways to look at old historical problems. We need now to turn briefly to some of the historical reinterpretations that have resulted from the cultural approach to legal history. One important aspect of this new work has been its focus on the role legal regulation of marriage and sexuality have played in racial formation, relying on local court records from the colonial era through the twentieth century.

The Rise of Racism and the Origins of Slavery

Many U.S. history students begin their study of slavery by reading the famous Degler-Handlin debate over whether Europeans' enslavement of Africans followed from their early beliefs in racial inferiority and associations of "blackness" with evil, or whether modern racism derived from the experience of slave relations that had grown out of economic imperatives.[45] The question of how much weight to accord to race and to class in shaping the course of southern history and the institution of slavery has animated many seminar rooms and lecture halls. Building on the magisterial work, *White Over Black*, in which Winthrop Jordan demonstrated both the early racial attitudes of English and early Americans, and at the same time the gradual invention of the modern ideology of racism within an international and institutional context, legal historians have tried to add specificity to the study of the origins of race, racism and slavery, thereby endeavoring to avoid a race vs. class debate.[46] Walter Johnson suggests that "descriptions of the relation between economic exploitation and racial domination might be sharpened by attention to everyday life, to the specific historical sites where race was daily given shape," including church pulpits, medical and agricultural journals, as well as courtrooms and slave markets where buyers and sellers "marked" race in their discussions of the bodies and character of slaves.[47] Cultural legal histories emphasize the importance of the courtroom as a site of race-making.

Kathleen Brown's study of race and gender focuses on colonial Virginia. It was in Virginia that Bacon's Rebellion occurred, a pivotal moment in the transition to slave labor. The tobacco farms of the Chesapeake provided the earliest testing ground for plantation slavery. Brown's great contribution to the study of the beginnings of race and slavery is to forcefully inject gender into the analysis. She accomplishes this "engendering" of the history of race by focusing on law. Indeed, legal records have allowed historians as never before to bring together the study of race and gender. Brown essentially argues that gender relations provided the template for discriminatory race relations; the "subordination of African women to the needs of English labor and family systems . . . ultimately provided the legal foundation for slavery and the future definitions of racial difference."[48] For example, the first treatment of Africans as different under law in Virginia was a 1643 tax on African women. Even English women who worked in the tobacco fields were legally classed as dependents, on the assumption that, like children and old men, they were too weak to produce much; African women were classed as "tithables" (individuals who performed taxable labor).[49] A 1668 statute clarified that even "negro women set free . . . ought not in all respects to be admitted to a full fruition of the exemptions and impunities of the English" and still had to pay the tax. Thus lawmakers gave English exemptions "an explicitly racial meaning."[50] Brown examined tax-exemption petitions in several county courts and found that a free black woman had to "demonstrate dependent status by proving her physical disability" in order to "enjoy the privileges of English women."[51]

Legal regulation of sexual relations and childbirth further contributed to the sharpening of racial difference. While fornication cases in the mid-seventeenth century appear to have been handled similarly whether the offenders were African, English, or an "interracial" couple, "[t]he real test for the applicability of English family law to enslaved Africans was . . . cases where women serving life terms became pregnant."[52] Beginning in 1662, legislation decreed that children followed the condition of their mother, and in the same act, that "if any christian shall committ fornication with a negro man or woman, hee or shee soe offending shall pay double the fines imposed by the former act."[53] "Christian" did not long remain adequate as a legal marker of difference; by 1667, baptism was no longer enough to free one who was born a slave.

The earliest restrictions on sexual activity aimed their discipline at white women; in 81 percent of the cases enforcing the 1662 law banning interracial intimacy, white women bore the brunt of the expense and punishment for the transgression.[54] But existing laws regulating white women's sexuality were increasingly used by lawmakers "to refine the legal meanings and practical consequences of racial difference."[55] Over the course of the late seventeenth century, a shift occurred in punishments for bastardy, from penance rituals to secular punishments, especially money damages to masters, treating sexual wrongdoing less as a sin and more as a crime. There was a "growing overlap between patriarchal privilege and racial domination."[56] In rape cases, women lost their suits against white men, but won against black men.[57]

Early evidence in the court records of racialized ideology already shows the linkage made between race and sexuality, for example, in the insult that a woman was "such a whore that she would lye with a negro." Over the course of the seventeenth and eighteenth centuries, the typical sexual slander suit changed from a white man suing a white woman because she claimed he had slept with her and abandoned her, to a white woman suing someone, often another white woman, who alleged that she had slept with a black man. Allegations of interracial sex were enough to threaten the white status of an English woman.[58]

Yet Brown does not portray law as a hegemonic force in creating the meaning of racial difference. She argues that "[r]acialized patriarchy and sexualized concepts of race created new ways for white men to consolidate their power in a slave society but did not suppress individual negotiations of behavior and identity."[59] Brown devotes a close reading to the case of Thomas(ine) Hall, a seventeenth-century Virginian of ambiguous sexual identity, who at different times in his/her life, passed as a man or a woman. Hall deeply disturbed the residents of Warraskoyack, Virginia, where he lived as a male servant to John Atkins. His dressing as a woman spurred Atkins and other neighbors to petition the General Court to punish Hall "for his abuse."[60] Hall told the justices of the General Court that he had lived his first twenty-four years as Thomasine in England, then dressed as a man to become a soldier. When he returned to England, he resumed his female identity, but became a man again in order to emigrate to Virginia in 1627. "For Hall," Brown writes," "the social expression or performance of gender identity was as malleable as a change of clothes and seems to have been partially motivated by opportunities for work."[61]

Hall was not the only one who sought to determine his gender identity; his neighbors in Warraskoyack also had strong opinions about who he was. When plantation commander Nathaniel Bass ordered Hall into women's clothes after physically inspecting him, the married women of the neighborhood strenuously objected and demanded to make their own inspection, claiming that he was a man. It was they who insisted his case be taken to the General Court. The justices reached a different conclusion than the women, Bass, or Hall himself: they sentenced him to a "permanent hybrid identity," wearing man's breeches but women's "Coyfe and Croscloth with an Apron before him."[62] Hall's identity, then, was determined by neither biology nor a single top-down definition, but by a long negotiation among officials, neighbors, and the individual himself. That does not mean that Hall succeeded in fashioning the gender identity he chose for himself; indeed, the justices' sentence was doubtless a humiliating punishment. But his performance, and the narrative he gave the court describing his performance, was an important part of the process of creating his identity.

In a variety of contexts, legal regulation of sexuality, and legal differentiation between African and white women helped to construct racial difference and enforce racial boundaries at the same time that the distinctions between slave and servant were becoming more pronounced. Kathleen Brown's work suggests that law was central to the process of negotiating racial identity, and that women played a crucial role in the negotiations. She asks us to turn our attention away from the question of which came first, slavery or racism, to take a closer look at the way deepening racial differentiation in law and changing meanings of servitude reinforced one another, often through the regulation of sexuality and gender.

Those who have argued that slavery preceded modern racism claim that racism and the category of "race" as we know them only emerged in the nineteenth century. Historians of racial ideology such as George Fredrickson and Reginald Horsman have read literary sources and the writings of the master class, to chronicle a shift in the justifications for slavery from "a necessary evil" to a "positive good" as southerners felt themselves under attack by abolitionists beginning in the 1830s and 1840s; the positive-good defense of slavery rested on a new articulation of race as a scientific category.[63] This account, while extremely persuasive, equates nineteenth-century racism almost exclusively with a medical and scientific discourse of "racial science"—vague and antique notions of a "Chain of Being," the study of African and European crania, and so forth. My study of trials of racial determination suggests that this story of the social construction of "race," emphasizing the rise of racial science, is incomplete. Because, until recently, the role of law in the culture of race and racism has been obscured, important aspects of race have remained in the shadows.

A variety of disputes litigated claims of whiteness, from suits for freedom on the basis of whiteness to criminal cases in which the defendant raised whiteness as a defense to an indictment, to inheritance disputes, suits for slander, witness disqualification cases, or suits against transportation companies who carried off runaway slaves who passed for white. In these cases, litigants, witnesses, lawyers, judges and jurors wrestled with the determination of an individual's racial identity and with the proper basis for such a determination—in other words, not only with the question of who was black, white or Indian, but what made them so. In the courtroom, both medical experts and laypeople spoke of race as science, recounting their views of an individual's heels or hair follicles or fingernails as evidence of hidden African "blood"; but they also discussed race as performance, the way the person at issue held himself out, danced at a party, whom he married, whether he voted or sat on a jury. This discourse of race as performance rose *alongside* discourse of race as science, beginning in the 1840s, and retained its salience over the course of the nineteenth century. Science and performance evidence might work together in a particular case—Alexina Morrison, for example, had doctors testify to her whiteness along with lay witnesses talking about her performance at balls and her white character, while witnesses for her master saw her "negro blood" both in the shape of her heel and in her sexual transgression. Or performance might trump science, as in cases where documentary evidence of ancestry was less persuasive to a jury than reputation evidence. But this suggests that legal discourse operated in the same cultural field as medical and other racial discourses and all contributed to ordinary people's understanding of racial identity.[64]

Paternalism vs. Capitalism

Another debate that has bedeviled historians of slavery has been the longstanding controversy over Eugene Genovese's characterization of the South as a paternalist, prebourgeois society inserted into a world system of capitalist socioeconomic relations. Despite the fact that contemporary historians rarely endorse this view explicitly, and many take pains to revise or renounce it, it has been remarkably influential on work in fields outside southern history and its influence continues to this day. To take one example, Amy Dru Stanley's recent prize-winning work of legal history, *From Bondage To Contract*, which is centrally concerned with antislavery and Reconstruction, reproduces Genovese's stark contrasts between the South and the North in socio-economic relations as well as culture.[65]

A generation of historiography has been animated by the effort to prove or disprove the Genovese thesis, including much of the legal history of slavery exploring the relationship between southern law and economic development. Mark Tushnet, writing in 1981, presented the Genovesean position, arguing that southern jurists attempted to divide the law into separate realms of humanity, into which master-slave relations fell, and "interest," in which market relations resided.[66] A series of articles by other authors compared the development of particular legal rules in the South and the North; if they developed differently, this was evidence that southern judges sought to protect slaveholders rather than industrial developers, and that the South was in fact paternalist and pre-capitalist. If the rule developed similarly, then the South was capitalist like the North.[67] Either way, the fact that judges instrumentally chose rules to maximize the interests of the powerful class suggested the fundamental sameness of law in South and North. Thomas Morris's large study of slavery and the law seeks to show a movement *from* paternalism *to* capitalism in commercial and property law, interrupted by the Civil War, rather than the dominance of one system or the other.[68] A recent work by an economist on the subject concludes that in any given instance, no matter how the rule developed, it did so because that was the efficient result, and the common law tends towards efficiency.[69]

A cultural approach suggests ways to avoid this debate, by demonstrating what Walter Johnson has called the "obscene synthesis of humanity and interest."[70] As comparative historians of slavery have argued, "paternalism" is most usefully defined as an ideology rather than as a system of social relations.[71] It is an ideology that can be found in very different societies. And as Walter Johnson shows, within American southern society, paternalism was "something slaveholders could buy in the slave market."[72] In my research on breach of warranty cases, for example, I found that a capitalist legal rule, like caveat emptor ("buyer beware"), was justified by the most paternalist language. The argument most frequently made by slave sellers, that a slave's character reflected his master's character ("like master, like man"), depended on paternalist imagery of the master as prudent father of a family giving his slaves firm moral guidance and setting a strong example. Yet "like master, like man" suggested that the buyer of a slave should bear responsibility for the slave's character because he could mold the slave in his own image if he were master of his own household and his own character. Thus, the proper legal rule was "buyer beware," the sales rule that facilitated capitalist exchange, according to historians of nineteenth-century contract. So facile equations of legal ideology and economic development are dangerous.

What, then, does the new work teach us about the southern economy and its relationship to law? For the most part, it bolsters the efforts of historians like James Oakes to show the importance of market relations to southern culture and to slavery, but it also demonstrates that values of honor and patriarchy associated with paternalist ideology could co-exist comfortably with the marketplace. Looking at the culture of the slave market and the commercial dispute in the courtroom, rather than at particular doctrinal rules, makes it difficult to argue that the law could be separated into distinct realms of humanity and interest. The rule of caveat emptor was not experienced by slaveholders, sellers and buyers, simply in rational, wealth-maximizing terms—who will be the most efficient bearer of the risk of sale based on information costs? Rather, the rule grew up in the context of trial stories about the character of masters and slaves, and these stories were fought and felt more passionately—and more anxiously—than would make sense if we see these litigants as only rational economic actors. Unfortunately, slavery was all too compatible with market capitalism, but at the same time, market capitalism did not mean that everyone behaved simply as rational wealth-maximizers. They brought their culture of honor and whiteness into the courtroom with them.

Promise and Pitfalls

Perhaps the greatest promise of cultural approaches to law and slavery is their evocation of the rich fabric of local life, the messiness of law as it was lived on a day-to-day basis by ordinary people. This localism also poses the chief hazard of cultural approaches: how to reach conclusions or sustain theoretical frameworks about law, race, and slavery save that of "complete confusion." Walter Johnson, whose own work is a shining example of cultural-legal history, has argued in a recent review essay that the overarching theme of the study of law and slavery should be, neither contradiction (between liberal legalism and slave property regimes, or between capitalism and prebourgeois slave society, or between the slave as person and property), nor transformation (from equitable paternalism towards capitalist formalism), but rather "complete confusion."[73] Johnson despairs of reaching general conclusions about the legal history of slavery, because, he argues, "[e]very case was an open contest over the pressing question ... what is slavery?"[74] If hegemony was always locally contested, and rules articulated by high courts were always only partially enforced and locally negotiated, then how can historians identify any single pattern, whether a single contradiction, or a set of consistent transformations?

In part, Johnson's jeremiad for the field is the warning of the historian to the social scientist, insisting on the contingency of human agency against the determinism of any broad theoretical framework, whether it be Gramscian hegemony, neoclassical economic efficiency, or evolutionary functionalist legal history of economic development. Yet historians have generally provided synthesis through a master narrative of change over time. "Bottom-up" local studies in many fields have challenged our ability to fashion such a master narrative. In some fields, like civil rights history, where new local histories revised the earlier narrative periodized in terms of the lives of great leaders and national organizations, it seems possible to replace these with a newly periodized history reaching farther back in time and emphasizing the local roots of civil rights protest and organization.[75] Cultural-legal histories of race and slavery have not yet provided a new master narrative of change over time, perhaps precisely because they have been so concerned with challenging the historiographic emphasis on origins stories.

A related concern to that of complexity regards causation. If earlier answers to the relationship of law and culture were too simple and overarching, at least the causal arrows usually pointed in one direction: law reflected economic interests or racial ideology; alternatively, legal developments influenced people's lives; or both at different times. But cultural histories of law resist the language of causation, at the same time as they repeatedly make claims that sound to many listeners like causation claims. Most cultural legal history is committed to the "mutual constitutiveness" of law and culture. Throughout this essay, I have made arguments about cultural narratives that *shaped* trials, or stories told in the courtroom that had cultural *influence* outside the courtroom. On the one hand, this sounds at least similar to a "mutual causation" language, describing some kind of legal-cultural feedback loop. On the other hand, the work described here strives to avoid viewing "law" and "culture" as separate realms with causal arrows pointing from one to the other, even from each to each. How to avoid this dilemma, to portray law as truly part of culture, yet a distinctive institution within a particular culture, with its own language and tradition and ritual?

One strategy is to distinguish between "constitutiveness" and "causation." For law to be constitutive of social relations suggests the following: law is part of the way people conceive of their identities, which make sense to them only in relation to others; those relations (husband-wife, parent-child, master-slave, black man-white woman) are regulated by law and understood (at least in part) in legal terms. As Hendrik Hartog wrote in his recent history of marriage in America, "Perhaps you didn't need law to fall in love. But you needed law to know that you possessed a 'private' life and the capacity to pursue a happiness or misery that was distinctively your own. . . . You needed law to know yourself as married 'really,' as committed beyond public conformity; you needed law to know that you possessed rights unasserted, legal opportunities forgone, virtue unqualified by strategic advantage."[76] Trials as a cultural ritual are part of that constitutive process. People create identities through the performance(s) of trials. While there are causal elements to this process of constituting identity, it is a fundamentally different *kind* of causation claim than those made in traditional law-and-society scholarship (both specific claims such as "the law changed because powerful people lobbied the legislature" and more general ones such as "law reflects elite interests").

This approach to causation is not wholly satisfying to those who yearn for a null hypothesis. The skeptic asks: How could one disprove the "mutual constitutiveness" of law and culture? Of course, if one finds a legal phenomenon and a similar phenomenon in the wider culture, it is easy to say that they are "mutually constitutive"; but how would one know if they were not? Isn't this just a self-fulfilling prophesy?

And, if that were not enough, there is the more general problem of proof that comes with any narrative approach to history. How are we to know that these examples are the right ones? Isn't this history merely anecdotal and unverifiable? This is perhaps the easiest of the objections to answer, so I will start here. Briefly, the strongest aspect of the new cultural legal work is its breadth of research. The mining of county-level archival data, the research into a broad range of sources, and in many cases, the rigorous quantitative analysis accompanying the narrative history, obviate these concerns. By looking at large numbers of records, and going to other sources such as manuscript census schedules and tax rolls, it is possible to give some backing to our claims of typicality and representativeness when we talk in depth about particular examples. Of course, historians still make choices about which examples to highlight in a narrative and which stories matter, but our choices can be informed by a large database of cases, and complemented by quantitative analysis of the cases. For example, Christopher Waldrep has been able to compare types of crimes before and after the Civil War, participation in Warren County courts by race, and to reconstruct literacy rates and property holdings of grand jurors over the course of the postbellum period.[77] In Adams County, I discovered that the majority of petit jurors in civil cases were nonslaveholding townspeople, and that they were two and a half times less likely to give a verdict for a wealthy planter who sued in circuit court than for one of more modest means; this quantititative finding influenced my readings of trials involving planters.[78]

As for complexity, confusion and causation: there will not be a single, satisfying answer here. Cultural legal histories will not give general maxims of prescription or even of description on the level of "law reflects the interests of the elite." Yet cultural histories offer real insights precisely because they break down easy assumptions based on monolithic models. And if there are no over-arching mantras to be applied to every problem, there are some generally useful heuristics: approach legal processes as cultural narratives and performances; attend to the negotiations between higher-level and lower-level actors; look for the ways that the relatively powerless nevertheless influenced the law. These ways of writing legal history do more than simply throw monkey-wrenches into others' carefully-conceived dichotomies (race/class, hegemony/resistance, capitalism/paternalism). Instead, they allow scholars to move to another level of exploration: assuming that both race and class played a role in shaping the beginnings of slavery, what part did gender play? How, specifically, did legal regulation evolve to distinguish between African slaves and white servants? No matter what you believe about the primacy of race over class or vice-versa, it is important to know that the regulation of African *women* in particular played such a crucial role.

A cultural approach allows us to see that slavery (and, by implication, other forms of racial inequality or institutionalized racism) is unfortunately all too compatible with market capitalism and with "white men's democracy." By restoring people of color and white women as agents of historical and legal change, even as they faced tremendous obstacles, a cultural approach also makes clear that law cannot be understood outside its interpretations by ordinary actors in their daily lives, and that means taking into accounts all perspectives, not only those of white male judges and legislators. Enslaved and free African-Americans initiated lawsuits, influenced cases to which they were not parties, and reacted creatively to legal developments they were powerless to influence; colonial white women shaped cases involving rape, miscarriage and slander through their gossip networks and their control over the examination and investigation of women's bodies. And cultural approaches demonstrate that through the regulation of sexuality and marriage, as well as in litigation, law played an important role in forging racial categories and identities.[79]

* * *

Commentary

LAURA F. EDWARDS

Ariela Gross's paper is structured around the refutation of dichotomies. She begins with the one binary—legal history vs. social history—that she battled as a graduate student. But questioning such fundamental assumptions is like opening Pandora's box. Only in Gross's paper, the result is not pandemonium. Instead, she shows that rethinking that basic dichotomy recasts a whole series of other historiographical oppositions: hegemony vs. agency, paternalism vs. capitalism, fluidity in race vs. the hardening of those categories. Reading the paper is like watching a row of intellectual dominos falling in chain reaction. Like the painted, wooden dominos that children used to play with, each of these southern history dominos appeared as separate, distinct entities while standing. Only after the first one wobbled, tilted, and fell in the right direction, was it clear that they were all connected. Therein lay the attraction of the game. Therein lies the power of this paper.

Gross does not trifle with details. At stake are virtually all the issues that have defined the history of the nineteenth-century South. Gross does a brilliant job of laying bare the false oppositions that have structured the literature, and then shows how and why southern historians' attentions might be more profitably directed elsewhere. I am sympathetic to this approach and enthusiastic about the results. My comments are critical in another sense. They engage some of the key ideas in Gross's paper, elaborating on their implications and then pushing them a bit further. In keeping with Gross's central theme, I will begin with the separation of the legal from the social and consider what the fusion of the two means for southern history. Then my focus turns to three related issues: 1) historical agency; 2) connections among topics previously considered separately in the literature; and 3) synthesis.

Since Gross has opened up the door to back-when-I-was-in-graduate-school-experiences, I will succumb to the temptation and begin there as well. Gross's account of her own encounter with the separation of legal history from social history hits home in a number of ways, except that the legal side was singularly absent in my case. I was trained in the what now appears to have been the last wave of the "new" social history—although the literature is no longer "new," as graduate students now remind me, with a little more glee than I consider necessary. I counted things in the census, and was proud of it. In fact, I did not know a single soul in graduate school who even wanted to do legal history. If they did, they kept it to themselves—probably for fear of what might happen if they admitted it publicly. This situation seems more than a little ridiculous now. It also seems more than a little odd, because of the yawning, unexamined contradiction in the dismissal of all things legal. For even as my cohorts and I rejected the law, we were all interested in power. More specifically, we were critical of the way that much of the "new" social history isolated ordinary people from politics, broadly defined. And we believed that the connection between ordinary people and politics could unlock the mysteries of power dynamics. Yet no one imagined that the law had anything to do with the issue.

Social history nonetheless led me to legal sources for evidence. Local court records, in particular, yielded fascinating information about people who did not appear elsewhere in the documentary record. They also shed light on the interactions of such previously anonymous people with the people and institutions that exercised power over them. As Gross points out, using these local court records was hardly path breaking. Historians in other fields have long relied on this kind of material to find information about people who did not appear in traditional archival collections. Yet, as Gross also notes, few southern historians had tapped these sources at that time, and so the information that was uncovered was new in the field of southern history. But any insight into the period stopped at information. Leaving basic historiographical categories in place, I used that information to answer questions as they had been framed by social historians. As strange as it now seems, it never occurred to me nor did anyone else suggest that I might need to understand the law to understand the legal sources I was using. Gross's paper explains why that was. Legal history and social history were distinct, unrelated fields. More than that, law and society were two separate arenas of life. With that assumption firmly in place, I did not see any need to understand the law because I did social history, not legal history.

That intellectual divide held until after I finished my dissertation. After the first flush of victory wore off and I began turning the dissertation into a book, I ran up against a brick wall. Local court records yielded example after example of people doing all sorts of things that they were not supposed to do. I shaped this evidence into an impressive history of defiance, assuming that any action that brought someone into court was, by definition, a defiant confrontation with "power." But I had no way to explain why such actions were important, other than to insist that defiance, by definition, was important. The analysis became increasingly unsatisfying and its tautology became increasingly difficult to ignore. I was left with a history of continual defiance that never really made any difference in power relations, a conclusion that undermined the importance that I so insistently and energetically ascribed to these defiant actions. In the midst of this crisis, Michael Grossberg made a comment that I will never forget. Don't you think, he asked me with a smile that I now recognize as one of amusement, that you ought to know something about the law if you're going to able to understand what people are saying and doing in their cases and why? You can't just do any old thing in court. There are rules that structure that arena, you know. His remarks stopped me dead in my tracks, and changed everything. I found myself in the position Gross describes, trying to explain why the law was relevant to southern historians who identified themselves as social, not legal historians.

I tell this story both to emphasize and elaborate on Gross's opening point about joining law and society in southern history. The conceptual implications are key, and they may get lost given the empirical grounding of Gross's paper. She does emphasize what new evidence has done to change our view of the slave South. As a result, it may seem that her primary point is about evidence: that recent work in legal history is important because of the new information that it uncovers. That information, in turn, alters the way we understand the period. But that is only part of Gross's argument. Her paper also shows the limits of uncovering new information to fit within existing historical frameworks. Such an approach can actually be counterproductive if historians do not know how to handle the evidence. That was the point of Michael Grossberg's comment to me about how important it is to understand the laws that shaped what people were doing in the courts. Gross knows this as well, and she is taking us further, inviting us to see the slave South in fundamentally different terms. She is pushing us to break down the intellectual barriers that make us think of legal history and social history as distinct fields and, then, to rethink the connections between law and society. Doing so, she argues, will change the questions that we bring to the past and what we see in our evidence. She is talking about a fundamental shift in our thinking.

Gross justifies this conceptual shift by demonstrating the specific results for key historiographical debates. But here Gross both undersells what she is doing and ducks some difficult questions about the stakes involved. By way of explaining some of the impetus for the new work that unites the social and legal, she briefly alludes to current trends both within and outside the academy, including celebrity trials that highlight the cultural power of courtroom proceedings and academic work on agency and performance. The sources of the changes in the historical literature, however, run much deeper and involve larger questions about the way we understand power and politics both today and in the past. Those questions, I think, are why the connection between law and society seem so relevant to historians now. To take myself as an example, it was my concern with power that first drew me to legal sources. Then, with some prompting, it was a nagging sense that I was not quite getting what the evidence in those legal sources had to do with the operation of power that led me to study the law proper. Considering the growing literature that moves in this same direction, I do not think I am alone here. Clearly, other historians see the law as a profitable route to understanding power.

At the same time and for the same reasons, the sense that we still do not understand power hangs over both Gross's paper and much of the work that forms the heart of her historiographical critique. And the effort in that work to grapple with power in the past comes from the sense that we do not have a handle on it today. That ambiguity–confusion, even—manifests itself in a certain analytical tentativeness. In both Gross's paper and the work that she critiques, there is a reluctance to universalize beyond the specific, often local historical context to a larger, linear narrative of change over time. Where others may construe that reluctant quality negatively, it strikes me as extremely productive. It is precisely what allows Gross to think in conceptually innovative ways about the history of the slave South. Moreover, despite Gross's own unwillingness to replace the master narrative with a new one, the combination of wary reluctance and bold innovation does suggest directions for a creating a new kind of narrative synthesis.

Those possibilities are evident in the historiographical issues that Gross covers. The first one that figures prominently in her analysis is the question of historical agency. As Gross argues, "Re-conceptualizing law as an element of culture, a source of cultural narratives and rituals, has allowed legal history to catch up with social history in recognizing slaves and white women as agents; in turn, this work challenges the idea that day-to-day resistance took place only on a private or unconscious level with no public or political dimensions." Gross's catalog of examples, beginning with James Oakes's path breaking work showing how the actions of runaway slaves figured into the battle over fugitive slave laws, is impressive. Then she deftly links these examples together to demonstrate the point that ordinary people, and slaves in particular, did influence the shape of the law and its application.

As Gross argues, the unintended and indirect consequences of slaves' actions were as important as those that were conscious and direct. "What is equally, if not more important, to emphasize," Gross writes, "is the evidence of the fear and anxiety white Southerners felt and expressed about slaves' resistance and moral agency, and their capacity to control their own fate, and the way this *fear* of slaves' agency shaped litigation. That is, trials demonstrate not so much slaves' direct ability to influence the law, but their indirect influence through the efforts of judges as well as masters to *control* slaves' agency." In her analysis, slaves' actions outside the institutional legal arena *always* shaped the law and, in a larger sense, governance more generally. As Gross's analysis suggest, slaves' power cannot be measured by their ability to influence the outcome of particular cases. Nor are the lines of causality always linear and direct. Yet, even though they could not always control the larger political implications of their actions, slaves still played a decisive role in the governance of southern society. Such a perspective, then, opens up the possibility of analyzing slaves' connections to the southern polity in ways that include actual slaves and the substance of their daily lives, instead of focusing on the institution of slavery in the abstract or dramatic moments of slave unrest, as the literature tends now to do.

I am pushing the implications of Gross's analysis here. These implications, moreover, are troubling. Despite the sophisticated literature that now surrounds the concept of hegemony and resistance, historians of the antebellum South still tend to evaluate resistance in terms of the victories of the agents. Successful resistance occurs when slaves get what they want. Attributing agency when that does not happen seems akin to blaming the victim. Nonetheless, as recent work in other fields suggests, the implications are worth pursuing. The fact that slaves did not achieve intended, let alone beneficial results for themselves does not make their actions any less important to the history of the slave South. At the very least, those defeats shaped the next round of battles. Moreover, if we count only moments of victory as historically significant, then it will always be impossible to include any marginalized group within the dynamics of history in any sustained way.

More importantly, Gross's analysis of slaves' agency moves the issue beyond the historiographical debates in which it has long been mired. At first glance, it may sound exactly like the kind of dynamic in Genovese's concept of paternalism. Genovese's antebellum South was the world the slaves made. In his analysis, slaves' actions were central in the construction of paternalism and the maintenance of planters' hegemony, both of which worked to maintain slavery. Yet Gross's analysis points in a new direction, because it is based on a fundamentally different conception of the connection between law and society.

That she does posit a different connection brings me to the next main issue, that of connections among topics previously considered separately in the historiography of the antebellum South. As Gross points out, Genovese's analysis rests on an instrumental view of law. That approach to the law is deeply ingrained in the literature, even among those who reject Genovese's concepts of paternalism and hegemony. This approach presumes a particular kind of separation between law and society, based on a particular understanding of power. In this approach, law and society are connected only to the extent that slaveholders used the law to maintain their position of power. The unstated assumption is that slaveholders' already established that position prior to entering the legal realm. That victory is what allows them to use the law. By extension, only slaveholders have the power to mount the barrier between law and society. Slaves and other people without power in the social realm cannot, and thus are largely irrelevant in law, except as objects. Such a perspective renders the law merely instrumental in the sense that it is a tool that those already in power can use to maintain their power. While important in that sense, the law is unnecessary in understanding the actual dynamics between slaveholders and slaves that produced slaveholders' power and slaves' lack thereof in the first place. To the extent that the law reveals conflict at all, it is between those people in power—a clash between the interests of individual slaveholders and the collective interests of slaveholders represented in the state. In fact, the logic is circular: it is possible to demonstrate that slaveholders did have power by showing that they consistently "won" in the legal arena. Such logic, alone, should give us pause about the assumptions underlying the instrumental view of law and its application to southern history.

By contrast, Gross sees the law in fundamentally different terms. In her analysis, the law is not an instrument that can ever be completely captured by one group. Rather, it is a complex ideology that can exist independently of any particular group, that contains a number of different meanings, even contradictory ones, and that can be taken in a number of directions. Even when the law is theoretically consistent, as Gross also points out, it can have multiple, unforeseen outcomes in practice. As in the case of determining racial identity, legal definitions break down when they have to be applied to actual people who do not necessarily fit neatly into pre-existing categories. From this perspective, the effects of the law on society and of society on law are always complicated and contingent.

Gross's view of the law is partly the result of evidence: where southern historians once stopped at statutes and appellate cases, Gross focuses on local court records. Looking at daily practice makes the law look less definitive and less unified, by emphasizing actual people and all the contradictions that made up their lives. At this level, we see the law constantly mediating conflicting ideas, values, and practices that historians have so often posed as dichotomous contradictions: the culture of honor versus the rule of law; the tenets of liberal legalism versus a regime that defined some people as property; the denial of slaves' agency versus the acknowledgment of it; the economics of capitalism versus those of a pre-bourgeois society; adherence to static racial categories versus the indeterminacy of race; the affirmation of patriarchal power versus the limitations on it; the distinctions among different household dependents versus the similarities in the logic of their subordination. At this level, we can also see how the mediation of all these seemingly contradictory constructs did not amount to a zero-sum game where the victory of one side meant the total defeat of the other.

Yet Gross's view of the law is not just a matter of evidence. Gross is positing a different relation between law and society, based on a different understanding of power. In her analysis, "society" always intrudes on "the law." The people involved all participated in shaping the content of law, even if they never intended to do so. They all brought their notions of justice with them into the courtroom and tried to manipulate the law to advance their own immediate interests. Conversely, "the law" is always part of "society. " It is so in the direct sense that local court cases were a public, highly symbolic means of working through the rules of appropriate communal conduct. And it is so also in the indirect sense that "the law" included both the legal culture of all those involved and accepted rules of conduct not found in law books. Gross uses the evidence in local court cases to question the dichotomous categories that have defined southern history, because of the way she sets up the relationship between law and society. She does not just present us with quirky exceptions at the local level that get ironed out as cases moved up the system and the law reasserted the unified interests of slaveholders. If anything the legal system magnified the multiple, conflicting values that defined slaveholders as a group and southern society as a whole. Gross is thus presenting us with a view of southern society that is defined *through* contradiction. Examples of contradiction are not exceptions to the rule. They are not challenges that occasionally present themselves to a pre-existing, unified power structure (however that might be defined) and that must be contained to maintain the integrity of that structure. Instead, contradictions are the constant, dynamic tension that defined power dynamics. They are the essence of the antebellum South.

That said, Gross could be more clear about the kind of relationship that she is positing between law and society. On the one hand, she reconfigures the relationship between the two arenas. On the other hand, in reconfiguring the relationship she still maintains the very distinction that she seeks to refute. In the end, law and society speak to each other differently. But we still have law and society, and we still have legal history and social history. That is often the case when questioning dichotomies, because it is difficult to engage the categories without using them and affirming them. It is even more difficult to come up with new categories to replace the old ones. In fact, those new categories often become new oppositions with their own intellectual limitations. Not all dichotomies, moreover, are bad. To the contrary, they can be useful tools for organizing evidence and understanding the past. Perhaps those oppositions between law and society, legal history and social history are ones that we want to keep. But it would be interesting to explore the issue instead of assuming it.

The final point is the issue of narrative synthesis. Having torn down so many of the intellectual edifices that have structured so much of antebellum southern history for so long, Gross is left with the inevitable question of what she is proposing to replace them. What is the new overarching synthesis? She rejects "complete confusion," an idea that Walter Johnson recently floated with perhaps a little more flippancy and humor than can be communicated in the pages of a historical journal. To Gross, "complete confusion" offers nothing coherent to replace the dichotomous frameworks that have defined historical work on the antebellum South which she also rejects, namely contradictions *in* time, such as those between capitalist and pre-bourgeois values, or those *over* time, such as the transition from a pre-bourgeois society to a capitalist one. Yet Gross ultimately avoids the issue by listing her findings in a way that suggests tinkering around the edges of existing paradigms.

Tinkering, however, does not do justice to the power of Gross's analysis. If not taken quite so literally, "complete confusion" does offer direction, although not a final resting place. The idea that constant tension is what characterizes the antebellum South does not lend itself well to a linear narrative—the kind of narrative that most historians associate with a coherent synthesis. The emphasis on conflict and contradiction means that there is no identifiable, unified "essence" of southern society. Nor does that unified "essence" change over time and to become a different, but still unified "essence." Given expectations of what constitutes a satisfying historical narrative, the result may seem like "complete confusion." But, from another perspective, "complete confusion" could be a leap necessary to move out of existing frameworks. "Complete confusion" could be productive, *if* it could lead somewhere else. Only when we let go of what is familiar will we be able to set off in new directions. Accepting the confusion and working through it will make that journey rewarding and exciting. It is what will ultimately allow us new insight into the past. Of course, that conclusion dodges the question of where we are going and what the destination will be. And, admittedly, I do not really know the answers to those questions. But I think that Gross's analysis has underscored the necessity of this journey and pointed out paths that we might pursue. We might, for instance, look for new terms through which to gauge change over time, instead of focusing on whether the South becomes more or less liberal and capitalist over time. We might abandon conceptual frameworks that define the South primarily in terms of its difference from or similarity to the North. If we do, we may find that the South becomes "more" or "less" something entirely different over time. Or we may find the process of change to be far less linear. We may find, in the specific context of the antebellum South, that capitalism and liberalism produce changes that are not exactly what we have come to expect. Perhaps the more liberal and capitalist the antebellum South became, the less like other liberal, capitalist societies it became. We may find ways to abandon the trappings of linear narrative altogether, with its emphasis on opposition of A to B or the transformation from A to B over time, although I find it difficult to imagine what such an analysis might look like, let alone come up with an example. Nonetheless, the possibilities that might present themselves if we open ourselves up to "complete confusion" are the most exciting parts of Gross's paper. If we accept "complete confusion" as a challenge, Gross's insights become starting points for rethinking the entire historical terrain of the antebellum South.

Rape in Black and White: Sexual Violence in the Testimony of Enslaved and Free Americans

NORRECE T. JONES, JR.

In light of the culture of racism that English and European elites began to codify legally in the second half of the seventeenth century and the dominance of men both preceding and long after this, it comes as no surprise that scholars looking back at the more than two centuries of bondage in North America have seen fit only to examine at length the sexual violence for which there is the least and most exceptional evidence. That they have relied primarily on the testimony of free people with the greatest interest in upholding the vision of slavery as enslavers saw it, rather than on the evidence from those enslaved, should not be a revelation but probably will be for some. The distortions inherent in this historiographical tradition provide a panoramic view of why the study of slavery in America is such a complex exercise filled with more than its share of the emotional clamors and chilling silences that historians must face.

Pick up any broad or specialized work on slavery and search its index, table of contents, or elsewhere for the word "rape" and you probably will not find it.[1] If you do, it will typically be an overview of what scholars today as well as contemporaries from the colonial period through the Civil War consistently have affirmed was an atypical occurrence: the rape of an English, European, or European American woman by an enslaved African or African American man. So uncommon was this sexual violence that when James Hugo Johnston wrote his doctoral dissertation in 1937, he found: "It is a common belief that the crime of rape committed by Negro men against white women was nonexistent before the Civil War; . . ."[2] As Johnston and others have established, this was a myth.

Not only did such rapes take place, but before the idea of race—and its progenitor, white supremacy—had dug deep roots throughout colonial America, blacks accused of sexually attacking white women could sometimes get a fair hearing and possibly a lenient verdict if the woman alleging to have been violated was of low status and, most important, were she known to have had non-coercive contacts with African or African American men.[3] But before any discussion of how the social construction of race affected the peoples interacting with each other in British mainland North America, we need to return to the issue of testimony.

One may reasonably ask why historiographical attention has been so intensely focused on the rape of white women when both indirect and direct evidence from a period of two centuries overwhelmingly points to a preponderance of rapes by English and European men—whose identities eventually would be subsumed into the powerful classification, "white race"—of enslaved women whose primary identification ultimately would be lowered and reduced into a membership designation no less significant, "black race."[4] From my perspective, the primary source for the most accurate assessment of this and any other type of sexual violence should be that of those victimized. Such testimony, that is, from the enslaved women who were raped, is rare. And, in the most literal sense, so too is that of enslaved Americans.

Only if one loosely defines "slave testimony," no document other than that written by or recorded for someone still in bondage should be so classified. Such testimony does exist. A number of people who self-emancipated themselves and fled to free territories were "legally" still enslaved when they wrote or dictated their accounts of bondage to amanuenses. Fortunately, the most extensive and detailed account of the sexual violence to which enslaved women were subjected was written in part while its author was still, at least in law, a slave. Writing under the pseudonym, Linda Brent, in hopes of keeping her prominent North Carolina owner off her trail, Harriet Jacobs published, *Incidents in the Life of a Slave Girl*, in 1861. Finding the courage to overcome both her fears and the societal dictates of what was considered acceptable public discourse, Ms. Jacobs recounted what was nothing less than psychological warfare between herself and her master. Beginning in adolescence and lasting until she was physically beyond his reach, the physician who owned her, Dr. James Norcom, subjected her to mental torture that he sometimes augmented with physical violence, all to convince her to have sexual intercourse with him.[5] She succeeded in never doing so, but what one historian describes as "mute evidence" reveals that most enslaved women who were targeted in this way, lost that particular battle.[6]

As I have argued elsewhere, the best way to understand relations between and among enslavers and those that they enslaved is to view slavery as a state of war.[7] The appropriateness of this analogy is given added force when one considers that in the long annals of human ingenuity in brutalizing and dehumanizing each other, rape has been a terrifyingly persistent one of men at war. To signal the vanquishing of their enemies, soldiers frequently have invaded the bodies of their counterparts' women and occasionally those of young men as the crowning declaration of an absolute victory. It is sometimes forgotten that all of the men mingling on the soils of America were from patriarchal societies in which women were held as possessions and where men dominated through their control of the most valued political, economic, and social power. With this in mind, the legislative cordoning off of women throughout the colonies by elite males for themselves takes on new significance.

The women who fared worst in this formal process of possession were African or African-descended females. Those enslaved were made tempting prey by laws that declared one's status followed from one's mother. Such legislation made it possible for a master to escape any fiscal or legally-enforced moral responsibility for a slave that he owned, raped, and impregnated. And, if she bore him a child, he was able to add at no additional cost another chattel to work or simply to hold for possible sale. Apparently overlooking this and other benefits, Maryland legislators—perhaps in their haste to keep any more white women from marrying or engaging in sexual relations with black men—failed to realize the implications in a 1664 law that read in part:

> *Bee itt Enacted . . . That . . . all Children born of any Negro or other slaue shall be Slaues as their ffathers were for the tenure of their lives[.] And forasmuch as divers freeborne English women forgettfull of their free Condicon and to the disgrace of our Nation doe intermarry with Negro Slaues . . . Be itt further Enacted . . . That whatsoever free borne woman shall intermarry with any slaue from and after the Last day of this present Assembly shall Serue the master of such slaue dureing the life of her husband And that all the Issue of such freeborne woemen soe marryed shall be Slaues as their fathers were[.]*[8]

They soon corrected themselves and revoked that portion on paternal status descent, since failing to do so would among other things, increase the free mulatto population (the "mute testimony" alluded to earlier) "at the same rate," in the words of historian Willie Lee Rose, "that white men impregnated slave women." Rose concludes: "Thus rapidly did an important fundamental of English law give way before the combined forces of racial antipathy, sexual license, and the need of an exploitable labor force in the new plantation country."[9]

Until the late eighteenth century, much speculation and inference is needed to determine the nature of interracial sexual relations and violence. No less than today, those who raped tended not to leave written trails. And those victimized by rape rarely were in positions to seek redress or even to tell who had raped them without the severest of consequences.[10] But the paucity of direct evidence during British colonialism does not mean that no exploration of this important topic is possible. With careful research, some imagination, and a modicum of common sense, much can be learned. There is no question, for instance, that the women who faced enslavement in crossing the line that was being drawn to racialize America had more than a little affection for the men with whom they chose to connect. Because the unfree desired nothing more than freedom, it is reasonable to assume that those granted liberty—particularly women who had borne children by their masters—were more than objects of pudendal pleasure. This would not of course necessarily speak to the mother's feelings. What we do know is that while the majority of colonial free blacks were mulattoes, most mulattoes were slaves.

By the last third of the seventeenth century, a broadening spectrum of nonblack males were privileged as men in a patriarchal society that defined power at the most rudimentary level as owning property, one's own labor, and being in control of all those within his household, including his wife, children, and any servants or slaves. No matter what their status in other areas, white males were advantaged by membership in the ruling race, extending the phrase historian James Oakes has used to describe the planter elite and the slaveholders' aspiring to join it.[11] And while their sex denied them full privileges, white women were also beneficiaries by placement in this racial classification. However difficult it was for them to bring any male who may have sexually violated them to justice, they were increasingly able to do so successfully if whoever they charged with rape was black. In a world where such violence was seen as an offense against the man whose patriarchal authority had been trespassed and where free patriarchs were generally given full rights over and access to the women within their domain, this was no small achievement. It also explains the dramatically disproportionate number of black men in comparison with white men who were executed after being charged with rape.[12]

Just as white women and white men were being advantaged in a widening array of ways, black men and black women were being disadvantaged. What already had been decidedly narrow avenues for non-English women to seek legal and social redress for sexual attacks, began to close completely in colony after colony. In fact, the wheels of white supremacy were moving ever faster in the direction that would eventually make the rape of a black or enslaved woman a juridical impossibility. The worldview guiding this movement received clear articulation from a Reverend T. T. Brown in 1762. Intervening on behalf of a fellow white accused of "abusing a 'Mulatto wench,'" he communicated to the New York Attorney General that, "If Negro's are protected in their insolence . . . but an old Country man indicted for every little Crime, twill be time for us to leave this Country, & leave it to its old Inhabitants."[13]

In what had become so unwaveringly a white man's country, Native American, African, and African American women were open territory. None suffered more than those women who were socially, politically, and racially least free. Some hint of this can be gleaned from the "humorous" disregard for the sexual rights and marital commitments of enslaved women. Encouraging a proposal to stock East Florida with more human chattels, slave trader, agent, and merchant John Graham wrote the Governor in 1765 that a "few likely young wenches must be in the parcell, and should their Husbands fail in their duty, I dare say my friend Sweetinham and other publick spirited Young Men, will be ready to render such an essential service to the Province as to give them some help."[14] Just how widely such services could be rendered, this time in the name of nothing more than opportunity, was indicated that same year in the Georgia *Gazette*. Angered not by what it would be difficult to imagine were anything other than wholesale rapes, a Georgia patriarch fumed that a white in his employ during the course of his "four month stay" had "infected every negroe wench on the plantation with a foul, inveterate and highly virulent disease."[15] Exactly how many other overseers damaged property as this one did is unclear, but there are more than ample records of those who left in their wake a number of mixed-race sons and daughters whom they had fathered without the invitation of the enslaved women in their charge.[16]

In *Stolen Childhood: Slave Youth in Nineteenth-Century America*, historian Wilma King writes: "As an instrument of terror, rape generally accompanies war. . . . If slavery were indeed like war, then it follows that rape occurred."[17] For African Olaudah Equiano, slavery was a state of war. He wrote in 1792, "When you make men slaves, you deprive them of half their virtue, you set them, in your own conduct, an example of fraud, rapine, and cruelty, and compel them to live with you in a state of war. . ."[18] This perspective no doubt was shaped by his observations during the years that he was enslaved.

An Igbo captured as a young boy in what is present-day Nigeria, Equiano experienced enslavement first-hand in Virginia, in various islands of the Caribbean, and in Great Britain before being permitted to buy himself and thereby to secure his freedom. Recounting what he saw on ships with captive females, he recorded this: "While I was thus employed by my master, I was often a witness to cruelties of every kind, which were exercised on my unhappy fellow slaves. I used frequently to have different cargoes of new negroes in my care for sale; and it was almost a constant practice with our clerks; and other whites, to commit violent depredations on the chastity of the female slaves; and to these atrocities I was, though with reluctance, obliged to submit at all times, being unable to help them. When we have had some of these slaves on board my master's vessel to carry them to other islands or to America, I have known our mates commit these acts most shamefully, to the disgrace not of christians only, but of men. I have even known them gratify their brutal passion with females not ten years old. . . ."[19]

When Olaudah Equiano wrote his autobiography, he was not a slave; obviously not a woman; not an African American, and, at least to our knowledge, not a victim of rape. Nevertheless, he, as so many others after him throughout the nineteenth and early twentieth centuries, left invaluable documentation of the pervasive subjection of enslaved daughters, mothers, sisters, wives, aunts, and nieces to rape and to a boundlessly ingenious multitude of other forms of sexual violence. Apparently choosing to accept the testimony of more than a few racist scholars during the first half of the twentieth century who dismissed the written words and oral histories of those most intimately familiar with bondage as little more than abolitionist propaganda, instead of examining the autobiographies, pamphlets, interviews, and recollections in which those antislavery accounts appeared, historians have barely tapped the priceless insights and knowledge contained within the treasure-trove, that for convenience sake, we may call "slave testimony."

Until the truths of slavery as the enslaved understood them are fully mined, our understanding will be for just that long incomplete. To date, what has been written—or perhaps more accurately, not been written—about the aspect of slavery that is the focus of this paper can be explained by the obfuscations inherent in any examination that pays more attention to the oppressor than to the oppressed.

Nothing captures more starkly the danger in such a skewed view than the decision of more than a few scholars to accept the logic of free patriarchs or supporters of slavery on matters of rape. Because in laws dating back to the seventeenth century, those who owned human property had the right to do with it almost anything they desired, sexual violence had long been a matter beyond the concerns of any secular court; white supremacy had effectively made questions of morality moot for all but the unfree and an always small minority of free abolitionists. Following white-majority thinking during bondage and expressing a not uncommon contemporary outlook, historian Ruth Mazo Karras concludes, "Sexual use of slaves could be violent or coercive but was not considered rape: the slave was the master's property to be used as he wished."[20] The enslaved thought differently.

One example of this opposing way of seeing comes in the rare testimony of a rape victim who was still in slavery when she gave it. Despite the illegality of testifying against a white, she was presented an opportunity to do so when called upon as a witness for her husband, a bondsman named Alfred on trial for murder in 1859. According to the court records of this Mississippi case, Charlotte, the only name we have for her, revealed that in retaliation for their overseer's rape of her, Alfred killed him. That act, referred to by the court as "adultery," neither justified the black man's action nor should or would be considered. The court declared: "Adultery with a slave wife is no defense to a charge of murder. A slave charged with the murder of his overseer can not introduce as evidence in his defense, the fact that the deceased, a few hours, before the killing had forced the prisoners wife to sexual intercourse with him."[21]

It is striking how reluctant even those scholars who recognize and acknowledge the sexual violence that bondswomen frequently endured have been to apply the word "rape." This omission has stemmed in part from their tendency to treat all forms of interracial fornication as a single phenomenon. But it is also a result of their focus usually on free white men. In a book he completed in the late 1970s, historian Joel Williamson made "mixing" his word of choice in *New People: Miscegenation and Mulattoes in the United States*. According to

Williamson, "The rate of mixing by slaveholding white men appears to vary from time to time. As one approaches the 1850s, however, it seems to be rising to a crescendo. Apparently whole families of planter men here and there surrendered sexually and fell over the race line. Whole clans of mulattoes, more slave than free, were created, to the almost inexpressible horror of their white neighbors."[22] At about the same time and in the same way, Bertram Wyatt-Brown, in his acclaimed *Southern Honor: Ethics and Behavior in the Old South* (1982), wrote of what he described as "sexual misconduct." "In the American South, as in England and France," he avows, "sleeping with a woman was an informal rite of virilization. The obvious way was to pursue a black partner. If the initial effort were clumsy or brutal no one would object, in view of the woman's race and status. Moreover, black girls were infinitely more accessible and experienced than the white daughters of vigilant, wealthy families."[23]

"Accessible," how? "Experienced," why? Horrifying, to whom? Were these questions to be answered from the perspective of female chattels, a very different history would be written concerning what historians have called "sexual liaisons" and the women they continue to label "concubines" and "mistresses." While all of these expressions suggest volition, what better captures the essence of most interracial sex is found in Wilma King's *Stolen Childhood*. There she reminds us, "With or without the analogy" of slavery as a state of war, "an untold number of enslaved females became pregnant through forced cohabitation and exploitation."[24] We must remember that not every rape produced a pregnancy and that many pregnancies were no doubt the result of multiple rapes.

Unwilling to wait until he got his fourteen-year old purchase home, Robert Newsome, a sixty-year old Callaway County, Missouri, man, stopped and raped the young girl named Celia whom he had just bought sometime in 1850 from an adjoining county. There is no way of knowing what family or friends she may have been torn from as a result of that sale or what might have been on her mind when she set out on the journey to her new owner's home. That she had two children by Newsome and was subjected to repeated rapes by him for the remaining years of his life are documented in the records of her 1855 murder trial for killing and confessing to have killed this particular rapist. For her crime, she was hanged.[25] Buying slaves for more than their labor and reproductive capacities was hardly foreign in slaveowning America. An 1805 letter to an affluent and unmarried Virginian verifies his reputation concerning a specific category of domestic trade. Of the pickings available on the current market, one procurer wrote: "Girls are more frequently for sale than boys—would you object to a very likely one—*a virgin*—of about 14 or 15."[26]

The enslaved had decidedly few options once masters established their aim. If they were violent, one could resist and possibly be spared the intended assault—or run the risk of being killed in the process. A slave woman could scream for help in hopes that someone would assist her. But she would have been only too aware that the consequences would be potentially life-threatening, if not on the spot, certainly later for any nonwhite—free or unfree—daring to intervene. By the antebellum period, the will of masters, wherever it took them, had become a sacred right and self-explanatory justification, for it had evolved into a worldview so all-encompassing and satisfying that its shadow still obscures the realities of slavery today.

Four years before secessionists attacked the United States military, southern intellectual George Fitzhugh was hardly introducing any new or original thought when he declared in his *Cannibals All! or, Slaves Without Masters*, that "Within the family circle, the law of love prevails, not that of selfishness. . . . Besides wife and children, brothers and sister, dogs, horses, birds and flowers—slaves, also, belong to the family circle. . . . The interests of master and slave are bound up together, and each in his appropriate sphere naturally endeavors to promote the happiness of the other."[27] In this fanciful world, enslaved women were especially privileged: they had to "do little hard work," and were "protected from the despotism of their husbands by their masters."[28]

Despots had long found in patriarchy a divine model; why various reformulations of it—whether called patriarchalism or paternalism—remain the most accepted and widely adopted means of understanding American slavery is more difficult to explain.[29] Whatever else the historians of patriarchs may offer, they have yet to provide any substantive discussion of the impact that their much-proclaimed mutual bonds of loyalties and obligations between enslavers and the enslaved had on slave women and men when they cohered figuratively and sometimes literally into incest.

Just under a year before a brilliant slave abolitionist and visionary named Nat Turner decided to take matters into his own hands and Harriet Jacobs was plotting to secure freedom for herself and her child, two other unfree Americans bound in Virginia made a fateful decision.[30] Two lovers who were willing to risk all for each other were affirmed in their decision to kill a particular father. When their deed was done, a witness said the following about the slave murderers, Peggy and Patrick:

> *The deceased to whom Peggy belonged, had had a disagreement with Peggy, and generally kept her confined, by keeping her chained to a block, and locked up in his meat house; that he believed the reason why the deceased had treated Peggy in this way was because Peggy would not consent to intercourse with him, and that he had heard the deceased say that if Peggy did not agree to his request in that way, he would beat her almost to death, that he would barely leave the life in her, and would send her to New Orleans. The witness said that Peggy said the reason she would not yield to his request was because the deceased was her father, . . . The witness heard the deceased say to Peggy that if she did not consent, he would make him, the witness, and Patrick hold her, to enable him to effect his object.*[31]

That her father was willing to speak publicly of what civilizations the world over have condemned, suggests something not only about the idea of race, but how far it and absolute power could degrade the civilized.

More than three decades ago, historian Winthrop Jordan courageously probed a delicate area of the white male psyche. Finding a pattern of English, European, and American scientific and popular interest in the black male's reproductive anatomy, he speculated that those men whose primary identity eventually became "white," may have feared defeat in an imagined phallic war.[32] If there is any validity to this psychological matter, it would warrant a closer look at the belief by whites—male and female—that enslaved men who conspired to gain their freedom through armed rebellion had no such aim. What they really wanted, so some declared, was to kill white men in order to take their wives.[33] But here again attention shifts to bondsmen rather than to bondswomen. It is not without significance that a number of scholars have found priapean dimensions more noteworthy than the fact that any were in public view. Both boys *and* girls wore sack-like shirts that became equally revealing as those wearing them physically matured. Through such clothing, traditions of punishment, and customs at slave auctions, white girls, boys, women, and men were able to paint sexually a group portrait of the enslaved among them.

It is now well established that one's sex was no safeguard against partial or complete denuding when being whipped by masters, mistresses, or anyone else in their network of controllers.[34] Although normally neither men nor women were forced to strip beyond the waist, this was not always the case. After escaping from slavery in South Carolina during the 1830s, six feet, five inches tall Moses Roper, a mulatto, described how his owners, a Mr. and Mrs. Hammans, were especially cruel in the lashings following his unsuccessful flights for freedom. Comparing the two, he said, Mrs. Hammans was the worst: "She used to tie me up and flog me while naked."[35]

To determine whether their prospective purchases were a "troublesome property," or in some other way less than healthy, those mounted on auction blocks were forced to undress in varying degrees so that buyers could make closer inspection. Such degrading displays of black flesh—and the active participation of mistresses in it—point to another problem with paternalism: its focus on patriarchs deflects attention from the matriarchs with whom they shared racial power. Although the testimony of the enslaved suggests that they found no more attractive any fictive contracts negotiated through the wives of patriarchs than they did those consummated through their husbands, new insights about bondage can be gathered from further study of slaveholding women—particularly if done not wearing paternal lens. An appreciative comment made by a free black man hints at why.

Freed through a daring 1848 escape that he and his wife made from Georgia, William Craft commended the former mistress of the woman he married. Whereas some female enslavers who preferred not to whip their slaves themselves would send them to the local jailhouse for chastisement, she never did. Why both he and Ellen Craft, his wife, were so appreciative is suggested in what he disclosed about the fate of some female slaves who were sent out for their lashings. In reference to this "common practice of ladies," he wrote, "it is a fact, that the villains to whom those defenceless creatures are sent, not only flog them as they are ordered, but frequently compel them to submit to the greatest indignity."[36] If he was alluding to rape and that it was known to those who ordered their punishment, then a closer scrutiny of slave testimony may reveal much more about plantation mistresses than we now know.

No aspect of slavery, other than ownership itself, was more widely and consistently condemned by former slaves—or those most familiar with them—than the sexual violence that so many of them had to endure. The full range of that violence has yet to be explored. Although there is no direct evidence of homosexual and lesbian sexual attacks, for instance, does not mean that they did not occur. Indeed, there is no reason to assume that these slaveholders were any less predatory than their heterosexual counterparts.[37]

In a similar vein, the paucity of testimony concerning the rape of slave females by enslaved men is hardly proof of its nonexistence. There are accounts both explicit and suggestive of sexual exploitation by slave men of slave women.[38] It is probable, however, that because resistance to a black was safer in some ways than opposing a white and that anyone victimized by such violence could likely count on retaliation from various segments of the enslaved population, there were checks against black male rapists. Much remains to be examined in regard to sexual violence and slave men. And there are more than a few complications in this area of research. The case of Sam and Louisa Everett, two "pitifully infirm" Florida residents, who were interviewed in 1936 exposes just one.

No doubt because the interviewer was a woman and an African American, the Everetts shared a painful chapter of their lives which began approximately in 1846 for Louisa and 1850, for Sam. Even then, the worker from the Negro Writers' Unit of the Federal Writers' Project,

Pearl Randolph, commented that "it was with difficulty that they were prevailed upon to relate some of the gruesome details recorded here."[39] What Randolph heard were the circumstances of their union. Both were owned by a planter called "Big Jim" McClain near Norfolk, Virginia. In addition to inviting his friends over for their choice of young women—married or single—and sometimes raping them in front of their husbands or lovers, he also compelled chattels whom he thought would produce large and profitable children to mate. The Everetts were such a pair.[40]

In the words of Mrs. Everett, whose name during bondage was "Nor," this was how it happened:

> *Marse Jim called me and Sam ter him and ordered Sam to pull off his shirt—that was all the McClain niggers wore—and he said to me: Nor, 'do you think you can stand this big nigger?' He had that old bull whip flung acrost his shoulder, and Lawd, that man could hit so hard! So I jes said 'Yassur, I guess so,' and tried to hide my face so I couldn't see Sam's nakedness, but he made me look at him anyhow.'*
>
> *'Well he told us what we must git busy and do in his presence, and we had to do it. After that we were considered man and wife. Me and Sam was a healthy pair and had fine, big babies, so I never had another man forced on me, thank God. Sam was kind to me and I learnt to love him.'*[41]

Not all men were like Mr. Everett and there are accounts of those who used the authority of masters to compel women to marry them without the consent of those women. And while we know there were husbands and lovers who lost their lives in defense of the women they loved, we cannot ignore what Harriet Jacobs had to say about some men: "Some poor creatures have been so brutalized by the lash that they will sneak out of the way to give their masters free access to their wives and daughters."[42]

In his essay, "Professing History: Distinguishing Between Memory and the Past," Elliot Gorn warns that Americans are becoming "a people without history," holding on, instead, to memory—thus clouding inevitably our ability to see. As historians, he argues, we must "bear witness to the past, including its horrors, in order to battle the amnesia that would sweep away all that is difficult or repugnant."[43] What historians with rare exceptions have virtually ignored is the reality and significance of the hundreds of thousands of African and African American mothers and fathers during the course of slavery in North America who raised, lovingly by almost all accounts, the sons and daughters of white rapists as their own.[44] Thanks to a British actress, Frances Kemble, who provided a brief window of opportunity for a number of enslaved women to tell of their sufferings safely, and to the careful research of William Dusinberre, we have the details of one such couple.[45] One year after a slave woman named Betty married her husband, Frank, and she gave birth to their first child, Betty was raped by the overseer's son. His father, Roswell King, Sr. had raped at least three women himself and impregnated each. One can only imagine the anguish that the young parents experienced during the nine months that Betty carried the young King's child. How they managed during the years of raising their second-born and several others after Roswell, Jr. became overseer, replacing his father in 1819, is unimaginable. This is all the more the case when one considers that Frank held a position of authority on the plantation as a driver, that is an assistant to the overseer. This meant that on the vast and demanding Georgia plantation of the extraordinarily wealthy absentee patriarch, Pierce Butler, Headman Frank, as he was known, would have encountered on a daily, weekly, monthly, and yearly basis the man who had so brutalized his wife. But this black man with his black wife made their union and all of Betty's children a family.[46]

With more clarity than I will ever possess about sexual violence and enslaved Americans, allow me to close with the testimony of what one free woman who had been a slave never forgot during her estimated one hundred years of living in America, from birth as a human chattel in Powhatan, Virginia to enslavement in Georgia and Louisiana, and old age in Alabama:

> *I was growed up when the war come, an' a mother befo' it closed. Kain't til you nothin' 'bout dem days any more dan dey was Hell—Suckin' babies*

snatch' from dey mudders breas' an sol' to de specalators. Chillen separated from dey sisters an' brudders, an' never see dem any mo. . . . I could tell you 'bout it all day, an' then you kain' even guess 'bout the awfulness of it, belongin' to folks what own you, soul an' body.

    I was born at Po'hattan, Virginia, an' was the younges' of thirteen chillen an I never saw any of my brudders an' sisters except brother William, an' him, an' my mammy, an' me, was brought in a spec'laters drove to Richmon' an' put in a big ware-house, with a drove of other niggahs. Then we was all put up on a block an' sol' to the highest bidder. . . .

    I nevah saw brudder William again. Mammy an' me was sol' to a man by the name of Carter, who was the Sheriff of the County. . . . He was a widower fo' awhile, an' his daughter kept house fer him, an' I nursed for her. . . . One night Ol' Man Carter come in drunk, an' set at the table with his head alollin' roun', an I was waitin' on the table, an he look up an' see me, an he give me a funny look, an' I was scared an' showed it, an' that made him mad, an' he said to the overseer, 'Take her out an' whip some sense in her', an' I run. I run out in the night, an' kept a-runnin', but finally I run back by the Quarters, an' heard Mammy callin' me, an' I went in, an' right away they come for me, an' a hoss was standin' in front of the door at the house, an' I was took that very night to Richmon' an' sold to a spec'later again. I never saw my Mammy any more.'

    I has thought many times through all dese years how Mammy looked that night; an how she pressed my han' n bofe of hers, an said 'Be good, an trus' in the Lawd.'[47]

*   *   *

Commentary

JAN LEWIS

Every once in a while you hear a paper or read a book that changes the way you think. Someone goes over the same material that others have combed through and shows you just what you—and everyone else—have been missing. Often it is not a matter of new research so much as taking the sources that all of us know and looking at them in a way that is so fresh—and so obvious—that you are stunned. Why didn't I see that before, you ask. How could I have missed something so obvious?

It just so happens that the authors of two such works—Annette Gordon-Reed's *Thomas Jefferson and Sally Hemings* and Walter Johnson's *Soul by Soul*—are also contributors to this volume. And Norrece Jones's paper, "Rape in Black and White," is a work of this kind.

But of course—it was rape. Wherever did we think all the mixed-race Americans came from? Love between equals? What a lovely fantasy.

And what else did we think slavery was? A paternalist institution in which the powerful took care of the weak? I suppose some indulge in this fantasy as well, some very good historians among them.

Great history works its magic on the head and the heart. Great history should make you cry, because it makes the majesty and the horrors of the human experience come alive, because it makes you know that what is at stake is our capacity to render past lives in their complexity, to do justice to those who have gone before. And great history should make you shout with joy, from the sheer pleasure of seeing a skilled historian at work. There is a joy to understanding, and to learning what we did not know.

Norrece Jones's paper filled me with tears and joy. It is great history.

To a certain extent, it is a very simple paper, with one simple point: Slavery is warfare, and one of the typical acts of war is rape. Under slavery, ". . . Native American, African, and African American women were open territory."

The point is so obvious that Professor Jones asks, quite reasonably, "why historiographical attention has been so intensely focused on the rape of white women when both indirect and direct evidence from a time span crossing two centuries overwhelmingly points to a preponderance of rapes by English and European men." This is a good question, and I will return to it in a moment. For the time being, let me turn to his brief discussion of the way that racial mixing has been treated in the historical literature. He quotes Joel Williamson, who wrote,

"Apparently whole families of planter men here and there surrendered sexually and fell over the race line." Similarly, Bertram Wyatt-Brown wrote of "sexual misconduct": "If the initial effort were clumsy or brutal no one would object." In these two passages, as Professor Jones shows, the black women who were the objects of white men's lust are completely erased. White men "surrender" and "no one . . . object[s]." That is, no white person objects, for what we are talking about here, at least in some significant percentage of cases, is coerced sex. If, as Wyatt-Brown says, "black girls [sic] were infinitely more accessible and experienced" than white women, it was because they were slaves, without the power to refuse or object. In the historiography, it is all about (white) men's desire; black women are either erased entirely or made the willing objects of that desire.

Professor Jones does not consider, and I wish he had, Eugene Genovese's rather different approach, which is to minimize the degree of racial mixing in the United States and attribute it to a combination of black resistance and, even more important, white restraint. In the light of Professor Jones's paper, this statement now seems quite extraordinary: "Typically, the slaveholders could not take their black 'wenches' without suffering psychic agony and social opprobrium. . . . By the early nineteenth century many slaveholders had become prudes, with enough exceptions to torment the quarters. Even the prudes took their share, but with an uneasy conscience."[1] For Genovese, it is all about white men's lack of desire, and rape is about sex, or sexlessness, rather than power.[2]

Professor Jones makes two simple moves. One is to remind us that slavery was fundamentally about power, and the benefits that accrue to the powerful. Further, he looks at sexual relations between free white men and enslaved black women from the perspective of the enslaved. Suddenly, everything changes. Just look at the slave testimony, he instructs us. He gives us several examples, clear and moving, but this present paper is not a work of extensive research. Rather, it is a new perspective. Professor Jones offers us a new way of looking at old material. He gives us several examples to show us how this old material might look in a new light, and we can fill in the rest. The power of a paper like this is that it makes us reexamine our old understanding. It is a new framework. And thus, we begin to look again at the building blocks of our knowledge of slavery to see how they fit into this new frame.

I am reminded of the W.P.A. narrative of the ex-slave Rose. You are probably familiar with her account, of how Massa Hawkins bought her mother, her father, and herself, keeping them all together. He was, by Rose's account, what might be called a good master. But, Rose noted—and the narrative is in dialect—"Dere am one thing Massa Hawkins does to me what I can't shunt from my mind." He forced her to live with Rufus, "'gainst my wants." After she had been on Hawkins' plantation for a year, he told the sixteen-year-old girl that she was going to live with Rufus, but she had no idea just what that meant. She cleaned up the cabin and fixed dinner, even thought she didn't like Rufus "'cause he a bully." And she thought that was it, until he crawled into her bunk with her. She kicked him out of the bunk and held the angry young man off—"he look like de wild bear," Rose said—with a poker. The next day, Rose complained to Mrs. Hawkins, who explained that her husband wanted Rufus and Rose "to bring forth portly children." Still Rose resisted, holding Rufus off yet another night with the poker. The following day, Mr. Hawkins himself called for Rose and laid down the law: "'Woman, I's pay big money for you and I'd done dat for de cause I wants yous to raise me chillens. I's put you to live with Rufus for dat purpose. Now, if you doesn't want whippin' at de stake, yous do what I wants."

Rose thought about it. She asked herself, "What am I's to do?" She yielded. After emancipation, Rose never married, "'cause one 'sperience am 'nough. . . . After what I does for de massa, I's never wants no truck with any man. De Lawd forgive dis cullud woman, but he have to 'scuse me and look for some others for to 'plenish de earth.'"[3]

In describing this narrative, which she entitles "Rose Describes Being Forced to Live with Rufus," Willie Lee Rose says that "what is especially interesting is that Rose was less hostile to her owner for his action than she might otherwise have been. . . ."[4] That may be so, but Professor Jones reminds us that we should be careful not to discount the testimony of the slaves or make excuses for the actions of their masters. In Rose's narrative, we have a clear and chilling account of a girl, sixteen years old, holding off a man authorized to rape her. This is a girl with no knowledge of sex, being compelled to submit to a man she dislikes, which she does out of gratitude to the master who kept her family together and also—and this should not be discounted—to avoid whipping. Yet the trauma was so great that once she was free, once she could make her own, uncoerced choice, Rose never spent the night with a man again.

Willie Lee Rose reminds us that there is very little evidence of the commercial breeding of slaves, but what we certainly see, with Professor Jones's help, is that rape and coerced sex were intrinsic to slavery.

Professor Jones makes us ask why this basic fact of slavery—that all slave women were vulnerable to rape or coerced sex, either with white men or black men assigned as their mates—has been overlooked. As he did in his book, Professor Jones makes us question the model of paternalism, developed in the antebellum South by proslavery ideologues and accepted as an accurate description by too many twentieth-century historians.[5] "[W]hy various reformulations of [patriarchy]—whether called patriarchalism or paternalism—remain the most accepted and widely adopted means of understanding American slavery is . . . difficult to explain."

I think that such an explanation is complex, but not impossible. Professor Jones quotes a passage from Fitzhugh's *Cannibals All!*: "Within the family circle, the law of love prevails, not that of selfishness. . . . Besides wife and children, brothers and sister, dogs, horses, birds and flowers—slaves, also, belong to the family circle. . . . The interests of master and slave are bound up together and each in his appropriate sphere naturally endeavors to promote the happiness of the other." Slave women were "protected from the despotism of their husbands by their masters."

This view of slavery is almost complete fantasy. Walter Johnson has recently defined paternalism as a "peculiar mixture of ostensible moderation and outright threat," and he has illustrated that definition with the example of a slaveowner who had just bought a family of slaves from another man: "I govern them the same way your late brother did, without the whip by stating to them that I should sell them if they do not conduct themselves as I wish."[6] By this definition, Rose's Massa Hawkins was a paternalist, affording Rose the "choice" of cohabitation with the loathesome Rufus or the whip. Thus were slaves coerced and thus did masters maintain the illusion that they were paternalists.

Paternalism was an ideology—a mis-communication intended to make slavery appear other than it was. Fitzhugh's insistence that masters protected slave women from the despotism of their husbands would be laughable were it not so horrific. Yet I think that we must pay some attention to this ideology, for it is this ideology that distinguishes slavery from warfare. Professor Jones uses the analogy of war; he recognizes that slavery was not in fact warfare but that it was *like* war. But because slavery was not war, slave owners never justified slavery in the terms of the just war. A slight modification: In the seventeenth century, the principles of the just war had been used to rationalize slavery, but by the eighteenth century, that rationale was no longer invoked. At the time of the American Revolution, even American slave owners recognized, uneasily, that slavery was inconsistent with their ideals of liberty. Just listen to Patrick Henry: "Would anyone believe that I am Master of Slaves of my own purchase! I am drawn along by ye general Inconvenience of living without them; I will not, I cannot justify it."[7] He—and others like him—knew that on the scales of justice, "inconvenience" bore very little weight.

Slaveowners at the time of the Revolution were in need of an ideology, and they found it in the ideal of the sentimental family, just coming into being at the same time. Fitzhugh's vision of the family as a "circle" where "the law of love prevails, not that of selfishness" was sentimental and bourgeois. This was a new notion of the family, a realm of love that could serve as a counterweight to the acquisitiveness of the world of work. Once this new notion of the family was available, slave owners could appropriate it to help rationalize slavery. Slaveowners took slavery out of the world of work and placed it in the world of family, the world of love. This was the ideological move that they made in order to try to justify slavery.

It is easy enough to understand why slaveowners did this. Slavery needed an ideology, and one that used the common language of family sentiment was probably as effective an ideology as they could muster. Much has been written about the supposedly distinctive southern culture, which offered a contrast and rebuke to Northern bourgeois culture. According to this story, Southern culture had its roots in feudal society, with its God-ordained hierarchy and its sense of mutual obligation. Yet historians have generally not noticed that there was nothing feudal or premodern or anti-bourgeois about the southern notion of family—a "circle [where] the law of love prevails, not that of selfishness." This is the northern notion of family as well, and northerners just as much as southerners contrasted the warmth of the family to the coldness of profit-making.

The purpose of slavery was to make slaveowners rich. Walter Johnson has brilliantly demonstrated that slaveowners who defined themselves in the market tried to persuade themselves that they bought slaves in order to rescue them from the market—to bring them home where "the law of love prevails." This was ideology, whose purpose was to enable Americans, northern and southern both, to participate with a clear conscience in a market about which they had qualms.

So why, Professor Jones asks, have historians accepted this ideology as an accurate description of behavior? This is a complex question. Part of the answer is that we, too, have qualms about the market, and hence we are susceptible to critiques of it, even when the very purpose of those critiques was to enable men and women to participate in that market, even the market in other human beings.

Part of the answer, too, might lie in our complex feelings about race and sex. As Professor Jones has shown, we have failed to recognize the rape and coercion of slave women because we have not been able to recognize the humanity, the personhood of slave women. The story of slavery has been written as the travail of whites—those helpless white men who "surrendered sexually and fell over the race line." For too many years, to the extent that slaves elicited sympathy, it was primarily male slaves, the "Sambo" for whom slavery was primarily an exercise in emasculation. Not until the publication of Deborah White's *Aren't I A Woman?*[8] were we afforded a view of slavery from the female slaves' perspective. Not until we can see slave women as persons can we appreciate the toll that slavery took on them, too.

Part of the explanation may come, too, when we attempt to answer another one of Professor Jones's rhetorical questions. He says that "one may reasonably ask why historiographical attention has been so intensely focused on the rape of white women when both indirect and direct evidence . . . overwhelmingly points to a preponderance of rapes by English and European men. . . ." He cites Martha Hodes's recent book, and he might have mentioned, as well, Diane Miller Sommerville.[9] In her case, however, her purpose is not to study the rape of white women by black men but to question whether antebellum Southerners were obsessed by the threat of black male rapists. Her conclusion, to put it in the broadest terms, is that elite Southern men were more concerned with protecting accused black males, slave and free, than the poor white women and girls who accused them of rape. If we combine her conclusions with Professor Jones's, we begin to see that southern whites, no matter what the ideal of paternalism said, offered no protection and considerable danger to enslaved black women and poor white ones.

I have noticed two trends in recent writing about slavery. One, exemplified by Professor Jones and Professor Johnson, is neo-abolitionist; this group of contemporary historians is taking seriously again the critiques of black and white abolitionists. The other focuses on race mixing. I believe that one reason for the (general) public acceptance of the DNA evidence that Thomas Jefferson almost certainly fathered one of Sally Hemings's children is that, as our nation becomes increasingly less white and as interracial marriage becomes more common, we are better prepared to see—and value—voluntary sex across the color line in past times.[10] But this impulse, which translates sex as love, may to some extent be just a reformulation of the nineteenth century bourgeois ideal, which imagined that love could conquer all. If, that is, love could triumph across the racial divide, then personal acts of love—rather than more demanding acts of justice—might heal our racial wounds.

In his powerful paper, Norrece Jones speaks for justice. Like his fellow neo-abolitionist historian Walter Johnson, he reminds us that no matter the fantasies in which slaveowners and their latter-day apologists have indulged, slavery rested upon, indeed *was* an abuse of power. But because the antebellum South was a world born out of the American Revolution, with its ideals of liberty and its suspicion of power, power could never be its own justification. Love, figured as the antithesis as power, became the rationale, and hence, slaveowners must have loved their slaves as they loved their families. It is this obfuscation, compounded by sexism and racism pure and simple, that has hidden the sexual violence of the slave system from us for so many years.

Professor Jones has pierced the fantasy, to show us what we should really have known already. This is history as it should be written, and it makes us cry.

The Long History of a Low Place: Slavery on the South Carolina Coast, 1670–1870

ROBERT OLWELL

Most people living in the South Carolina lowcountry today would probably agree wholeheartedly with William Faulkner's famous (and perhaps over-cited) aphorism that in the American South, "the past is never dead, it's not even past." Certainly, anyone who spent time in Charleston in the last year of the twentieth century could not escape the fact that not only is the region's past refusing to die; at times, it almost seems to bury the present. In the summer of 2000, lowcountry inhabitants were engaged in a heated and bitter statewide debate as to whether the Confederate battle flag should continue to fly from the dome of the South Carolina Capitol in Columbia and a local struggle concerning a proposal to erect a statue of Denmark Vesey in Charleston's Hampton Park (which itself is named in honor of a Confederate general whose red-shirted vigilantes violently wrested control of the state from black majority rule in 1876). In August, the region's past literally rose from the grave when a sunken confederate submarine was lifted from the seabed off the coast and brought into Charleston harbor, its crew still entombed inside. As the barge carrying the rusted wreck slowly proceeded up the Cooper river, the city's waterfront was lined with confederate "re-enactors" saluting the return of this "lost patrol" of the "lost cause."

Nor have all of South Carolina's struggles over the meaning of local history been entirely homegrown. Charleston residents reacted with a mixture of pride, embarrassment, or outrage to the premiere of *The Patriot*, a Hollywood epic of the American Revolution, filmed in and around Charleston, and which was purportedly set in eighteenth-century South Carolina. The film very graphically depicts the brutality of the war and the sacrifices that white Carolinians made for their liberty. Yet, although a large majority of the region's eighteenth-century population was comprised of African or Afro-Carolinian slaves, many of them denied their liberty by those same white patriots, slavery is almost completely absent from the film, and black Carolinians themselves are only slightly less invisible. In some instances, this historical revisionism required that considerable artistic license be taken with the truth. In one scene, for example, a British patrol arrives at the plantation of the movie's patriotic hero (Mel Gibson) and offers freedom to the blacks at work in the fields. The workers however, give the indignant (and preposterous) reply that they are already free and are working for wages! Gazing dumbstruck at the screen, I hardly knew whether to laugh or cry—if only the actual sins of the past could be so easily washed white and forgotten.

It is, of course, current academic fashion to declare soberly that all visions of the past are subjective, and that both historical documents and historians' descriptions of them are but the interpretation and the perspective of individuals who are (or were) themselves the products of larger cultural and ideological forces. In this guise, *The Patriot* says more about American society, and selective historical memory, at the end of the twentieth century than it does about the complex realities of the revolutionary era. In coastal South Carolina however, the idea that all history is contested, and that the meaning of the past depends upon where you stand, does not require graduate study. It has long been a matter of simple common sense and everyday life.

As the examples I have just related suggest, some parts of South Carolina's past are livelier and more contested than others. The skeletons whose bones rattle most loudly in South Carolina's historical closet are those of slavery, and its attendants: secession and civil war. There is a very good reason why the ghosts of slavery haunt the lowcountry, for no other place in the United States has had as long or as close a relationship to the institution.

Of all of the thirteen British colonies that later formed the United States, only in South Carolina was slavery present from the very start. In the lowcountry, the emergence of slavery was not the tragic result of an "unthinking decision" made forty and fifty years after settlement, as was the case for late-seventeenth-century Virginia, nor was it a conscious fall from grace as in mid-eighteenth-century Georgia.[1] In the 1660s, when the Carolina colony was still only a dream in the minds of its proprietors, slavery was written into its future and into its "Fundamental Constitutions" (authored by Lord Shaftesbury's private secretary, John Locke). If there were not slaves on board the three small ships which arrived to establish Charles Town in March 1670 (and there well might have been), the first surviving record of the presence of slaves in the colony dates from only five months later.[2]

Not only was the South Carolina lowcountry linked to slavery from the start, no other colony/state had such a profound commitment to the institution. In comparing slave regimes across the early modern Atlantic world, scholars have lately begun to make a useful distinction between "societies with slaves" and "slave societies."[3] In the former, slaves are present in small numbers and slave property is legal, but the institution is of only marginal economic, social, or political significance. According to these criteria, a list of "societies with slaves" would encompass all of colonial America (and indeed, the entire Atlantic world) prior to the last quarter of the eighteenth century. In a slave society, on the other hand, large numbers of slaves constitute a critical mass (usually depicted as at least one fifth or one fourth) of the local society's population, are the most important form of wealth, and the institution of slavery (or better, the perpetuation of masters' ownership of slaves' bodies and expropriation of slaves' labor) is the central focus and pivot around which the entire economic, social, and political order turns.

By this definition, South Carolina was the first slave society on the North American continent. A 1672 account of the then two-year-old colony's population already put the proportion of slaves at greater than one person in four.[4] By contrast, Virginia, while always the largest slave colony/state in purely numerical terms, did not obtain a comparable ratio of blacks to whites for a further fifty years (until about 1720), more than a century after the first slaves arrived at Jamestown.[5]

Early in the eighteenth century, the number of black slaves in the lowcountry already surpassed that of free whites. The region's "black majority" continued to grow until by 1740 black slaves outnumbered free whites by almost two to one. In the generation before the American Revolution, with increased slave imports and expanding rice production, the imbalance tipped ever further. By 1775, when the Revolutionary war began, black slaves comprised almost eighty percent of the lowcountry's population. In the nineteenth century, the natural limits (and continued high mortality) of rice and sea-island cotton cultivation combined to slow the increase of the region's slave population. Around 1830, the number of slaves in the lowcountry reached 140,000 and stalled. It remained approximately at this level for the next thirty-five years. (The continued stasis probably required a small but steady migration of slaves out of the region through this period). This fact, combined with the continued slow growth of Charleston, which was always about half white, to forty thousand people by 1860, tipped the racial balance slightly backward. But the lowcountry never came close to racial equilibrium. At the start of the Civil War, the region was still home to more than twice as many black slaves as free whites.[6] Nowhere else in the American South did a slave majority appear so early, continue for so long, or form such a persistently large proportion of the local population.

As the concept of a slave society asserts, these demographic facts had profound social and cultural consequences. As the *ne plus ultra* of American slave societies, the lowcountry's entire world (white and black) was dominated by the presence or shadow of slavery. In no other state in the nineteenth-century United States did the ideology of slavery so dominate political life or meet with such small opposition or mitigation. Left to themselves in their small slaveholder's republic, the masters of South Carolina were free to indulge their fantasies and neuroses to the fullest. It is therefore no accident that these same men ultimately would lead the South into secession and precipitate a civil war in defense of slavery.[7]

Given the prominent role played by the South Carolina coastal region in America's long and tortured involvement in slavery and in the origins of the most traumatic single event in American history, it is not surprising that the subject of slavery in the lowcountry has attracted a good deal of historical scrutiny. The resulting studies are full of fascinating detail, imaginative research, and compelling argument. Perhaps, more than any other similarly sized region, the South Carolina lowcountry has become a recognized locale in the historical geography of American slavery. But while these studies have inculcated a powerful sense of the lowcountry as a "place," they have not, as yet, constructed an equally compelling sense of the lowcountry as a place that existed through time.

The two-hundred-year-long reign of slavery in the lowcountry has rarely been incorporated as a central concept in studies of the subject. Perhaps the human tragedy that eight generations of human bondage encapsulates has simply overwhelmed scholars' powers of analysis and narrative abilities. In this regard, it may be no accident that Edward Ball, the only person who has thus far taken on the project of writing a history of lowcountry slavery from start to finish, (or at least from the late seventeenth century through emancipation) is not an academic pursuing scholarly objectives. Ball's study follows his own ancestors' part in the "slave business" from 1698 to 1865. The resulting book is more about Ball himself, his guilt about his ancestors' "crime" and his own inheritance of racial privilege, than it is an investigation of the past on its own terms.[8]

Consequently, although historians have begun to point out that slavery indeed has a history (that is, that it changed over time and in relationship to other factors and forces) and have called upon scholars to treat the subject accordingly, there has been as yet, little effort to follow up upon this insight in the study of particular places such as the lowcountry.[9] Most scholars of the subject, myself included, have instead continued to define their studies in ways that put little or no emphasis on issues of development or change, and our research design seldom extends beyond a few decades or a single generation. In adapting such a synchronic approach, we have in most cases chosen to ignore or at least down play questions of causation and have seldom endeavored to account for change over time. Rather than try to digest the "total history" of the subject, most scholars of lowcountry slavery have bitten off and chewed upon only one small piece of slavery's two-century long reign in the region. Nor have scholars been indiscriminate as to what part of this history they chose to study. Until quite recently, studies of lowcountry slavery crowded together at one end of the temporal spectrum, and focused on slavery's last few decades. The last generation of slavery's existence in the South Carolina lowcountry, that is, from about 1840 to 1865, has inspired and informed as much (and until the last decade quite a bit more) research and writing as the previous seven generations put together.

One benefit of this concentration of effort has been the lively debate that these works have been able to conduct with each other and with larger historiography of slavery in the antebellum American South, which has also been hugely concentrated upon this final chapter. But because only a few of these works devote more than a quick backward glance (or perhaps an opening chapter) to slavery in the lowcountry prior to 1840, the resulting image, extraordinarily rich and complex as it seems in every other way, is as regards historical change, often quite simplistic. The impression gained from these studies is of a place that is almost "timeless," where neither the past that came before nor, since the world that they describe ends abruptly in 1865, a future that will come after, can intrude upon a perpetual present.

Only in the last ten years, and especially with the publication of Philip Morgan's long awaited comparison of slavery in the eighteenth-century lowcountry and Chesapeake, (as well as my own, far more modest study of the relationship between colonialism and slavery in mid-eighteenth-century South Carolina—which was also long-awaited, at least in my own household) has it become possible to flesh out a portrait of slavery and slave life in the mid-eighteenth-century lowcountry that is rich and complete enough to be usefully be compared and contrasted with that of the mid-nineteenth century.[10]

Similarly, it is only now, I think, that by drawing connections between these individual studies, and by comparing the portrait of lowcountry slavery in the eighteenth century that is emerging, to the already substantial (albeit still growing) literature on the nature of slavery and slave life in the nineteenth century, that we might begin to construct a "genealogy" of slavery in the lowcountry from its birth in 1670 to its death two centuries later. At last, enough monographic signposts may have been built to allow us to take the measure of the entire landscape of lowcountry slavery and we might finally undertake to make a survey of the entire subject.

However, as any surveyor can tell you, the first step in mapping a territory is to draw the boundaries. So, having just described how we might plot a "total history" of lowcountry slavery, I will immediately divide this totality into more usable and comprehensible parts and to decide upon the grid that will guide my mapping. Previously, the historiographic boundary markers of the subject have been vague at best. For example, few studies of slavery in the nineteenth century, have long pondered, let alone problematized, the chronological parameters of their research. When, one might ask, did the "Old South" begin? And, how was this nineteenth-century South different from that period (the pre-Old South?) that had come before?

Perhaps because they stood outside the mainstream, studies of lowcountry slavery before 1800 (i.e., the pre-Old South), have generally been more attentive to situating their studies in the context of time. In 1974, in his pioneering study of slavery in the early colonial lowcountry, Peter Wood divided the first seventy years of lowcountry slavery into two periods: a frontier era covering the years from 1670 to 1720, and a second era during which South Carolina "evolved from a frontier outpost to a staple-producing colony" that spanned the decades between 1720 and 1740. Although his own study ended with the Stono Rebellion in 1739, Wood's conclusion argued that the post-1740 era should constitute a third (and perhaps final) period. More recently, both Philip Morgan and Ira Berlin, in their studies of American slavery before 1800, suggested that the history of early slavery should be divided into three parts or phases.[11] Morgan's recommendations for the lowcountry specifically were for three divisions consisting of a "frontier phase" (1670–1710), an "institution-building" phase (1710–1750), and a "mature" phase (1750–1790). Berlin's periodization was less defined geographically and chronologically than Morgan's but paid greater attention to larger historical events. Berlin broke the subject into "charter," "plantation," and "revolutionary generations." In none of the three cases, of course, did the proposed boundaries extend past the end of the eighteenth century. Thus, there remained a gap, or at least a "lost generation," between the end of their studies (and periodization) in 1800 and the commonly accepted genesis of the "old South" (sometime between 1820 and 1840). In fact, that Morgan's proposed "mature phase" ends in 1790, posing the unanswered question of what, in this schema, the last seventy five years of slavery's existence in South Carolina might be called, "post-mature"? (or perhaps "rotten")?

Following on the trail of these periodizing pioneers, but carrying on past 1800 to slavery's end, let me now suggest that the long history of slavery in the lowcountry might be usefully divided into seven distinct periods:

1) A "frontier" or settlement period that lasted from 1670 to approximately 1720—a date which I, like Wood, tie to the end of the Yamassee war as much as to the colony's decisive turn to the rice staple. (The two events were, as I will point out, closely related.)

2) A "plantation building" era from 1720 to 1740 in which the region made a decisive economic transformation, vastly enlarging its slave labor force, and redeploying its economic and coercive energies to the construction and cultivation of rice in the lowcountry swamps.

3) A period of relative stability and "maturity" that lasted from 1740 until the outbreak of the American Revolution. In my own work, I have termed the lowcountry in this period a "colonial slave society," in part to distinguish it from the slave regime of the nineteenth century. While I have some important disagreements with Wood about the nature of this post-Stono regime (a theme only briefly sketched out in the closing pages of Black Majority*), I nonetheless agree with Wood that 1740 marks an important watershed in the lowcountry's history.*

4) In concurrence with Berlin (and contra Morgan), I also believe that the era of the American Revolution and the post-war restoration of order on the plantations, deserves to be considered as a distinct period with a unique set of possibilities and perils for slaves and masters alike.

5) The next era, which I would begin about 1785 or so, is the least studied era of all in the entire two centuries of lowcountry slavery. The four decades following the American Revolution constitute something of a missing link between the suddenly robust historiography of the eighteenth century and the older established literature of the antebellum era. Yet this period poses a number of interesting questions. Like the "plantation building" phase of eighty years earlier, these decades also saw massive slave imports into the region (approximately 140,000 Africans arrived in Charleston between 1785 and the closing of the trans-Atlantic slave trade in 1807) and a greater than fifty percent rise in the lowcountry slave population. This growth coincided with a dramatic transformation of lowcountry agricultural practices and labor relations—including the shift from inland to tidal rice cultivation and widespread introduction of rice pounding mills (replacing the toil of pounding rice by hand with mortar and pestle), the almost complete abandonment of indigo (in the colonial era the region's "second staple"), and perhaps most dramatic of all, the development and rapid expansion of cotton culture after 1790 on a gang rather than task based labor system throughout the sea islands and on lowcountry land not suited to rice.

6) After 1830, according to the demographic evidence (or to give Denmark Vesey his due, perhaps we might say 1822), this new regime was largely in place and the lowcountry slave society entered upon a second plateau, or "mature" phase, which would last until the outbreak of the Civil War. To draw a distinction and also a parallel between this last period (which we might otherwise, following historiographical custom, term the "old South"), and the earlier, eighteenth-century mature phase (or perhaps "older South") of 1740–1775, an era which I have described in the lowcountry as a "colonial slave society," I would denote the era from 1830 to 1860 as that of the "republican slave society."

7) And finally, the ten years that followed upon the firing of the first gun at Fort Sumter, and that saw the destruction of slavery and the beginnings of a new post-slavery (if not entirely free) society in the lowcountry constitute a seventh and final act in the drama, and require a separate consideration.

Divided this way into seven parts, the "long history" of the lowcountry may appear to be a mere chronicle, too long, and too awkward, to be of much analytical value. Like the blind man's description of the elephant, it seems to be just one damn thing after another. But taken collectively, these seven chronological territories suggest that the long history of lowcountry slavery contains a provocative paradigm. With the exception of the first fifty years of frontier settlement, the long history of the lowcountry slave society reveals two cycles, each approximately three generations in duration, between 1720 and 1870. In each cycle, a painful and transformative period of plantation development and economic intensification (as well as Afro-Carolinian cultural development) was succeeded by a era of "mature" stability, which was followed in turn by a revolutionary crisis.

Seeing their history in this way offers some credence to lowcountry slaves' common comparison of their plight to that of the ancient Israelites in bondage to pharaoh, and of equating their historical experience with scripture. As in a typological interpretation of the Bible, events presaged in the lowcountry's "old testament" of the eighteenth century, or colonial period, appear to be both reenacted and "fulfilled" in the "new testament" of the nineteenth, and the republican era. The most obvious example of this "providential" foreshadowing is how the slaves' final redemption from bondage in the Civil War was presaged in the temporary and in illusory liberty offered by the British in the Revolution. Not surprisingly, the idea that the long history of lowcountry slavery can best be articulated as a typological narrative has been most clearly expressed in studies of lowcountry Africans' religious experience. Studies of this subject, such as those of Margaret Creel and that of Sylvia Frey and Betty Wood describe a sequence in which the seeds of Christianity sown by Anglican missionaries and Methodist evangelicals in the first "Great Awakening" of the mid-eighteenth century fell upon stony ground, only to bear fruit in the conversion of the slaves and the creation of an unique African Christianity in the second "awakening" of the nineteenth century.[12]

Parsing 150 years of lowcountry slavery into two consecutive cycles of transformation, plateau, and crisis, allows us to perceive patterns of how lowcountry slavery may have changed through time, and to ask how lowcountry slaves may have understood and made sense of those changes in their own lives. But this tidy compartmentalization also will allow comparisons to be made between each of the phases so that the differences as well as the continuities between the two centuries might be brought into sharper relief. Perhaps the long history of the lowcountry should not be depicted in straightforward linear fashion but as a meandering track that at times bends back upon itself, so that some social forces and effects seem to have occurred before.

An examination of the earliest, frontier, phase of the lowcountry's history suggests some of the difficulty inherent in narrating a history of slavery over a long time span. Such problems of narration may explain why, despite its enormous reputation and very important role in drawing attention to lowcountry slavery as a subject, Peter Wood's *Black Majority* still stands as the sole study of this early period, more than a generation after its publication. Despite Wood's hope, expressed in the book's preface, that *Black Majority* might serve to "open up" the field to further research, the truth has come closer to the prediction of one of Wood's Harvard professors, that *Black Majority* would serve to "wrap up" the subject.[13] Why has this happened?

To understand *Black Majority*'s paradoxical impact, receiving much well-deserved praise and a wide readership (it has never gone out of print) but yet inspiring very little historiographical engagement (contrast this reception with that given two other 1974 works: Eugene Genovese's *Roll, Jordan, Roll*, and Robert Fogel and Stanley Engerman's *Time on the Cross*) we must consider the context of its creation.[14] The time and the place in which *Black Majority* was first conceived and written (Cambridge, Massachusetts in the early 1970s) was at the center of a project of early American history that was centered upon the intense scrutiny of small New England towns. In 1970 alone, no fewer than four such works appeared.[15] These studies drew upon the then new techniques of social history and the wealth of documentation of the everyday lives of ordinary people that could be found in the local records of New England. Combined, these books were enormously influential in the field of early American history, and they soon sparked an outpouring of similar "community studies."[16]

Most of these community studies shared a "declension narrative," that is, their authors described the gradual process through which a world based upon a traditional, cooperative, community gave way to a "modern" ethos of competitive, capitalistic, individualism.[17] Along with demographic pressures, the dynamic force that produced this transformation was generally depicted as some form of merchant capitalism or market-intensification. The paradigm was closely related and intellectually indebted to the sociological concept of "modernization."[18]

As he began his graduate work in early American history at Harvard in the late 1960s and began to cast about for a research topic, perhaps the only question Peter Wood was asked was which New England town did he intend to study? By instead choosing to examine a different region, and another people, Wood boldly broke with the historiographical orthodoxy then prevailing in Massachusetts. But, in other ways, *Black Majority* is surprisingly compatible with the New England town studies in whose company it was first conceived and written. Like them, *Black Majority* examines an immigrant population as they create a community in the new world, and then traces how that community was transformed and diminished through the last half of the seventeenth and first half of the eighteenth centuries.

Moreover, like the town studies with which it was contemporaneous, *Black Majority* clearly follows a narrative of declension. For example, of the first decades, Wood writes that "servants and masters shared the crude and egalitarian intimacies inevitable on the frontier," and that "common hardships . . . put the different races . . . upon a more equal footing than they would see in subsequent generations."[19] Eventually, however, the impact of the market, in the form of the lure of profits to be gained from rice cultivation, altered and destroyed this racial commonality, so that after 1720: "where blacks and whites had previously shared most activities distinguished only by the fact that the latter gave the commands and took the proceeds, workers were now . . . set apart by race."[20] Finally, after the bloody aftermath of the failed Stono Rebellion of September 1739, "the new social equilibrium which emerged in the generation before the revolution was based upon a heightened degree of white repression and a reduced amount of black autonomy."[21]

It is hardly surprising that despite breaking with the New England town studies in terms of its subject, *Black Majority* was nonetheless strongly influenced by the historical narratives that they had employed and developed. In saying this, I do not mean to suggest that Wood was entirely wrong to depict the black experience in South Carolina in the three generations between 1670 and the Stono Rebellion as tragedy. The construction of a fully-fledged plantation slave regime was indisputably tragic and imposed immense costs in terms of lives lost and blighted. Moreover Wood's portrayal of the contingent and inter-dependent nature of black and white interactions on the lowcountry "frontier" is one of the most important and persuasive aspects of his work. It has been echoed by most subsequent depictions of slavery in seventeenth-century America.

It also serves however to separate his study, and this period, from the work of scholars studying slavery in the following centuries. Accepting plantation slavery and codified racism simply as a given, and not as tragedies whose origins need be explained, these scholars have pursued a different line of analysis, studying the slave family, slave religion, slaves' economic activity, and the dynamics of slave resistance and masters' power. While *Black Majority* does, in fact, suggest most of these lines of inquiry, Wood does not fully develop any of them, and subsequently, *Black Majority* is seldom cited as anything more a than an inspirational pathfinder in these ongoing debates. Consequently, for over twenty-five years, *Black Majority* has stood at the threshold of the history of lowcountry slavery—an intellectual achievement that cannot be ignored, but which also has never been fully engaged.

Now, perhaps, the time has at last come to take another look at this frontier period, taking seriously the argument that South Carolina was a slave society from the start. By discarding the narrative of a tragic declension implicit (or explicit) in any description of slavery's origins, several questions immediately suggest themselves. Was, for example, slavery in the lowcountry's first fifty years actually less terrible, or just terrible in different ways (and perhaps for different people)? There is certainly evidence for such a dystopian view. For instance, rather than see slaves who labored to turn pine trees into turpentine and tar as woodland "pioneers" as Wood does in *Black Majority*, perhaps a more accurate analogy would be to workers in a primitive, and hazardous, chemical factory. And unlike the large, kin-ship based, slave communities that could be found on most rice plantations by the last half of the eighteenth century, the black men who worked in the turpentine industry generally labored and lived alone, or in small, impermanent, camps, with little or no ability to find wives and form families.[22]

Moreover, only recently have scholars begun to devote any serious attention to the presence and effects of the Indian slave trade in early America. Throughout the frontier phase of the lowcountry's history, one of the region's most important, albeit illegal, commodities were Indians captured in wars or obtained through trade with other Native American groups. In fact, it was not until approximately 1720, the end of Wood's frontier phase, that the lowcountry became a net importer of slaves. In South Carolina's first fifty years, the twelve thousand Africans who were imported from Africa or the Caribbean were balanced by an estimated twelve thousand Indians who were exported from the colony.[23] Thus, the Yamassee war of 1715–1720 marks a fitting end to the frontier phase for two reasons, for not only did the destruction of the lowcountry's Indians territorial claims literally clear way for the expansion of rice production, as Wood and others have argued, but the sale of captured Indians' bodies (including 700 Yamassee) directly helped defray the purchase of Africans.

Black Majority also dominates the second phase of the lowcountry's history, the plantation-building phase of 1720 and 1740. Here, Wood again sets the terms for historiographical debate in this period with two important questions: the trajectory of slavery's history and the impact of Africans on subsequent lowcountry culture. *Black Majority* depicts the events of the 1720s and 1730s as a destructive and tragic cycle in which slaves' growing initiative inspired a mounting anxiety among whites. In *Black Majority*, Wood portrays a vicious dynamic in which masters' desires for a greater exploitation of their slaves, and for more slave workers led them to seek a tighter rein on slaves' lives, which in turn only provoked a rise in black resistance, which finally culminated in the Stono Rebellion in the fall of 1739. For Wood, the rebellion was "a high water-mark, and its ruthless suppression represents a significant turning of the tide."[24] He described what followed, the passage of a new slave code the following spring and other repressive measures, as "a new chapter in the history of South Carolina and ... the end of an era for the Negro in the colony."[25]

But, in light of work by Morgan and others, one might ask whether the Stono Rebellion actually caused a significant alteration in the ways that whites and blacks interacted in the lowcountry society. In many ways, little changed. In the post-Stono decades, blacks continued to enjoy most of the petty liberties that Wood first described. In many cases, they may even have expanded upon them. Likewise, whites continued to exercise their dominion over slaves—often with extreme violence. Yet, as most of the lowcountry population, black and white, became native born (for whites, this transition occurred in the 1740s, for blacks a decade later), more complex and varied forms of both resistance and repression emerged, and the "culture of power" became for both a way of life.

Comparing Wood's portrait of the "plantation building" era of the 1720s and 30s, with Joyce Chaplin's study of the period from 1785–1815, is a reminder that the meaning of history is a matter of perspective.[26] Although in significant ways, Chaplin argues that the post-revolutionary period was undergoing a similarly dramatic and painful transformation, her study—undertaken largely from the view of the planters—is a tale of successful innovation and economic development. South Carolina planters living in 1740 could, and did, tell a similarly progressive of their achievements in building a profitable rice plantation system. One wonders if a study of the post-revolutionary era focused more intently than Chaplin's on the experience of the lowcountry's black population, both newly arrived Africans and creoles, would offer a different impression of this era.

Moreover, subsequent work upon a hypothesis first proposed in *Black Majority* about the African roots of South Carolina culture, has both confirmed and questioned some of Wood's themes. In 1981, Daniel Littlefield examined the African origins of colonial South Carolina slaves and offered powerful evidence that lowcountry rice culture derived from African roots.[27] Margaret Creel's study of the Gullah culture, and its origins in this period, also owed a lot to Wood's initial exploration of the subject.[28] But John Thornton's work on the African origins of the Stono rebels suggests that the rebellion was probably a response to the dislocation and violence of enslavement and the horrors of the middle passage rather than to worsening conditions for slaves within the lowcountry.[29] The proper context for the Stono Rebellion, Thornton argues, is the Atlantic slave trade and the early-modern Atlantic rather than the "small world" of the mid-eighteenth-century lowcountry.

Interestingly, the post-revolutionary generation is similarly depicted by most scholars of nineteenth-century lowcountry African-American culture as a extremely formative one. During the crucible of plantation building in which they were thrown between 1720 and 1740, lowcountry Africans constructed a new culture: Gullah. Likewise, during the transformations and dislocations at the end of the eighteenth and early-nineteenth centuries they created a new faith. It was in these decades that a distinctive African-influenced Christianity emerged and soon encompassed the majority of the lowcountry's slave population. This new, shared, faith formed the basis for a new sense of community and identity, and ultimately a new forum for resistance for lowcountry blacks. Denmark Vesey's conspiracy for example, was rooted in Charleston's African Methodist Episcopal church. As Sylvia Frey and Betty Wood have recently noted, "the conversion to Protestant Christianity was a, perhaps *the*, defining moment in African American history."[30]

The two "plateaus": the "colonial slave society" of 1740 to 1775, and the "republican slave society" (or "Old South") of 1820 to 1860, also offer interesting ground for making comparisons and contrasts. Each of these periods is dominated by a single work around which all subsequent (or preceding) work has been (or will be) measured. For the eighteenth century, the touchstone is Philip Morgan's 1998 *Slave Counterpoint*. For the nineteenth century the key work has long been Charles Joyner's 1984 *Down By the Riverside*.[31] Although the publication of these two books was separated by fourteen years, and their subjects are separated by a century, they nonetheless, belong to a similar historiographical tradition and period. In fact, the 1998 publication date of *Slave Counterpoint* is somewhat deceptive, for the project that culminated in Morgan's book began as a doctoral dissertation that he completed in 1977, and much of the research and conceptualization that informs the book found in its way into numerous influential articles that Morgan published in the intervening years.

Morgan's study is extraordinarily well-researched and is truly exhaustive in its archival breadth. There can be few documents on slavery in the eighteenth-century lowcountry that Morgan has not consulted. Morgan's book probably tells us as much about the structures of everyday life for blacks in the early lowcountry as we will ever know. But although the work provides a wealth of information on topics from slaves' diet, housing, clothing, work patterns, family size, linguistic ability, and so forth, Morgan's enormous whole is not equal to the sum of his many parts. Despite the large scope of the study, one hundred years of slave life in the lowcountry (and Chesapeake), and despite Morgan's division of the century into three periods in the introduction, causation, change over time, and development, are not dynamic principles in the book. The American Revolution passes by with hardly a tremor. The only change Morgan details is a shift from an "infant" to a "mature" slave society, a process that is itself so imperceptible in his text that after six hundred pages he has to remind us in the conclusion that it has happened at all.

Joyner's portrait of the slave community on Waccamaw Neck in the mid-nineteenth century is far more focused. Using the memories of slavery collected during the 1930s as a key source, Joyner provides a thick and vivid texture to slaves' ordinary life. But like *Slave Counterpoint*, the historical vision in *Down By the Riverside* is essentially static. The lack of change is perhaps less surprising in Joyner's case as his focus is only on a few decades rather than an entire century. But it is plain that Joyner, as much as Morgan, deliberately constructed a study of slave life where time, or contingent events, would not be an important factor. In a final chapter, Joyner follows his slave community through the Civil War and the beginnings of freedom, but even here his emphasis is more on what persists from the old regime—on continuity rather than change.

Why this predilection for forces of stability and stasis, rather than violence and change? In their introductions, both Morgan and Joyner (the latter more forthrightly than the former) trace the methodological and intellectual underpinnings of their work to two modes of social science that were very influential among American historians in the latter 1970s and early 1980s, that is, at the same time that both Joyner and Morgan began their research.

The French *Annales*, the first influence they cite, emphasized the "deep structures" of social, cultural, and economic life in a given geographic environment over a long time period. The sympathies and focus of the *annalistes* tended toward peasants rather than princes, and they sought to recapture the *mentalite* (or world view) of ordinary people whose lives were lived close to the earth, well below the froth of politics. At this level of analysis, as Fernand Braudel wrote, the passage of history "is almost imperceptible" and the individual is "imprisoned within a destiny in which he himself has little hand."[32]

The second influence for both Morgan and Joyner, was cultural anthropology, and in particular the method employed and expounded by Clifford Geertz. Both authors also acknowledge a debt to a 1976 essay co-authored by the anthropologists Sidney Mintz and Richard Price which theorized how discrete African cultures evolved in the new world into a shared African-American culture.[33] But while Mintz and Price argued that culture be viewed historically as a process, Geertzian anthropology stressed the interpretation of repetitive rituals, and thus depicted culture primarily as a static practice. Like the *Annales*, with whom he was closely linked, Geertz sought to approach the experience of the ordinary people who did not write the documents that historians use, and was equally uninterested in historical processes or causation. Geertz's method of "thick description" was far better suited to explicating social exchange than to explaining social consequences.

One can readily see the attraction that these methods had for scholars of slaves and other subaltern groups. Both Joyner and Morgan, and many social historians of the late 1970s and 1980s desired to look at slave societies from the "bottom-up" and to emphasize slaves' experience and agency rather than the masters' power. But equally, one can today more easily recognize the limitations of this method and approach. Other recent work on lowcountry slave society during the mid-eighteenth and mid-nineteenth centuries has taken a different tack—one that has sought to reassert the presence and effect of the masters' power on shaping slave life, and to insist upon the importance of politics and other "contingent" events in dictating and transforming the history which slaves lived.

William Dusinberre's *Them Dark Days*, published in 1996, was a direct challenge to the implications (if not the overt conclusions) of the prevailing "slave community" scholarship.[34] Where Joyner, and others like him, had sought to uncover slaves' ability to build viable communities and cultures within the crucible of slavery, Dusinberre, as his title suggests, demanded that our attention be drawn back to the horrors of the regime. Dusinberre's focus upon only a few truly hideous examples (in particular the Manigault's Gowrie estate on the Savannah River) provided a powerful and nightmarish glimpse of how truly terrible slavery could be and actually was for some.

But Dusinberre's narrow lens cannot provide the whole story of how slavery perpetuated itself as a social and economic system. Simply put, if the mortality of Gowrie plantation were indeed typical, neither lowcountry slaves nor lowcountry slavery would have long survived the end of the Atlantic slave trade. For every Gowrie-like death camp, there had to have been a Silk Hope, or a Chicora Wood, if only to replace the lost workers. Is there room therefore for both Joyner and Dusinberre's depictions of slavery in the nineteenth-century lowcountry? In their basic facts the answer must be yes, but in the larger implications of their works and their portrayals of the effect of slavery on the slave, the two studies are utterly incompatible.

In a similar fashion, my own work also seeks to problematize the image of the mid-eighteenth century as an era of stability—even while I also make use of it. My work is focused upon the public (and political) rather than the private worlds of slaves and undertakes to examine how slaves and masters interacted in these relatively well-documented arenas. The result might seem to merely complement Morgan. If *Slave Counterpoint* details the private details and demographic facts of eighteenth-century slave life, *Masters, Subjects, and Slaves* attends to slaves' public life. But I also hope to suggest that slaves did have a public life, and a political role, and that slaves' actions and choices in these arenas did alter the world they lived in and did make history, in the sense of effecting larger historical changes. The crisis of the revolution, I would argue, was not merely something that happened to slaves, but also something that they played a role in instigating and in directing the course of historical change. Mention of the revolutionary crisis brings us, at last, to the final comparative pairing: that of the events of 1775–1785 (the American Revolution) and 1860–1870 (the American Civil War). Here the similarities in terms of events and actions, by whites and blacks alike, are often remarkable. Perhaps this may simply be a case of like symptoms producing like effects. For example, the actions of the British during their invasion and occupation of the lowcountry in 1779–1782 are a remarkable foreshadowing of the policies later adopted by the Federal government eighty years later. In both the American Revolution and the Civil War, armies invading the lowcountry were beset by fugitive slaves seeking freedom and refuge. At first, the British and later United States military leaders sheltered (and made use of) the fugitives under the guise of confiscated enemy property. But, of course, the British never issued an Emancipation Proclamation, and never declared war on slavery. Thus the first revolutionary crisis stopped well short of becoming an internal lowcountry revolution.[35]

Another profound difference exists in the origin of the two crises and in the behavior of the lowcountry's master class in each period. I and others have argued that the South Carolina elite in 1775 were very reluctant revolutionaries forced by events outside their colony, and more especially by their fear of a British inspired (or influenced) slave revolt, to join in the armed struggle against the king. By contrast, in 1860 the lowcountry's republican slave masters lit the fuse of secession and fired the first guns of the war that would bring about their own downfall. How might one explain this shift and the apparent paradox of a slaveholder turned revolutionary? Perhaps, the mere fact of their victory in the revolutionary crisis, and the resulting eight decades of lowcountry republicanism, played a part. Without an imperial power to constrain their ambitions and pride, South Carolina's leadership may have become too accustomed to having their way. If, as it is said, "those whom the Gods would destroy they first make Mad," the first step toward madness might well be home rule. But I also suspect that the emergence of abolitionism after 1830, played a part in the lowcountry elites' descent into madness. The North of 1860, may not have been abolitionist per se, but it was surely anti-slavery in ways that King George and his ministers were not (at least before 1775).

Comparing the actions and demands of black Carolinians in the two periods is also very revealing. In both instances, when left to their own devices, or allowed to follow their own preferences, lowcountry blacks sought to pursue small-scale, self-sufficient agriculture. Sidney Mintz has described this mode of life as a "reconstituted peasantry," and argues that its emphasis on family farms and independence both from masters and the market makes it the ideal anti-thesis to the plantation.[36] The promise of landed independence that was contained in the forty-acres and a mule which lowcountry slaves were granted in General Sherman's famous field order number 15 in February 1865 (or in the original charter of the Freedmen's Bureau one month later), was first enacted informally in the lowcountry in the summer of 1780. After the British conquered Charleston and destroyed the established authority in the state and many masters fled their plantations, those lowcountry blacks who "remained at home" grew their own provision crops and became "quite their own masters." (Why isn't that scene in *The Patriot*?)

Inevitably, however, in both 1782 and 1865, when the fighting ended, the masters and (law and order) returned. In the eighteenth century, masters reimposed slavery and crushed fugitive slaves who attempted to preserve their defacto freedoms in maroon encampments. In the nineteenth-century "restoration," lowcountry blacks' freedom may have been de jure, but through a mixture of violence and legal control over property (the latter supported by the Federal government, which in 1866 rescinded the "Sherman Reserve"), lowcountry whites were still able to turn the lowcountry's post-war settlement into something far less than the landed independence and self-control that blacks' had long desired.

Certainly, the slaves' dreams of freedom, self-mastery, and deliverance were as old as lowcountry slavery itself. As early as 1759, a century before the first guns of the Civil War, a slave executed for conspiring to lead a revolt was said to have promised his black listeners that "the Sword should go through the land, & it should be no more White King's Governors or great men but that the Negroes should live happily & have laws of their own." Likewise, when the revolution began, slaves were quick to interpret the struggle as one in which their freedom was the central issue in the struggle between their masters and their king.

This long march through the long history of the lowcountry suggests some of the possibilities of viewing the subject comprehensively over the course of two centuries. But it also reveals some of the difficulties and pitfalls in trying to comprehend and make collective and insightful sense of such a large and long (in chronological terms) subject. One might consider for instance whether the history of slavery in the lowcountry over the course of two centuries is primarily a story of change or of continuity. To what extent were changes in the lowcountry shaped by internal factors and to what extent were they imposed from without?

Pondering the lives and deaths of slaves and masters over the course of eight generations also raises questions about the utility of the concept of "everyday resistance." Can activities that, over the course of two centuries, failed to destroy (or even demonstrably weaken) the slave regime be usefully termed resistance? To what degree did lowcountry slaves shape their history and that of their region? If the long history of the lowcountry is a study of the dialectic between authority and resistance, what was the course (or progress) of this dialectic? That is, were slaves becoming more or less resistant, more or less influential over time?

The danger when one weighs the effect of any individual human life, of any single act of resistance (or collaboration) against the infinite sands of time is that all human agency, all humanity, can appear futile. But the fact that people can not control their history, does not mean that they have no part in its making. The challenge for historians of the lowcountry, is to preserve the complexity of the dynamic relationship between the individual and the society, between the specific locale and the larger world, and between the particular possibilities of a moment and the passage of time. Pondering the long and tortured process of historical change, the nineteenth-century English socialist William Morris once wrote of "how men fight and lose the battle, and the thing they fought for comes about in spite of their defeat, and when it comes turns out not to be what they meant, and other men have to fight for what they meant under another name."[37]

Today in the lowcountry, the struggle continues.

* * *

Commentary

WILLIAM DUSINBERRE

I shall comment only indirectly on Robert Olwell's stimulating paper. He persuasively suggests that historians should analyze how lowcountry slavery changed over time; he proposes a periodization well-suited to that purpose; and his commentary on recent historiography is illuminating. But I seek instead to complement his paper by taking the same group of recent books he has discussed, and indicating what this research may add up to if we emphasize *continuities* from 1720 to 1860.

A central contention of these books is that lowcountry slaves gained considerable autonomy from their masters. The most powerful statement of this view, for the eighteenth century, is in the splendid work of Philip Morgan. In stressing the slaves' autonomy, however, Morgan and the astute synthesizer Ira Berlin may present an unbalanced picture.[1] I wish to look at a dozen elements of the slave system, starting with the masters' power, then examining the extent of the slaves' autonomy, hoping thus to suggest where the balance lay between masters' power and slaves' autonomy.[2]

Rice culture produced an extraordinary concentration of wealth. Rice planters were by far the richest people in late-colonial North America.[3] And the size of their plantations grew ever larger. During the 1740s the median South Carolina slave had lived on a plantation of thirty-five slaves. By 1860 the median lowcountry rice slave was owned by a planter holding just over two hundred slaves.[4] These estates were huge compared to those elsewhere in the South. A slave in the Rice Kingdom was likely to be part of an estate more than eight times as large as those elsewhere.[5]

Rice culture undermined the slaves' health more than anywhere else in North America (except perhaps on sugar plantations). In the mid-nineteenth century about two-thirds of slave children on rice plantations died before age fifteen. This was even worse—a lot worse—than the 46 percent of slave children elsewhere in the South who died before age fifteen.[6] And conditions on rice plantations were probably no less horrific in the eighteenth century.

Yet despite these frightful conditions the slave population of the Rice Kingdom soon reproduced itself naturally, and even achieved a small growth rate. But even Jamaica had *nearly* achieved a naturally self-reproducing slave population by 1817, once the number of women matched the number of men.[7] The important question is not, "Was the slave population growing?" but "How fast was it growing?" Was it growing at the rate of about 27 percent every ten years (as it was in most of the nineteenth-century South[8]), or was it growing at only about 4 percent every ten years (as seems to have been true on rice plantations[9])? A historian should *not* say, I think, that the Chesapeake and the lowcountry both could "boast" self-reproducing slave populations.[10] We need instead a strong statement that health conditions remained so dreadful for rice slaves—especially as reflected in child mortality rates—that the slave population's natural rate of growth was tiny, as contrasted with that in the Chesapeake and elsewhere in North America.

The governing of lowcountry slaves probably was even harsher than that elsewhere in the South. The masters were particularly anxious to control their slaves because slaves outnumbered them so heavily. And since masters normally left their rice plantations for six months each year, they could not readily monitor the severity of their overseers.

No doubt brutality toward slaves declined somewhat after the eighteenth century; thus the last slave burned alive by public authority in South Carolina seems to have been in 1830.[11] But here again, I think we should emphasize continuity: Ever since rice plantations became rooted in South Carolina, about 1720, the governing of slaves there was always particularly harsh, and it remained so until 1865. This view is documented in Norrece Jones's *Born a Child of Freedom*, which convincingly shows that severe punishments of slaves were common in the nineteenth-century lowcountry.[12]

The lowcountry slaves' overt resistance primarily took the form of fleeing a plantation (at least for a few days or weeks) rather than of striking out violently at the masters.[13] And while the number of insurrections and conspiracies may have been greater in the lowcountry than elsewhere in the South, the number, and the scale, of these conspiracies was small compared to those in the Caribbean. Lowcountry slaves almost always realized that the white people—even in areas where slaves greatly outnumbered them—would rapidly gather overwhelming military power to crush any hint of rebellion. Of course lowcountry slaves were *not* contented: their discontent was profound, as was shown by the frequency of temporary flights, the ubiquity of "day-to-day" dissidence, and the hostile spirit of their folk tales. Thus the relative infrequency of violent resistance is testimony to the severity of the regime which lowcountry masters imposed on their bondspeople.

Where does this emphasis on the masters' power leave us with the question of the slaves' agency?

Charles Joyner and Philip Morgan, with other historians, have demonstrated that lowcountry slaves gained considerable autonomy— probably more than rural slaves achieved anywhere else in the South.[14] This result flowed principally from two sources: the "task system" and the lowcountry slaves' relative isolation from white people. The task system arose from negotiation between masters and slaves, where slaves pushed to gain control over their time in the late afternoon (after a speedy slave could complete the day's task). This system was accepted by rice planters because of the shortage of white overseers, and because a field hand could tend so many acres of rice land—spread over such a large distance—that no overseer could carefully supervise the labor of more than a relatively few field hands. The slaves' pressure alone was *not* enough to achieve a task system: doubtless slaves in Jamaica (where there was also a shortage of white overseers) would have preferred a task system too, but their pressure could not gain it for them. The reason—as Philip Morgan has argued—was that a slave on a sugar plantation could tend only a relatively small patch of land; consequently a Jamaican overseer could keep his eyes on a large number of slaves, concentrated together in gang labor.[15] This is a salutary reminder that pressure from the slaves could often gain significant results only when other circumstances favored their achieving their goals.

Lowcountry masters limited what the slaves could gain from the task system by denying them a regular meat ration, so that the slaves would have to use much of their so-called "free" time in hunting or fishing. And at certain times of the year masters suspended the task system. Nevertheless, this system *did* give lowcountry slaves more control over their time than was common in the rural South. Many slaves used this time to work their provision grounds—or to do craft work—not only to supply their families with food, but to produce a surplus. Masters often tried to confine this marketing to the plantation itself. But a substantial number of slaves—especially near Charleston or Savannah—evaded such restrictions, managing to get their produce to buyers other than their own masters. These activities improved the slaves' material conditions; and even more important, the slaves built, with this work, their self-esteem and their family solidarity. Although they had no legal right to own property, slaves acquired for themselves a customary right to do so; and they commonly owned chickens, household goods, Sunday clothes, and sometimes pigs. A handful acquired a cow, or even a mule or a horse. Such possessions were more widely held by lowcountry slaves than by bondspeople elsewhere in the South.[16]

The shortage of white overseers meant that enslaved "drivers" were granted more authority in the lowcountry than elsewhere. These drivers—by sometimes turning a blind eye to "misdemeanors" committed by field hands—enhanced the relative autonomy in working life which the task system offered to lowcountry field hands.[17] But two caveats may be entered. The despotic power entrusted to drivers surely corrupted some of them. And Julie Saville—who does *not* romanticize the Reconstruction period—nevertheless observes that the autonomy in working life enjoyed by lowcountry *freedpeople* after 1865 was hugely greater than that which the slaves had possessed. Saville urges us not to exaggerate the amount of autonomy slaves could acquire from the combined effects of the task system and the system of black drivers.[18]

By contrast, the autonomy lowcountry slaves enjoyed in their religious life was immense, especially in the eighteenth century when masters discouraged the Christianization of their slaves. And when Christianization did finally come, it often came via black preachers, who gave their own spin to a Christian message. Even after 1830, when white evangelicals modified their earlier tune and preached to slaves a version of Christianity intoning obeisance and submissiveness, lowcountry slaves proved remarkably resistant to this message. I think Margaret Washington Creel has best conveyed the tone of rural lowcountry Afro-Christianity in the nineteenth century; and she persuasively argues that African influences saturated that amalgam, at least as late as the 1860s. *This* variant of Afro-Christianity was by no means the profoundly Christian alloy (however much adapted to the slaves' interests) which gripped slave communities elsewhere in the South.[19]

The lowcountry slaves' distinctive Gullah language was less intelligible to most whites than the black English prevalent elsewhere in the South, and this helped lowcountry slaves to hide their thoughts from surveillance. And as Charles Joyner has also shown, trickster tales served complex needs of the slaves, while again disguising their thoughts from their masters.[20] Because lowcountry slaves' language and folklore retained more African elements than slaves could preserve elsewhere, their culture was more autonomous than elsewhere; and this surely sometimes benefited lowcountry slaves. But this cultural autonomy may not have been an unmixed blessing; and I think some historians will say so, as the years go on. (Indeed, Robert Olwell's book has already presented interesting evidence on this subject.)[21]

The conventional view has been that the family life of lowcountry slaves was less disrupted than that of slaves elsewhere in the South, because relatively few lowcountry slaves were sold in the interstate slave trade, and because fewer slaves there than elsewhere had to resort to abroad marriages. Nevertheless, a flourishing *intra*state slave trade did disrupt some lowcountry slave families, while others were smashed when a master punished an indomitable fugitive by selling her or him out of the state. And against whatever advantages remained to lowcountry slave families must be set a huge disadvantage: the lowcountry's devastating child mortality meant that even more families lost loved ones—children—than elsewhere. Which was worse—to see one's child sold to a slave trader at age twelve, or to witness that child's death at age twelve (or earlier)? Slave parents in the Rice Kingdom who had six children saw four of them die—on average—before age fifteen.[22] I doubt whether the slaves' family life was less unhappy in the lowcountry than elsewhere.

During the nineteenth century about 12 percent of lowcountry slaves lived in Charleston and Savannah, where life could be substantially less oppressive than on the plantations.[23] Even here, however, there were countervailing forces. For example, the excess in the number of urban female slaves over males, and the employment of many of these women in domestic service, reduced the opportunities of these slaves for stable family life; and it exposed the women to even more sexual exploitation by white men than they were likely to encounter on the plantations.

A higher proportion of lowcountry plantation slaves held specialized positions than elsewhere in the South.[24] Yet the long lists of specialized workers on a rice plantation can give a misleading impression. A "plantation cook" or an "overseer's cook," for example, would normally have worked as a field hand for most of her life, and she was made a cook only when too old to do much field labor. The majority of carpenters were not *highly* skilled, and they spent many months of the year doing field work, turning to carpentry only during slack times in the agricultural cycle. A fraction of the specialized workers did nevertheless constitute an occupational elite, including the drivers, some of the "trunkminders,"[25] and the most skilled of the artisans and domestic servants; but these may have constituted less than half of all those plantation slaves who held specialized positions, and therefore only perhaps 10 percent of all adult plantation slaves.[26]

Finally, the masters' ideology needs consideration: it served an important function in shaping the masters' self-image. When the stern patriarchalism of the eighteenth century was later transmuted into paternalist ideas,[27] this altered ideology influenced the conduct of some masters, making their treatment of slaves somewhat less harsh than it had been in the eighteenth century. But, as Clarence Walker reminds us,[28] we should not look at the lowcountry through a romantic haze. The conditions which slaves experienced there in 1860 were still appalling; and I think our emphasis should be on what was actually happening on the plantations, only secondarily on the ideology with which—like a gas mask—masters sought to protect themselves from inhaling the "miasma": the contaminated air surrounding lowcountry slavery.

If a glass is half empty, it may nevertheless be described as "half full." Many of the best recent books on lowcountry slavery—for example, Philip Morgan's and Ira Berlin's—seem sometimes to argue that the lives of the slaves were indeed half full. But suppose that the glass was *90 percent* empty—that health conditions on lowcountry plantations were dreadful, and remained so; that most slaves were at some time subjected to excruciating pain, and to terrifying acts of despotism, successfully aimed at deterring almost all violent resistance. Suppose that many masters, many overseers, and some enslaved drivers were corrupted by their despotic powers, so that they abused those powers. Suppose that nearly all lowcountry masters deprived their slaves of a regular meat ration, in order to curtail the free time which the slaves might have gained from the task system. Suppose that—despite the development of skills among some slaves—an overwhelming majority of female plantation slaves, and a vast majority of male plantation slaves were obliged to perform mind-numbing drudgery in often wet, and sometimes perishingly cold, swampland for most of their working lives, without pay, with only brief opportunities to leave the plantation, and with no chance whatever of being manumitted. Suppose, furthermore, that only a small proportion of lowcountry slaves lived in towns, where they might hope to escape the worst constrictions of plantation life. . . .

Perhaps we historians should vigorously affirm that the glass, which had once been 95 percent empty, remained 90 percent empty even in 1860, despite the slaves' heroic efforts to make better lives for themselves. *Was* the glass half full by 1860, or did lowcountry slavemasters indeed successfully continue depriving the slaves of most of the meaning of life?

Paul Robeson and Richard Wright on the Arts and Slave Culture

STERLING STUCKEY

> *The glory of my boyhood years was my father. I loved him like no one else in the world. His people, among whom he moved as a patriarch for many years before I was born, loved him, too. And the white folks—even the most lordly of aristocratic Princeton, had to respect him.*
>
> –PAUL ROBESON, *Here I Stand* (1957)

> *A quarter of a century was to elapse between the time I saw my father sitting with the strange woman and the time when I was to see him again, standing alone upon the red clay of a Mississippi plantation, a sharecropper, clad in ragged overalls holding a muddy hoe in his gnarled, veined hands . . . [H]e was standing against the sky, smiling toothlessly. . . . I stood before him, poised, my mind aching as it embraced the simple nakedness of his life, feeling how completely his soul was imprisoned by the slow flow of the seasons, by wind and rain and sun, how fastened were his memories to a crude and raw past, how chained were his actions and emotions to the direct, animalistic impulses of his withering body. . . .*
>
> –RICHARD WRIGHT, *Black Boy* (1937)

After escaping from slavery in North Carolina, Paul Robeson's father eventually moved to Princeton, New Jersey. Though illiterate at the time of his escape, by the time he arrived in Princeton, he had graduated from college with honors in Greek and Latin. Small wonder that he expected Paul, who was born in Princeton in 1898, to meet the highest standards in every field. And small wonder that he was a respected leader of the tiny black community in Princeton that covered but a handful of blocks. Many of the Robeson relatives, ex-slaves and former sharecroppers from North Carolina, lived there and formed a close family at the center of which was Paul's father. The Reverend William Drew Robeson disdained any airs of superiority toward his largely illiterate kin, some of whom worked as caretakers and coachmen in town, as laborers at farms nearby, or in brickyards in Princeton.[1]

Since Princeton was a magnet for the privileged sons of the white South, southern Negroes who moved there found little relief from racism. As Paul put it, the sons of the masters were there as the South extended its reach over time. The controlling mind of the Princeton of Robeson's youth was Wall Street, and he explained that Bourbon and banker were one in the town where "the decaying smell of the big house" blended with "the crisper smell of the countinghouse." He thought Princeton "spiritually located in Dixie," and added, "the theology was Calvin, the religion cash." In addition, Paul remarked that historically, "the great university drew a large part of its student body and faculty from below the Mason-Dixon Line, and along with those sons of the Bourbons came the most rigid social and economic patterns of White Supremacy."[2]

Southern black culture moved North with migrating former slaves and sharecroppers. The flock shepherded by the Reverend Robeson was said to have "consisted almost entirely of rural Negroes from the South" who "might as well have been in Alabama even then," according to Paul. In part, the preservation of southern black culture in the North owed much, certainly in Princeton, to the fact that the education so crucial to Paul's upbringing did not extend into most other homes which, in a number of instances, included those of his own relatives.[3] The extraordinary bond that he later had with southern, working-class blacks appears to have developed from such associations in youth.

In those early years, his father never discussed slavery with him. No doubt the tragic death of his wife in a fire contributed to the father seeking to harbor the youth—six at the time of her death—from unnecessary pain. Despite his mother's death, Robeson found a nurturing, wider home in the black community. Moreover, other blacks seemed to think him fated for great things. "Somehow they were sure of it, and because of that belief they added an extra measure to the affection they lavished on their preacher's motherless child," he remarked, and "wondered at times about this notion that [he] was some kind of child of destiny" whose "future would be linked with the longed-for better days to come."⁴

Despite their poverty, he found among the ex-slaves and sharecroppers folk wit and tale and the joy of laughter. Theirs was a world in which the home was concert stage, theater, and social center where the whole range of Negro music was heard: songs of trials and triumphs, of love and longing, hymn-song and ragtime ballad, gospels and blues, and the "healing comfort of the illimitable sorrow of the Spirituals." The Robesons, together with others, cherished spirituals and blues at a time when many in the black middle class, seeking approval from whites, shunned them. That they sang blues as well as spirituals was by then exceptional, especially in the home of a preacher. During slavery, the two musics enjoyed a closer relationship than is generally conceived today, and Paul's father continued that tradition, so Paul did not conclude, as some students of slave music have, that the spirituals were sacred, while the blues were profane and the devil's music.⁵

Paul's earliest conception of slave character was drawn from his father's example. Consequently, the extremely negative association of blacks with slavery that were so troublesome to many blacks, especially to educated ones, did not seem to affect him. His father's qualities as a human being served to undermine any defense of slavery or attack on the humanity of slaves. Such qualities did not end with William Drew Robeson, for his church on Witherspoon Street in Princeton "still stands with one of the stained-glass windows glowing 'In Loving memory of Sabra Robeson,'" Reverend Robeson's slave mother to whom Paul referred with respect deep into the twentieth century.⁶

The impulse that led him to escape from slavery caused the Reverend Robeson to champion freedom for his people in Princeton and in other New Jersey communities. In so doing, he won the respect of whites even as efforts were mounted to curb him. The editor of a local newspaper wrote that Reverend Robeson "was very familiar with the characteristics of his race and was always interested in their welfare. He quickly resented any attempt to belittle them or to interfere with their rights." It was said that Reverend Robeson "had the temperament which has produced so many orators in the South and he held his people together in the church here with a fine discernment of their needs." Paul has written: "Though my father was a man of ordinary height, he was very broad of shoulders and his physical bearing reflected the rock-like strength and dignity of his character. He had the greatest speaking voice I have ever heard. It was a deep, sonorous basso, richly melodic and refined, vibrant with the love and compassion which filled him. . . ."[7]

Paul's father impressed on his teenage son that he should never assume that any success achieved was just for himself, or that his burden should be less than that of others. "I had a very dear father," he once stated, "whom I often heard talk from the pulpit and say—it is a very simple text—when you go into the vineyard you do your job the same as everybody else." Apparently Paul did just that, working beside others "whether it be a brickyard or a hotel. . . ."[8] Still, his burden in the vineyard was harsh because his labors extended beyond the normal ones. As tender in age and sensibility as he was, his father expected him to withstand any assault upon his dignity in the interest of his people who were thought not to have proven themselves. As a boy, he recalled looking at his father, whose father had been a slave, possibly born in Africa, and thinking: "Is someone going to tell me my father is a savage, that my father is not a human person? I should say not!"[9]

In addition to being Phi Beta Kappa at Rutgers, Paul was All-American in football, a champion debater, and gave the commencement address. Walter Camp, the dean of football authorities, said that he was the finest end, on defense and attack, ever to play the game. Paul also took a law degree from Columbia University, won fame as a singer and actor, and was a top student at the London School of Oriental Languages.[10] There could not be a clearer indication of his intellectual ends than his commencement address at Rutgers, in which his discussion of the "sacred duty" of educated blacks to go forth to help their people shows the influence of W. E. B. Du Bois.[11]

Eschewing a career as a lawyer, almost simultaneously he achieved national attention as a singer and actor. In 1925, the critic for the *New York World* said of a Robeson concert in New York: "All who listened last night to the first concert in this country made up entirely of Negro music . . . may have been present at a turning point, one of those thin points of time in which a star is born and not yet visible—the first appearance of this folk wealth to be made without deference or apology. Paul Robeson's voice is difficult to describe. It is a voice in which deep bells ring." The Greenwich Village concert also was lauded by the *New York Times* critic, who reported, "His Negro Spirituals have the ring of the revivalist; they hold in them a world of religious experience; it is their cry from the depths, this universal humanism, that touches the heart." "Sung by one man," he continued, "they voiced the sorrow and hopes of a people."[12]

Paul's association in youth with relatives constituted his primary means of contact with the singing of ex-slaves, which was immensely important in his case because he sang slave music exclusively over a period of years, a unique development for a concert artist. His sense of the worth of Negro dialect was in marked contrast to negative pronouncements on the subject by critic James Weldon Johnson and, later, by novelist and critic Ralph Ellison.[13] While the focus of Johnson and Ellison was on creative writing, their bias betrayed an unease with dialect on principle that caught on, virtually unchallenged, among black intellectuals and artists.

Robeson knew that Negro dialect was the language of the slave artist/field hand, an aspect of slavery not yet touched on by students of slavery. Like W. E. B. Du Bois, he rejected the view, popular among some Reconstruction historians, that modern black culture owes more to developments from Reconstruction than to slave culture. As explicitly and precisely as Du Bois in *Black Reconstruction*, Robeson, recognizing himself as a direct and natural beneficiary of vital aspects of the artistic heritage of his ancestors, remarked: "The spirituals and Negro dialect were also part of my earliest background. My father was the minister of a small Negro community, and so the spirituals must have been known to me before I was born. I 'learned' Negro dialect and the spirituals as I learned to talk and walk and breathe and sing."[14] Apparently no attempt by others to encourage him to sing spirituals like a white man made much of an impression. Thus, in his voice as he sang spirituals, the world came to hear, perhaps without knowing it, the projection of slave vocal potential and fulfillment, of which his ex-slave father's voice provided a prime example.

Robeson sang both spirituals and work songs as he wrote about them, as though more than language was at stake: "These songs reflected a spiritual force, a people's faith in itself and a faith in its great calling; they reflected the wrath and protest against the enslavers and the aspiration to freedom and happiness."[15] He appreciated the poetic beauty and revolutionary thrust of "I Got A Home in Dat Rock," which was an early and lasting favorite:

Poor man Laz'rus, poor as I,
Don't you see (2)
Poor man Laz'rus, poor as I,
When he died he found a home on high,
He had a home in dat rock,
Don't you see?

Rich man Dives, he lived so well,
Don't you see? (2)
Rich man Dives, he lived so well,
When he died he found a home in Hell,
He had no home in dat Rock,
Don't you see?

God gave Noah de rainbow sign,
Don't you see? (2)
God gave Noah de rainbow sign,
No more water but fire next time,
Better get a home in dat rock,
Don't you see?[16]

In 1926, Carl Sandburg compared Robeson to Roland Hayes, the great Negro tenor, observing that "Hayes imitates white culture and uses methods from the white man's conservatories of music, so that when he sings a Negro spiritual the audience remarks, "What technic; what a remarkable musical education he must have had!" When Paul Robeson sings spirituals, the remark is: "That is the real thing—he has kept the best of himself and not allowed the schools to take it away from him!"[17]

It must have seemed unusual, given his success in *Othello* at the young age of thirty-two in 1930, that Robeson did not begin distancing himself from the speech of the southern Negro, especially since his command of Shakespeare's English won much praise. In London for the *Othello* opening, a *New York Times* critic, G. W. Bishop, stated: "Robeson lives the part imaginatively and, of course, his greatest asset is his magnificent voice, which he uses perfectly." Bishop reported that not only was "the curtain raised and lowered twenty times before the frenzy of applause subsided" but that seasoned "playgoers searching their memories [could] recall no such scene in a London theatre in many years."[18]

Rather than distance himself from slave language and culture, Paul considered the uses of language in other cultures to further drive his point home: "Let us take a concrete example. What would have become of the genius of Marie Lloyd if she had been ashamed of being cockney? Would Robert Burns have been as great a poet if he had denied his ploughman speech and aped the gentlemen of his day? Do not misunderstand me. Do not think I am trying to say that those who are born to inequality cannot become cultured people. I mean exactly the reverse. I am attacking the impulse which drives such people to hide their true value under a false foreign culture, applied from the outside, when, instead, they could encourage a graceful, natural growth from within. It is not as imitation Europeans, but as Africans, that we have value."[19] Building on his concern about a false culture being imposed from without, he stated: "Only those who have lived in a state of inequality will understand what I mean—workers, European Jews, women . . . those who have felt their status, their race, or their sex a bar to a complete share in all that the world has to offer." Those disadvantaged groups could understand what makes Negroes want to demonstrate, "on the white man's own ground," that they are equal. Still, "only a few will recognize that the very impulse which drives them to copy those with the desired status . . . is killing what is of most value—the personality which makes them unique."[20]

Though he believed the artistic value of the spirituals was "universally acknowledged," he did not deny European influences on them or on Negro folk music generally, observing that the folk songs of various immigrant people, of the Irish, the Scots, and the Spanish, were influences. "But they did not determine the distinctiveness and universal significance of the folk-song culture of the American Negroes," he argued. Including the spirituals in the broader context of slave folk song, he asserted: "The power and beauty of Negro songs, the indigenous features which distinguish Negro folklore from the songs of all other peoples in the world, stem from ancient African culture, from the remarkable musicality which the Negroes inherited from Africa."[21]

Rejecting any conception of high or low culture, Robeson thought the music of Duke Ellington as important as that of Marian Anderson, and he thought Count Basie the equal of any piano player in the world. This is not to say that he did not respect classical music, for he did, and he sang a great deal of it. Rather, having placed near or at the top of many fields, with command of a number of languages, and having lived abroad and moved in the highest intellectual and social circles, he had the confidence to "challenge any opera singer to take those ball parks like Mahalia Jackson and Sister Rosetta Thorpe."[22]

Although he was one of the great bass-baritones of the twentieth century, there are countless reviews but no systematic treatment of this aspect of Robeson's art. We have relatively brief critical reactions to his concerts, but no scholarship on his training; it is often assumed that it was mainly classical. In the most comprehensive work on Robeson, Martin Duberman evaluates his singing from the perspective of classical music critics and musicians who sometimes appear to know little or nothing of the shaping of Robeson's art. Thus, Duberman, in *Paul Robeson*, writes that Paul "proceeded on the basis of natural gifts alone" while "worrying about his lack of training. . . ."[23]

Equally misguided, novelist Ralph Ellison writes that classical exposure was *all* that Robeson knew, referring in *Shadow and Act* to Robeson's "development" having resulted "from an extensive personal contact with European culture, free from the influences which shape southern Negro personality."[24] This astonishing statement indicates that there were serious gaps in Ellison's knowledge of the black folk tradition, that he greatly underestimated the value of its language and its degree of complexity and potential for grandeur. In addition, it is clear that his knowledge of the struggle for human rights in the South, both spiritual and social, was sadly inadequate.

Years before Ellison penned his thoughts on Robeson, Paul addressed an integrated audience in New Orleans, remarking that he "must come South again and again, again and yet again," that it was only there that he achieved "absolute and utter identity with [his] people." Foreshadowing protests beginning with the Montgomery Bus Boycott, he asserted: "I must . . . come South. I must do so to be with my people and to refresh my soul with their strength. . . . The firing line, the battle zone is here. . . . We must expose ourselves unremittingly to the source of strength that makes the black South strong!"[25]

Furthermore, to argue that Robeson lacked training is to overlook the fact that most of the great black musicians of the century, singers as well as instrumentalists, were under the influence of the music of the black church. Robeson addressed the matter: "Yes, I heard my people singing!—in the glow of parlor coalstove and on summer porches sweet with lilac air, from choir loft to Sunday morning pews—and *my soul was filled with their harmonies*. Then, too, I heard these songs in the very sermons of my father, for in the Negro's speech there is much of the phrasing and rhythms of folk song. The great, soaring gospels we love are merely sermons that are sung; and as we thrill to such gifted singers as Mahalia Jackson, we hear the rhythmic eloquence of our preachers, so many of whom, like my father, are masters of poetic speech."[26] In that statement there is a feature of black culture, during and since slavery, not often remarked—that sermon can become song and song sermon, a movement from one category to another that defies compartmentalization. What is involved is a flowing conception of reality in relating speech to song.[27]

Training among his people had prepared Robeson for a concert career before audiences no matter how sophisticated. He had heard, in the church and in the black community, their anguish and joy in the tones and accents of their speech and as they resonated in song. In the process, he developed a quality of voice remarkable for its ability to portray, much as a writer does through words, fundamental human emotion and experience. The absence of even a hint of artificiality in his sound, its naturalness, won it an honored place in much of world music, which he sang in many languages.

In his London years, from 1927 to 1939, he learned a number of African languages, among them Yoruba, Twi, and Swahili. Indeed, his efforts in this regard, about which so little is known, were the subject of a letter, in 1936, from Melville Herskovits to folklorist Lydia Parish. Herskovits wrote: "You will be interested to know, I am sure, that another person in the minority with us is Paul Robeson. He has worked out correspondences to his own satisfaction and to mine between the African music he knows and American Negro songs, particularly work songs, in rather remarkable fashion. The next time he comes through here [Evanston, Illinois] I am planning to have him record for me a West African war song followed by an American Negro railroad working song, which demonstrates the continuity of tradition in the most startling manner I have yet experienced."[28]

Herskovits asked one of Paul's professors at the London School of Oriental Languages if the rhythms of ex-slave speech to which Robeson was exposed gave him an edge, as Robeson thought, over other students in studying West African languages. The professor responded that Robeson was good in African languages because he was exceptional at learning languages. Still, it is well to recall that Robeson knew southern Negro speech far better than most professors of African languages. It could well be, as he thought, that his exposure to southern Negro speech helped prepare him for the study of West African languages. What is also important is that he came to understand, in academic and performance terms that suited him, that what was generally and mistakenly thought to be simply imperfect language spoken and sung by slaves was a reflection, in part, of African influences in grammar and syntax that David Dalby so brilliantly illustrated in his Hans Wolfe lecture at Bloomington in 1970.[29]

Paul was one of the first American intellectuals to study the speech and music of people of African descent on both sides of the Atlantic.

As he studied in London, he was at times particularly at home with his origins, declaring in the mid-thirties in a handwritten note: "I am a singer and an actor. I am primarily an *artist*. Had I been born in Africa, I would have belonged, I hope, to that family which sings and chants the glories of the tribe. I would have liked in my mature years to have been a wise elder, for I worship wisdom and knowledge of the ways of men."[30]

In an essay that anticipated the sea-change in scholarship on slavery fifty years later, Robeson argued that slave culture was fundamentally African. He asserted, "the dances . . . the songs, and the worship perpetuated by the Negro in America are identical with those of his cousins hundreds of years removed in the depths of Africa, of whom he is only dimly aware."[31] In his view, there was no evidence that slave dance, on the whole, was anything other than African. And though he did not say so, the most powerful evidence of the stamp of Africa on dance in North America was the counterclockwise movement in which the spirituals were born and developed, a movement associated with religious observances in black Africa. But most compelling was his argument that the American Negro's "peculiar sense of rhythm alone would stamp him indelibly as African. . . ."[32]

Paul's aesthetic and academic interests, which often dovetailed, were known to Africans in London, and his example of preparation in gaining knowledge of black Africa established heights toward which others might strive. He wrote that it is not an easy thing "to assume African nationality," that the process is complicated and "fraught with the gravest importance to . . . some millions of coloured folk." He declared that a nationality could not be assumed "as you would a new suit of clothes," adding that "patient inquiry" was needed.[33]

In 1937, together with Max Yergan, Robeson founded the Council on African Affairs, which became, after his return to America in 1939, the most important organization fighting for the liberation of Africa—with the focus on South Africa. Before he left England, a reporter asked him why he was so interested in his people and he responded: "My father was a slave. Can I forget that? Hell, I can't forget that! My own father a slave!" He added: "There can be no greater tragedy than to forget one's origin and end up hated and despised by the people among whom one grew up. To have that happen would be the sort of thing to make me rise from my grave."[34]

Richard Wright thought the slave a product of America, that Africa left no imprint. In fact, Wright could not have been more explicit, writing in his "Blueprint For Negro Writing" that the African's experience in North America marked "the emergence of a new culture in the shell of the old."[35] Stripped of culture, according to this view, the Negro brought nothing of value onto American soil. It might be argued that Wright thought slavery achieved its objective, destroying the Africans' sense of the past, rendering them "a new people" whose sense of humanity was derived from the shaping influences of others. According to Wright, it was "through the portals of the church that the American Negro first entered the shrine of Western culture. Living under slave conditions of life, bereft of his African heritage, the Negro found that his struggle for religion on the plantations between 1820–1860 was nothing short of a struggle for human rights. It remained a relatively progressive struggle until religion began to ameliorate and assuage suffering and denial."[36]

As black leaders such as Richard Allen and David Walker attest for the decade of the eighteen twenties, and Henry Highland Garnet, Frederick Douglass and Daniel Payne for the thirties, forties and beyond, the "struggle for religion," meaning Christianity, by slaves on plantations presupposes that slaves had no religion. Since slaves faced pervasive opposition from the master, high illiteracy, and lacked access to the Bible, how was a struggle for Christianity to be waged? With but dozens of missionaries working full-time among three million and more slaves after 1830, the main struggle concerned attempts by ethnically diverse slaves to find a common vision out of a multitude of African cultural differences. The effort was represented by the symbol of the circle, which was as pervasive as the determination of slave owners to prevent slaves from being exposed to Christianity.[37]

Three years after "Blueprint" was published, Wright qualified his stand regarding African culture, arguing that it was actually brought to America but could not last: "The Negro . . . possessed a rich and complex culture when he was brought to these alien shores. . . . What culture we did have when we were torn from Africa was taken from us; we were separated when we were brought here and forbidden to speak our languages. We possess no remembered cushion of culture upon which we can lay our tired heads. . . ."[38] Perhaps contradicting himself when one recalls his image of "a new culture emerging in the shell of the old," Wright also insists: "And the Negro, instead of being physically weak, is tough and has withstood hardships that have cracked many another people."[39] It would take Wright years to integrate the proposition that Africans brought culture with them into his thought on black culture in America.

Historians once adopted the view that Africans entered North America bereft of culture, the brutalities of the slave trade having stripped it away. A line of argument advanced in recent decades by anthropologists Sidney Mintz and Richard Price accords almost perfectly with this view. In *An Anthropological Approach to the Afro-American Past: A Caribbean Perspective*, they argue that slaves in the Americas were so devoid of African institutions and principles that "new cultures" had to be created from "crowds" of Africans, a position that finds support in Ellison's writings in particular.[40] He believed that slave culture was Americanized and that American pluralism was the midwife that helped bring slave art into existence.[41] Though Wright vacillated, sometimes concluding that Africans in America left their culture behind and sometimes arguing that they brought it with them, usually emphasizing the former, he never subscribed to Ellison's extreme position on pluralism and slave creativity.

Why was the Negro from the time of slavery, asks Wright, in such desperate straits culturally? He answers that question in *Black Boy*, stating that the Negro was never "allowed to catch the full spirit of Western civilization," living "somehow in it but not of it." As he brooded upon the emptiness of black life, he wondered "if clean, positive tenderness, love, honor, loyalty and the capacity to remember were native to man." It is difficult to avoid the conclusion that, with exceptionally broad strokes, he was generalizing from the tragic portrait he had drawn of his father. For he writes of him in his grim autobiography: "From the white landowners above him there had not been handed to him a chance to learn the meaning of loyalty, of sentiment, of tradition. Joy was unknown to him as was despair . . . I forgave him and pitied him as my eyes looked past him to the unpainted wooden shack."[42]

Wright refers to "channels of racial wisdom" as if they are not rooted in the past. Hence, he could not perceive the resilience and complexity of slave cultural life because he knew so little of its sources, and apparently did not discuss such matters with Robeson, for years a friend and occasional artistic collaborator. As Robeson's highly original comparative work with languages and music was under way, Wright was of the opinion that, some time back, two cultures "sprang up" among Negroes, "one for the Negro masses, crude, instinctive, unwritten and unrecognized," and another for the daughters and sons of "a rising bourgeoisie, bloodless, petulant, mannered, and neurotic."[43]

Once more, it is hard to avoid the conclusion that he generalized from his father in imagining the culture of the masses: "a creature of the earth," he described him, "hearty, whole, seemingly indestructible, with no regrets and no hope." Though he overstates the cultural division between middle class blacks and the masses, there is no doubt that the former, in large numbers, were reluctant to be associated with the spirituals and the blues in the opening decades of the twentieth century, many preferring, like Ellison, watered down versions of the spirituals.[44]

Wright, when reflecting on culture, was guided by instinct together with keen powers of observation and intellect. For much of his life he had no real conception of the sources of the folklore he at times so brilliantly represented, sometimes in ways that seemed to contradict his bleak conclusions about black culture. Because he did not know African influences on slave song, tale and dance, and how they related to slave religion, he did not explain what he meant by the "instinctive" culture of the mass of blacks "springing up," nor can there be an explanation, for culture does not spring forth like Athena from the head of Zeus. Painstakingly and communally created, it cannot be eradicated short of the destruction of a people. Wright's immersion in the work of the Chicago School of Sociology, with its thesis that the culture of the rural black was pathological, did not help his effort to understand either slave culture or African American culture since slavery.[45]

Growing up in Mississippi and spending time in Memphis, he could not escape the blues, jazz, and the Negro spiritual, and he found in the blues a bitter resonance with his own history. Hence, he wrote a blues lyric about Georgia that recalls his father standing in the red clay of Mississippi:

> *I miss that red clay, Lawd, I*
> *Need to feel it on my shoes.*
> *Says I miss the red clay, Lawd, I*
> *Need to feel it on my shoes.*
> *I want to see Georgia, cause I*
> *Got them red clay blues.*
>
> *I want to be in Georgia, when the*
> *Big storms start to blow.*
> *Yes I want to be in Georgia when that*
> *Big storm starts to blow.*
> *I want to see the landlords runnin' cause I*
> *Wonder where they gonna go!*
> *I got them red clay blues.*[46]

This was not the only blues lyric that Wright wrote. In fact, he wrote close to twenty and chose Robeson for "King Joe" (Joe Louis Blues), which was recorded in 1941. For Robeson to sing the blues seemed out of character for a man of his vocal gifts, but Wright could not have found a greater background for Robeson's voice than the Count Basie band. While it does not appear likely that Wright, when "King Joe" was recorded, thought the blues a product of slavery, it is possible that Robeson did. The structure of some blues and spirituals is close enough to suggest a common origin of which Wright may not have been aware. A superb but largely unsung poet, Wright had a feel for the blues. But "King Joe" is a blues more of sunlight than of shadows, which is why Robeson may have come to mind:

> *Rabbit say to Bee, what makes you sting so deep? (2)*
> *Bee say I sting like Joe and rock 'em all to sleep.*

They say old Joe just lays down sleeps all day long, (2)
What old Joe does at night, Lord, sure ain't done him no wrong.

Been in Cleveland, St. Louis, and Chicago, too (2)
But the best is Harlem when a Joe Louis fight is through.[47]

Whatever his reservations about the culture of the Mississippi Negro, Wright also wrote poetry in unmistakable dialect:

Mister, things ain't never been all stirred up this way be'fo!
It ain't never been that Ah couldn't place a stake.
An' all the folks talkin' 'bout something's goin' to break.
Ah feels it in mah bones![48]

An expatriate in Paris as Robeson had been in London, Wright was exposed to Africans, and to others, who were knowledgeable about the continent. France, an imperial nation like England, trained its citizens in universities to go into the colonies. Therefore, it was highly possible that a black person living in that atmosphere could hold an informed opinion of West African culture, much more likely than in the U.S., where there was virtually no interest among intellectuals in Africa.

Yet as late as 1946, when Wright moved to Paris, he had read nothing by African writers and knew little of African history and culture.[49] Not surprisingly, however, African intellectuals, artists and future leaders looked to Wright as "a representative man, an incarnation of black American genius in exile. . . ." Among those who sought him out in 1947, at the suggestion of Jean Paul Sartre, was Alioune Diop, who was launching *Presence Africane*, which soon became the premier journal of African culture.[50]

With his weak background in African culture, Wright was poorly equipped to represent, for *Presence Africaine*, at Diop's urging, English-speaking members of the African diaspora. No better evidence of this can be found than his having conferred with Roy Wilkins, the Executive Secretary of the NAACP regarding non-writers who might attend the First Congress of Negro Writers in Paris, for which preparation began in

1955. Also, Wright submitted not only the name of Ralph Ellison but that of E. Franklin Frazier, the steadfast opponent of the view that African cultural influences could be found in North America.[51]

A testament to his intellectual honesty and astuteness, Wright eventually distanced himself from, while insisting upon, the force of new and pathfinding discoveries. His drastically altered position, which appears in *Black Power* (1954), merits attention from students of black culture across a number of disciplines. But how does one account for the failure of scholars to treat his cultural findings? The timing of the book's appearance in the 1950s, a decade of almost frenzied interest in integration by many black intellectuals, partly accounts for its failure to make an impact on black cultural thought. In any case, within its covers are remarkable passages on how African culture relates to the culture of black Americans. The discussion is important enough to cast new light on Afro American culture in the twenty-first century and earlier. In fact, it should cause us to rethink the forms and significance of sacred dance in slavery and in the black church in America today.

In West Africa, Wright "was astonished" on seeing "women, stripped to the waist, their elongated breasts flopping wildly, do a sort of weaving, circular motion with their bodies, a kind of queer, shuffling dance . . . as if they were talking with the movements of their arms, necks, and torsos; as if words were no longer adequate as a means of communication." He experienced a flash of illumination: "And then I remembered: I'd seen these same snakelike, veering, dances before. . . . Where? Oh, God, yes; in America, in storefront churches, in Holy Roller Tabernacles, in God's Temples, in unpainted wooden prayer-meeting houses on the plantations of the Deep South. . . . And here I was seeing it all again against a background of a surging nationalistic political movement! How could that be? . . . Yet, what I was now looking at in this powerfully improvised dance of these women, I'd seen before in America!"[52]

Wright is referring to sacred dance in the rural and urban South, and in the cities of the North to which blacks had migrated in great numbers by 1950. Since he witnessed the dance in Accra, the dancers could have been Ga-speakers. However, they might well have been Akan-speakers, for he heard people around him give the Akan greeting "Akwaaba," meaning welcome in Asante Twi (a dialect of Akan). Thanks to him, we may be able to identify the ethnic group or groups with which the dancers were affiliated. Since American slavery was hardly unaffected by Africans from areas of present day Ghana, including Ga- and Akan-speakers, enslaved Africans must have brought the dance to North America during the Atlantic slave trade.[53]

Wright had one prepossession on traveling to Africa: he doubted that he would "be able to walk into the African's cultural house and feel at home and know [his] way around." There were for him problems in crossing the bridge thrown up before him. He found the dance "as astonishing and dumbfounding" as when he had seen it in America. What had bothered him about black dance in the United States bothered him in Africa, but he implies that a great many American Negroes would not have been upset, for many could dance and carry a tune and he could not. Moreoever, he wrote: "I'd long contended that the American Negro, because of what he had undergone in the United States, had been basically altered, that his consciousness had been filled with a new content, that 'racial qualities' were but myths of prejudiced minds. Then, if that were true, how could I account for what I now saw? And what I now saw was an exact duplicate of what I'd seen for so many long years in the United States."[54]

Here is an admission that Wright had thought the consciousness of the African slave a blank tablet. While in Ghana, however, a single question was enthroned in his mind and would not leave, he stated, until he "solved the riddle of why black people were able to retain, despite vast distances, centuries of time, and the imposition of alien cultures, such basic and fundamental patterns of behavior and response." He was beginning to understand the toughness of certain qualities of culture brought to America by enchained Africans. Still, his questioning regarding dance and music continued: "Why could I not feel this? Why that peculiar, awkward restraint when I tried to dance or sing?"[55]

But what he had discovered in some ways went beyond much of what anthropologists had argued regarding links between African culture and the culture of American Negroes, beyond survivals and vestigial remains, for he saw the dance style in all its fullness, in flowing, dynamic form. In fact, his description is such that the circularity of the dance he witnessed in Ghana establishes a tie with black dance in slavery, and its veering quality a tie to dance now seen in Daddy Grace's United House of Prayer For All People, and in the storefront churches of black America.[56]

"Last night," he wrote, "I hadn't had time to question myself closely regarding that snakelike, shuffling dance, that strange veering and weaving of the body." Recalling his years in the United States, he added, crucially: "A certain group of anthropologists had long clamored for a recognition of what they had quaintly chosen to call 'African survivals,' a phrase which they had coined to account for exactly what I had observed."[57] Hence, the connection was made between religious practices in West Africa and the religion of sizable numbers of his people in America—halfway into the twentieth century. In the process, Wright opened up a field that yet awaits treatment in comparative terms, for he has affirmed the existence of a major form of sacred dance that thrives today on both sides of the Atlantic.

Wright's testimony demonstrates that yet another form of sacred dance was not destroyed by slaveholders, who saw without understanding. For how else can we explain a form of dance, long prominent in churches, North and South, that apparently was not opposed during slavery, except to conclude that what was considered dance and sacred by slaves was not, in this case, regarded as such by slaveholders. But the problem is more complex, the key to its understanding still more elusive, for a distinguished line of students of African American dance failed to identify the dance described by Wright. The *veering* movement of this dance distinguished it from other slave dance in America and might have caused dance scholars, like whites a century before, to think it too odd in appearance to be called dance. That position, if ever held, has been undermined by Wright.

The music in Daddy Grace's churches is often the music of the blues. In his band in Washington, D.C., nearly a dozen trombonists at times play their instruments with a spirituality so taut that, when it snaps, the possession state is induced. The name "blues," does not apply in the secular sense at such times, for the instruments appear to be the trombones of God. Estimated to have some three million members alone, the United House of Prayer for All People is but one of numerous Pentecostal churches in North America, which means, it is likely, that more than three million African Americans know and practice the African dance described by Wright.[58] This is of particular interest when one takes into account Wright's views, following his trip to Ghana, on the blues and Negro spirituals, both of which he related, finally, to the African response to slavery.

Though Wright did not refer to dance in introducing Paul Oliver's *The Meaning of the Blues*, his brief but rich remarks, set down in Paris in 1960, were to some extent informed by what he had come to know of African influences in slavery. Indeed, in his Foreword he asserts that "shackled, transplanted blacks," "tribal men whose values differed dramatically from those of the Puritan Christian environment in which they were injected" arrived at their own estimates of their condition despite slave owners who thought them incapable of reflecting on their condition.[59]

Wright has a seventeenth-century Virginia planter struggle with his conscience and ruminate: "Now these black animals have human form, but they are not really human, for God would not have made men to look like that. So, I'm free to buy them and work them on my tobacco plantation without incurring the Wrath of God. Moreover, these odd black creatures will . . . leave no record behind of any possible suffering that they might undergo. Yes, I'll buy five of these to be slaves. . . ."[60] Wright appears to have undergone a radical departure from his position prior to going to West Africa, depicting slave holders as deluded in thinking slaves incapable of leaving a record of their longings and sufferings.

He states that slaves did indeed possess what he had earlier doubted, the capacity to recall, and he marveled at their ability to overcome the contempt of the master class. This was demonstrated to his satisfaction, he said, "in those astounding religious songs known as the spirituals," created by slaves "closest to the Big House" who caught "whiffs" of Christianity from southern whites. In a shrewd observation, he concluded that "the field slaves were beyond the pale."[61] That being the case, what happened to the kind of religious struggle for humanity on the plantations to which he earlier referred? Since it does not follow that those working in the big house created the spirituals—the songs were linked indissolubly to sacred African dance, which was loathed by slave masters—Wright appears to be arguing that field hands, from quarters nearest the big house, created the spirituals.

"It was from slaves and their descendants that the songs . . . called the blues came," he declared boldly and unconventionally, undoubtedly thinking of field hands. In locating the beginning of the blues as a musical form with slaves, he challenges us, brilliantly, to enter upon uncharted ground with all sorts of implications for the study of slavery. In an interpretation of the blues that is in some ways remarkably like those of Frederick Douglass and James Baldwin, Wright states that "the most astonishing aspect of the blues is that, though replete with a sense of defeat and down-heartedness, they are not intrinsically pessimistic; their burden of woe and melancholy is dialectically redeemed through sheer force of sensuality, into an almost exultant affirmation of life, of love, of sex, of movement, of hope. No matter how repressive was the American environment, the Negro never lost faith in or doubted his deeply endemic capacity to live. All blues are a lusty, lyrical realism charged with taut sensibility."[62]

Wright's position is radically at odds with the work of almost all historians, few of whom have given meaningful attention to the spirituals, let alone the blues, as a product of slave genius. And like Robeson on the spirituals, Wright notes that slaves, in the blues, created a form of music that has achieved the status of a universal art form. "In Buenos Aires, Stockholm, Copenhagen, London, Berlin, Paris, Rome, in fact, in every large city of the earth where lonely, disinherited men congregate for pleasure or amusement, the . . . wail of the blues, and their strident offspring, jazz, can be heard," he states.[63] In so closely linking the blues to jazz, in fact in finding the origins of jazz in the blues, Wright was among the first to argue that, in studying slavery, the blues *and* jazz should be treated, a position that should gain adherents as the interrelatedness of the spirituals, jazz and the blues is increasingly acknowledged.

Paralleling Robeson's interest in the language of slave song, Wright considers the language of the blues "terser than Basic English" and "purged of metaphysical implications," an unpretentious language tailored to the harsh realities of which slaves and their descendants sang. But such qualities of the blues will be of greater interest to literary scholars than to historians, who are likely to seize upon Wright's argument that "The most striking feature of these songs is that a submerged theme of guilt, psychological in nature, seems to run through them." They are likely to do so because Wright asks: "Could this guilt have stemmed from the burden of renounced rebellious impulse?"[64]

On the other hand, the blues symbolize disaffection. Brought into being and responded to by slaves, they provide a new optic on master-slave relations. Since they appear to be closely related in ancestry to the spirituals, which argues the complexity and depth of the slave aesthetic, one can ask what art came out of Roman slavery, or any other slave society, that rivals the spirituals and the blues? This is a particularly searching question when one bears in mind the indispensable role of the spirituals and the blues in the development of jazz, one of the modern world's great artistic forms.[65]

* * *

Commentary

ROGER D. ABRAHAMS

Sterling Stuckey makes eloquent testimony to the importance of two of the artist-heroes of the Civil Rights struggle of the 1930s and 40s, Richard Wright and Paul Robeson. Stuckey gets at the heart of the lives of the these giants, through forms of plaintive song, the *spirituals* and the *blues*. Juxtaposing these two men and these two forms of expression encourages him to draw on the entire range of song-dance which emerged from the Black Struggle. By all accounts since the Civil War, spirituals represented the lot of the enslaved more fully than any other.

They provided the vehicle for the community of celebrants to express their plight in common and to bring upon the congregation the ever-present promise of *getting happy* as the spirit of the Lord descended upon them. These song-dances channeled anxiety through Old Testament parables that the hardship engendered by enslavement might be transcended.

On the other hand, the *blues* became the focal secular genre of the early twentieth century, by which personal exile came to be expressed. Neither of these ineluctably African American inventions were placed in such a central symbolic position until artists and educators, writers and orators focused on them, for they had many other choices from other song-dances which originated in the slave quarter or the brush-arbor. Facing the need for visible and aural productions around which African American identity might be formulated, the more up-beat play songs such as breakdown and strut had been coopted by whites in blackface. Stuckey argues that the spirituals and the blues provided these heroes with forms through which they, individually, felt connected not only to the heritage of the plantation but, through time and study, to an African past. As such, Wright and Robeson, like DuBois early on and later Ellison, Baldwin, Angelou, Murray, and Morrison, drew upon a vocabulary of shared social complaint that audiences could recognize immediately as vehicles for taking social rupture and grief, finding in these forms the containing metaphors for these alienated states of being.

Happily, in the years since both Sterling and I were being directed to attend to the details of the transatlantic flow of culture by Melville Herskovits, the continuity of African practices, musical and otherwise, were maintained on both sides of the Atlantic. These continued developments may be traced in song and dance, as they are found in forms of worship, health maintenance, in the production of various kinds of pottery, woven baskets and other items of material culture, and work and play. The resulting wide and deep body of scholarship demonstrated that throughout the Atlantic World a common culture was forged drawing upon the consistent production of new popular styles which actually were predominately confected of old customary forms of behavior given a new spin. Within a wide range of vernacular practices were to be found layers of meaning and understanding that reestablished the links within the transatlantic world. The concept of the body and the soul was demonstrably shared, projected in forms of worship, healing, and popular entertainments.

Song and dance fads occurring in both Africa and the Americas reflected the operation of the same set of ethico-aesthetic features, and each has flowed both ways across the Atlantic. Just as jazz, swing, and today, rap and salsa have been major styles of song and dance among Africans on both sides of the Atlantic, so too the jubilees and shouts, the spirituals of African American worship practices have long been the staples of church singing throughout Christianized Africa, especially in those places missionized by African American ministers.

Even more complicated has been the impact of the blackface performance throughout this geographical expanse. Of course that theatrical form which came to be identified as *the* representative American form in the last half of the nineteenth century was initially a white imitation of slave entertainments. As such, it became a form of popular entertainment in many African entrepots, as it had become in European cities. Ostensibly a rendering of slave holidays and Saturday night dances, such imitations underscored the idea that everyone in the slave quarters was capable of bursting into song or cutting a caper.

When the emerging Christian churches, especially Methodists, attempted to "civilize" the leisure practices of the enslaved and then the emancipated workers, they introduced the tea party and dance, which was soon transformed into the Tea Meeting in the anglophonic West Indies, a more competitive and lubricious event; and in many African ports of call the Concert Party was spawned. Both Tea Meeting and Concert Parties drew upon the materials and the patterns of performance of the blackface minstrel stage, evolving into a contest of wits, of high oratory, of comic routines, and sentimental songs. In Africa, Concert Parties were performed in indigenous tongues in these multicultural urban settings. Thus, one could discover skits and sketches, songs and dances from five, six, even seven different language groups. The presumption was that the audience might understand everything. I mention these forms of entertainment only to underscore the portability and adaptability of African and Afro-American expressive forms. Such a history, of course, undermines the notion that everything of cultural importance was erased in the Middle Passage. Perhaps even more interesting for the present occasion, a number of these adaptable forms carried with them reminders of enslavement, of plantation culture, and of emancipation. Significantly, the two forms which Stuckey focuses upon, the blues and the spiritual, are not associated with the blackface show, but rather with actual black community responses to the dislocation experiences and the disenfranchisement of the slaves and their descendants.

Sterling and I have had a chance to marvel over the achievement of Paul Robeson a number of times over the last twenty-five years—or is it more? To me, a Jewish would-be athlete and singer whose family came from the left politically, Paul Robeson was both a god and a familiar voice. In 1947, coming home from basketball practice with the absolute knowledge that I would never make the first team, I threw myself on the couch and put my 78s of Paul Robeson on the record-player. I knew exactly what therapy I needed, and it was completely contained within that voice offering the balm of Gilead. What did I know of sin- sickness, but I knew that my adolescent soul was in need of ministration. Of course, it was his voice and not any salve that promised this healing. This was the only voice ever to visit earthlings that so totally addressed the sense of loss and longing that percolated through my imagination—a sense that had been forever cemented in my imagination when my parents took me to see the Robeson-Ferrer *Othello*. In the play, as in the spirituals, the combination of endurance and loss—maybe even endurance through loss—was wholly contained. He provided a perfect vehicle for an early adolescent's yearnings for some way of understanding rejection. How could a person of these talents and virtues be put through the political agonies of these immediate post-war years, when it was his recording of Ballad for Americans as much as any other social document that had given the nation a sense of historical wholeness and common endeavor during the wartime years?

To those of our generation and our political sensibilities, the figures of Robeson and Richard Wright were bound together in our moral universe because of their political rejection and subsequent exile. Their anger provided the necessary outrage for those on the left trying to figure out how a nation we had come to love so fully in those patriotic years could also produce the Scottsboro Boy outrage, and the other crops of Strange Fruit hanging over our yard.

After 1945, a post-war sense of the necessity of critical exile began to be felt by African American artists. Moving away as a means of forging the consciousness of the race seemed more and more attractive. Even though I knew Robeson's personal travails, for they were the subject of dinner table conversations, the very act of singing promised some kind of personal redemption. In my own family's set of legends, Robeson and Wright were emotionally connected with the stories of Josephine Baker, Inez Cavanaugh, Sidney Bechet , Billy Strayhorn and others jazz figures who had moved to Europe as acts of cultural disengagement and social disdain. These were very different in kind and intensity from that of the white exile community of the nineteen twenties. The figures of the '50s, as we viewed it, were getting away from America to have the requisite distance to hone their craft.

The very word, *spiritual*, as the name of a song-type, did not enter the American vocabulary, black or white, until just before the Civil War. It did not attain currency among the singers themselves until the escaped contrabands who encamped in the South Carolina low country had been observed and reported upon by the abolitionists William Allen, Charles Pickard Ware and Lucy McKim Garrison,[1] and even more, Thomas Wentworth Higginson.[2] The songs and the responsorial and jubilant style of their movement were already in place, of course, but referred to as "the hymns of the slaves" and "their *shouts* or *jubilees*." These songs provided the point of connection between that group of runaway slaves who became members of the "the Black Regiment" which emerged in the wake of the engagement at Fort Sumter, South Carolina. These soldiers made night come alive throughout the war in songs and speeches. Higginson wrote: "Every twilight the air is full of talking, singing, clapping of hands in unison & often of speeches. One of their favorite songs is very plaintive . . . they sing these at all seasons. . . . This evening after working themselves up to the highest pitch they suddenly all rushed off, got a barrel & mounted a man upon it who said "Gib another song, boys, & I'se gib you a speech."[3] This was followed by a song and a speech, and then seven more orations. "Every speech was good, without exception—with the queerest oddities of phrase & pronunciation" but phrased "with a perfect understanding of the points at issue" making them "perfectly thrilling."[4] Higginson took advantage of his position to write of this experience in a number of articles written from the front, including the early use of *spiritual* for the songs.

These inspired and spirited songs, then, were deeply associated with serious worship; but they had emerged in many other contexts. Higginson and others noticed them used as means of coordinating military drills, marches, and a number of different work tasks; Allen, Ware and Garrison (and Fanny Kemble and many other visitors) talked about them in connection with work tasks. That the songs were also recognizably one element of a worship service is significant, as it tied them to the elaborate speeches and sermons which caught the imagination of many other observers of slave and freedmen's churchly practices. These were the serious and respectable song-dances, different in tone and topic from the festive songs found in the slave's after dinner and Saturday night entertainments.[5]

After the war, as a number of institutions of higher learning serving the ex-slaves came into being, singing groups were formed displaying these musical capabilities. Perhaps beginning with the fund-raising efforts of the Fisk Jubilee Singers, groups from Hampton, Tuskegee and a number of other historically black colleges developed choirs. The Fisk group presented themselves in concert garb, and assembled on stages and in parlors much as abolitionist singing families had before the war.[6]

No group was more important in establishing the canon of these spirituals than the Fisk Jubilee Singers, as they not only performed widely in the United States and Europe, but sold songbooks wherever they performed. And this group also projected an image of high respectability, and sang them in musical arrangements composed for the group.

In this they departed from the more spontaneous feeling reported by Higginson and so many others, but they did so in the service of embodying a music as sublime and fully articulated as any other concert form of singing. While they maintained the sense of movement within the singing congregation, they did not leave the stage and join in the ring-shout. All of them had received classical music training at one time or another, and clearly they developed their presentational format with concert goers—and potential financial contributors—in mind.

In addition, their self-presentation was in direct contrast to those in blackface who engaged in the eccentric singing and dancing, and especially the Walkabout or Strut which provided the final moments of the "Ethiopian" ensembles' performances. Increasingly, the *Spiritual* provided an antidote to such social poison, but it did so without the holy dance of the *ring-shout* which Sterling Stuckey has drawn upon so nicely as the representative form of the retentions of African spirit and style in his work on slave culture.

As a folklorist, the most interesting development of the Spiritual and Jubilee singing movement occurred not at Fisk but at the Hampton Institute. For here, the faculty, under the leadership of the great black educator Capt. M. M. Moton, formed the Hampton Folklore Society in 1884. The recently formed American Folklore Society held their second annual meeting at Hampton, to the great enthusiasm of the founding members of the AFS represented by the founder and Secretary-Treasurer William Wells Newell. Indeed, Newell as well as Moton gave papers at that meeting, as did the remarkable independent black intellectuals Alexander Crummell and Anna J. Cooper.[7]

An even more interesting history is to be found in the emergence of the blues as a representative form. Under the rubric of the blues were included all kinds of disreputable, sinful songs. It was not until the last decade of the nineteenth century that the term was employed at all, and it didn't come into wide public notice until the second decade of the twentieth century. The use of blues as a term of art for songs about personal trials and alienation did not take hold until the 1920s, and then not among the singers themselves but writers who saw in the blues singer the epitome of the social dislocation of the now disenfranchised ex-slaves and their descendants.

Far from typical of African American expressive norms, the songs were sung by solo performers in dialogue not with other singers but with their accompanying instrument, usually the guitar. These other voices of the community of performers were subdued in favor the messages of personal isolation and social abandonment embodied in the figure of the stock figure of the *bluesman*. In fact, because such figures have been brought into the cosmopolitan marketplace of creative *types* (in the French sense), it is difficult to wring from the historical record just how the blues form and performer achieved this prominence.

In an earlier life, singing and collecting from performers throughout the lowland South, I ran with a number of old-time songsters who were regarded by folk-festival audiences as bluesmen. Many of these men were figures like Mississippi John Hurt, Bukka White, and Mance Lipscomb, born in the late-nineteenth and early-twentieth centuries, who found it amusing that they were called this by festival emcees. Repeatedly, they said that they were just *songsters*, scuffling musicians called on to play dance music of many different styles. Blues, they said, was just one of these, a popular dance fad that came to be used to describe a lot of other kinds of songs once it became a club and concert genre. Singing on street corners, juke joints, and rent-parties, they mainly provided the background music for carousers. They were not used to having the words to their songs actually listened to by such audiences. Backstage in folk festival contexts I heard a good deal of joking about how their discovery by white audiences had led to them into the spotlight more they were accustomed, singing songs that people took more seriously than they ever expected. Clearly, the songs of loss and abandonment fit into these new audiences' lives in ways that differed from what the singers had encountered before. To be sure, by the time they said this, many recording artists from Mamie and Bessie Smith to B. B. King and Bobby "Blue" Bland had been billed as blues singers and had prospered through such a designation. So these stories might have provided a way for one generation of musicians to talk about the old days, differentiating themselves from the tent show and bordello and club singers.

The creation of the blues as a culturally encumbered and deeply responsive form, from such a perspective, should probably be regarded as an artifact of Black Modernism. The attraction of Sterling Brown, James Baldwin, Albert Murray, Ralph Ellison, and the many others who wrote from the perspective of the alienation of the black artist is better understood, I think, through regarding them as modernist authors engaged, as James Joyce has it, in forging the conscience and the consciousness of "the race." Today, of course, the blues involve more than this, much more, but with that generation of writers this song-form provided them with a marked form of expression which was immediately understandable to their modernist European and Euro-American peers, much as generic *jazz* had been taken up in the 1920s, and *swing* in the 1930s.

My point is that African American communities continuously came up with forms and styles of expression which were potentially useful to artists far beyond those times and place of origin. Local styles and revived forms are taken up by popular culture, black and white, and made into a larger, often generational response to life. When they achieve this greater audience, they build a structure of sentiments which become an available symbolic form to that generation. The spiritual, born of Civil War and Emancipation, comes to embody African American respect norms as they went on to become vehicles for concert performance. Paul Robeson was born into a community of communicants that knew this intimately; he was able to take for granted then that this was a form which carried important social messages to blacks and whites alike. Did the blues operate in a similar fashion with Richard Wright? Sterling Stuckey makes a very persuasive argument that they do.

But more than this, Stuckey reminds us that it was often through these folk and popular forms of song-dance that public figures such as Robeson and Wright came to feel connected to those of African ancestry on both sides of the Atlantic. They came to this understanding, moreover, at the very time when this feeling of commonality was derided by the academy and the bourgeois public in general. In doing so, these figures take an even firmer place in our pantheon of heroes.

Notes

Notes to INTRODUCTION

1. The remark was by an historian at Berkeley whose field was Early Modern Europe. The seven papers at that Symposium were by John W. Blassingame, David Brion Davis, Carl N. Degler, Stanley Engerman, Eugene D. Genovese, William K. Scarborough, and Kenneth M. Stampp. They were published in Harry P. Owens, ed., *Perspectives and Irony in American Slavery* (Jackson, Miss., 1976).

2. George Washington Williams, *History of the Negro Race in America, from 1619 to 1880: Negroes as Slaves, as Soldiers, and as Citizens*, 2 vols. (New York, 1882–1883). See John Hope Franklin, "George Washington Williams, Historian," *Journal of Negro History* 31 (1946): 60–90; also the *American National Biography*.

3. For example, Jeffrey R. Brackett, *The Negro in Maryland: A Study of the Institution of Slavery*, Extra vol. VI, *Johns Hopkins University Studies in Historical and Political Science* (Baltimore, 1889).

4. W. E. B. DuBois, *The Suppression of the African Slave-Trade to the United States of America, 1638–1870*, vol. I, *Harvard Historical Studies* (New York and London, 1896).

5. *Journal of Negro History* 1 (1916): 163–216. Work on the new journal had begun the previous year.

6. Ulrich Bonnell Phillips, *American Negro Slavery: A Survey of the Supply, Employment and Control of Negro Labor as Determined by the Plantation Regime* (1918; reprint, New York, 1952), viii. Later, Phillips moved to Yale.

7. Samuel Eliot Morison and Henry Steele Commager, *The Growth of the American Republic* (New York, 1934), 415.

8. John Hope Franklin, *The Militant South, 1800–1860* (Cambridge, Mass., 1956).

9. Harvey Wish, "American Slave Insurrections before 1861," *Journal of Negro History* 22 (1937): 299–320.

10. Robert A. Gross, ed., "The Making of a Slave Conspiracy, part 2," *William and Mary Quarterly*, 3d ser., 59 (2002): 135–202. The forum was triggered by Michael P. Johnson, "Denmark Vesey and His Co-conspirators," *William and Mary Quarterly*, 3d ser., 58 (2001): 915–76 [pagination differs in some printings]; *New York Times*, Mar. 2, 2002.

11. Speech of James H. Gholson, *Richmond Enquirer*, Jan. 21, 1832.

12. Eugene L. Horowitz, *The Development of Attitude toward the Negro* (New York, 1936), which uses the term *attitude(s)* in both singular and plural; Charles K. Ross, *Outside the Lines: African Americans and the Integration of the National Football League* (New York, 1999).

13. Part of the subtitle, *The Negro Problem and Modern Democracy* (New York, 1944), was rendered anachronous by the text. For the review and a wider discussion, David W. Southern, *Gunnar Myrdal and Black–White Relations: The Use and Abuse of An American Dilemma, 1944–1969* (Baton Rouge and London, 1987), 74–75 and *passim.*

14. Kenneth M. Stampp, *The Peculiar Institution: Slavery in the Ante-Bellum South* (New York, 1956), ch. 4.

15. Especially on Abram Kardiner and Lionel Ovesey, *The Mark of Oppression: A Psychosocial Study of the American Negro* (New York, 1951). See also Stampp, "The Historian and Southern Negro Slavery," *American Historical Review* 57 (1952): 613–24.

16. Samuel Eliot Morison and Henry Steele Commager, *The Growth of the American Republic*, 5th ed., 2 vols. (New York, 1962), I, 524–25. (The front matter makes clear that Morison, not Commager, was responsible for this chronological portion of the work.) Morison, *The Oxford History of the American People* (New York, 1965), vii, 505.

17. Weld, *American Slavery as It Is: Testimony of a Thousand Witnesses* (New York, 1839); Richard Hofstadter, William Miller, and Daniel Aaron, *The United States: The History of a Republic*, 2d ed. (Englewood Cliffs, N.J., 1967), 347.

18. Stanley M. Elkins, *Slavery: A Problem in American Institutional and Intellectual Life* (Chicago, 1959), 82, 89.

19. Most notably, B[enjamin] A. Botkin, *Lay My Burden Down: A Folk History of Slavery* (Chicago, 1945).

Notes to "LOGIC AND EXPERIENCE: THOMAS JEFFERSON'S LIFE IN THE LAW"
by Annette Gordon-Reed

1. Jefferson to Short, Jan. 3, 1793, Julian Boyd et al., eds., *The Papers of Thomas Jefferson*, 27 volumes to date (Princeton, 1950–), 25: 15.

2. Alan Watson, quoted in Thomas D. Morris, *Southern Slavery and the Law, 1619–1860* (Chapel Hill, 1996), 10.

3. *Howell v. Netherland*, in Paul Leicester Ford, ed., *The Works of Thomas Jefferson*, 12 vols. (New York, 1904–05), 1: 373–81.

4. Dumas Malone, *Jefferson the Virginian*, Vol. 1, *Jefferson and His Time* (Boston, 1948), 121.

5. Ford, *Works of Jefferson*, 1: 379.

6. Ibid., 374.

7. Ibid.

8. Ibid.

9. Malone, 187; William Cohen, "Thomas Jefferson and the Problem of Slavery," *Journal of American History* 56 (1969): 506–07.

10. Thomas Jefferson, *Notes on the State of Virginia* (New York, 1964); Jefferson to Madison, June 17, 1783, in Boyd, *Papers*, 6: 277; Malone, 414; Cohen, 510.

11. *See* Robert Cover, *Justice Accused, Antislavery and the Judicial Process* (New Haven, 1975), 51–55, discussing Wythe's opinion in *Hudgens v. Wright*, in which Wythe tries to outlaw slavery in Virginia through judicial interpretation; *See generally*, St. George Tucker, *A Dissertation on Slavery: With a Proposal for the Gradual Abolition of It in the State of Virginia* (Philadelphia, 1796).

12. Cohen, 509.

13. Philip J. Schwarz, *Slave Laws in Virginia* (Athens, 1996), 37.

14. Joshua Rothman, "Social Knowledge of Interracial Sex," in *Sally Hemings and Thomas Jefferson: History, Memory, and Civic Culture* (Charlottesville, 1999), 96–97.

15. Jefferson to Francis Grey, March 4, 1815, in Andrew A. Lipscomb and Albert Ellery Bergh, eds., *The Writings of Thomas Jefferson*, 20 volumes (Washington, D.C., 1903–04), 14: 267–71.

16. Lucia C. Stanton, "'Those Who Labor for my Happiness': Thomas Jefferson and His Slaves," in *Jeffersonian Legacies*, ed. Peter S. Onuf, with a foreword by Daniel P. Jordan and afterword by Merrill D. Peterson (Charlottesville, 1993), 152.

17. Annette Gordon-Reed, "The Memoirs of Madison Hemings," in *Thomas Jefferson and Sally Hemings: An American Controversy* (Charlottesville, 1997), 248.

Notes to "COMMENTARY"
by Peter S. Onuf

1. The best recent biography, Joseph J. Ellis's *American Sphinx: The Character of Thomas Jefferson* (New York, 1997), puts Jeffersonian conundrums front and center. For reviews of the literature and further discussion of the problems of Jefferson biography see Peter S. Onuf, "The Scholars' Jefferson," *William and Mary Quarterly*, 3d ser., 50 (1993): 671–99; and Jan Ellen Lewis and Peter S. Onuf, "American Synecdoche: Thomas Jefferson as Image, Icon, Character, and Self," *American Historical Review* 103 (1998): 125–36.

2. *Thomas Jefferson and Sally Hemings: An American Controversy* (Charlottesville, 1997). See also Gordon-Reed's subsequent (post-DNA test) thoughts on her subject in, "'The Memories of a Few Negroes': Rescuing America's Future at Monticello," in Jan Ellen Lewis and Peter S. Onuf, eds., *Sally Hemings and Thomas Jefferson: History, Memory, and Civic Culture* (Charlottesville, 1999), 236–52; and "Engaging Jefferson: Blacks and the Founding Father," *William and Mary Quarterly*, 3d ser., 57 (2000): 171–82.

3. For a compelling discussion of this theme see Jan Ellen Lewis, "The White Jeffersons," in Lewis and Onuf, eds., *Hemings and Jefferson*, 127–60.

4. Jefferson described himself "as the most blessed of the patriarchs" in a letter to Angelica Schuyler Church, 27 Nov. 1793, in Julian Boyd et al., eds., *The Papers of*

Thomas Jefferson, 27 vols. to date (Princeton, 1950–), 27: 449: "I have my house to build, my fields to form, and to watch for the happiness of those who labor for mine."

5. Jay Fliegelman, *Declaring Independence: Jefferson, Natural Language, and the Culture of Performance* (Stanford, 1993), 94–107. My discussion of self-fashioning is indebted to this brilliant study.

6. Jefferson, "Summary View of the Rights of British America" (1774), in Merrill Peterson, ed., *Jefferson Writings* (New York, 1984), 116.

7. Peter S, Onuf, *Jefferson's Empire: The Language of American Nationhood* (Charlottesville, 2000), 147–88; Onuf, "Every Generation Is an 'Independant Nation': Colonization, Miscegenation, and the Fate of Jefferson's Children," *William and Mary Quarterly*, 3d ser., 57 (2000): 153–70.

8. Jefferson to Edward Coles, 25 Aug. 1814, in Peterson, ed., *Jefferson Writings*, 1344.

9. So described by Jefferson, in a letter to Gov. James Monroe of Virginia, 24 Nov. 1801, in Andrew A. Lipscomb and Albert Ellery Bergh, eds., *The Writings of Thomas Jefferson*, 20 vols. (Washington, D.C., 1903–04), 10: 296. In this letter, written in the wake of Gabriel's Rebellion, Jefferson imagined both American continents, though *not* the "island of St. Domingo" where black republicans struggled for their independence, free from either "blot or mixture."

10. Onuf, *Jefferson's Empire*, 109–46.

11. Query XIV (Laws), *Notes on the State of Virginia*, ed. William Peden (Chapel Hill, 1954), 138.

12. Jefferson to Samuel Kercheval, 12 July 1816, in Lipscomb and Bergh, eds., *Writings of Jefferson*, 15: 37.

13. Jefferson to Joseph C. Cabell, 2 Feb. 1816, in ibid., 14: 421. On the ward republics see Onuf, *Jefferson's Empire*, 119–21. For more sympathetic accounts, see Richard K. Matthews, *The Radical Politics of Thomas Jefferson: A Revisionist View* (Lawrence, Kans., 1984), 77–95; and Suzanne W. Morse, "Ward Republics: The Wisest Invention for Self-Government," in James Gilreath, ed., *Thomas Jefferson and the Education of a Citizen* (Washington, D.C., 1999), 264–77. Neither Matthews nor Morse makes any reference to slavery.

Notes to "The Peculiar Fate of the Bourgeois Critique of Slavery"
by James Oakes

1. Frederick W. Seward, ed., *William H. Seward: An Autobiography* (New York, 1891), 268, 806.

2. Quoted in Eric Foner, *Free Soil, Free Labor, Free Men: The Ideology of the Republican Party before the Civil War* (New York, 1970, 1995), p. 46.

3. *The Papers of Benjamin Franklin*, Leonard Labaree, ed. (New Haven, 1961), vol. 4, pp. 229–30.

4. Ibid., 230–31.

5. Adam Smith, *The Theory of Moral Sentiments*, eds. D. D. Raphael and A. L. Macfie (Indianapolis, 1982), VII. ii. I. 28; Smith, *An Inquiry into the Nature and Causes of the Wealth of Nations*, ed. Edwin Cannan (Chicago, 1904; 1976), p. 411. For perceptive commentary see David Brion Davis, *The Problem of Slavery in the Age of Revolution, 1770–1823* (Ithaca, 1975), 347–54. On the importance of political economy to the Scottish Enlightenment, see Istvan Hont and Michael Ignatiev, eds., *Wealth and Virtue: The Shaping of Political Economy in the Scottish Enlightenment* (Cambridge, Eng., 1983), esp. pp. 1–44. The best account of the influence of Scottish political economy on the Founding generation in America is Forrest McDonald, *Novus Ordo Seclorum: The Intellectual Origins of the Constitution* (Lawrence, Kans., 1985), pp. 97–142.

6. *Papers of Benjamin Franklin*, v. 4, p. 230.

7. Smith, *Wealth of Nations*, 412.

8. Quoted in Davis, *Problem of Slavery in the Age of Revolution*, 347.

9. Lee is quoted in Laurence Shore, *Southern Capitalists: The Ideological Leadership of an Elite, 1832–1885* (Chapel Hill, 1986), 6–7. Readers of Shore's excellent book will recognize my enormous debt to his pathbreaking work. To avoid confusion, however, it is best to state the points at which my interpretation diverges from Shore's. First, the studies referred to in the previous footnote suggest to me that political economy was a more widely established mode of analysis by the late eighteenth century than Shore allows. Second, and more importantly, Shore *accepts* the bourgeois critique of slavery, referring at one point to the "apparent prosperity" of the slave economy. I believe there is ample evidence to be suspicious of the bourgeois critique. Indeed, the very real expansion and prosperity of the slave economy presented almost all commentators with a major intellectual problem precisely because slavery did not die out the way the bourgeois critique predicted it would. This conceptual problem is the subject of this paper, and as such it departs significantly from Shore's impressive analysis.

10. Ibid., 4–5.

11. For an earlier formulation of this argument, stressing the internal weaknesses of anti-slavery sentiment, see James Oakes, "'The Compromising Expedient': Justifying a Proslavery Constitution," *Cardozo Law Review* 17 (1996), 2023–56.

12. John Taylor, *Arator: Being a Series of Agricultural Essays, Practical and Political: In Sixty-four Numbers*, ed. M. E. Bradford (Indianapolis, [1977]), 115, 120–25.

13. Ibid., 119, 125.

14. James Madison to Frances Wright, September 1, 1825, in Marvin Meyers, ed., *The Mind of the Founder: Sources of the Political Thought of James Madison* (Hanover, N.H., 1981), 329–30. For Madison the problem was the destruction of the individual's motivation to work, which he seemed to attribute as much to *gang* labor as to

slave labor. In theory his argument against the plantation system might have applied to free labor as well as to slavery. For Madison's views on slavery, see Drew McCoy, *The Last of the Fathers: James Madison and the Republican Legacy* (Cambridge, Eng., 1989), 253–322.

15. Alison Goodyear Freehling, *Drift Toward Dissolution* (Baton Rouge, La., 1982), establishes the context for the debates. Joseph Clarke Robert, *The Road from Monticello: A Study of the Virginia Slavery Debate of 1832* (Durham, N. C., 1941), contains the most readily available excerpts from the debate.

16. Robert, *Road from Monticello*, 62, 63.

17. Ibid., 64, 65, 109.

18. Ibid., 78, 79.

19. Ibid., 92.

20. Ibid., 99, 100.

21. Ibid., 67, 77. Charles Faulkner responded to Gholson by decrying the planters' "mere pecuniary claim" that slavery was profitable to the individual slaveholder even if it was, in Faulkner's view, detrimental to "the great interests of the common weal." Thus began the long tradition of distinguishing the short-term *profitability* of slavery from its larger, long-term *viability*. The problem with Faulkner's response was simple: in the long run of economic history almost nothing is "viable." Indeed, the fact that the southern slave economy flourished for over century and a half suggests that it was more viable than many other economic enterprises that have come and gone with considerably less longevity. In short, it is difficult to sustain the argument that an institution that remained profitable for centuries—and which was put to death while still vigorously profitable—was somehow not "viable."

22. Ibid., 91, 95.

23. Ibid., 107.

24. Ibid., 99, 100.

25. Thomas R. Dew, "Review of the Debate in the Virginia Legislature, 1831–1832," reprinted in *The Pro-Slavery Argument; As Maintained by the Most Distinguished Writers of the Southern States* (Charleston, S. C., 1852), 287–490.

26. On the diffusion of slavery see William Barney, *The Road to Secession: A New Perspective on the Old South* (New York, 1972), 3–84; Adam Rothman, "The Expansion of Slavery in the Deep South, 1790–1820" (Ph.D. diss., Columbia University, 2000). For an appreciation of Malthus's influence, see McCoy, *The Last of the Founders*, 175–76.

27. Thomas R. Dew, "Review of the Debate . . . ," in *The Pro-Slavery Argument*, 287, 292.

28. Ibid., 362, 388, 435.

29. Ibid., 447–48., 449–50.

30. Ibid., 482–83. Because he accepted the general rule of free labor's superiority as it applied to whites, he fairly gushed at the prospects for capitalist development in his

native Virginia. Toward the end of his essay Dew praised the state legislature and the city of Richmond for their recent support of internal improvements projects. They would "revolutionize the financial condition of the Old Dominion, and speed her on more rapidly in wealth and numbers, than she has ever advanced before." He foresaw the growth of towns and cities in eastern and southern Virginia, drawing in free laborers from the North and diffusing their influence throughout the countryside. Plantations would give way to "gardens" that would feed the swelling population of the towns and cities. And so, without the assistance of dangerous and impractical schemes for the abolition of slavery, slavery would eventually give way before the natural progress of free labor. As a defense of slavery this was nothing if not peculiar.

31. David Christie, "Cotton is King: or, Slavery in the Light of Political Economy," in E. N. Elliott, ed., *Cotton is King, and Proslavery Arguments*. . . . (Augusta, Ga., 1860), 19–267.

32. James Henry Hammond, "Hammond's Letters on Slavery," in *The Pro-Slavery Argument*, 147.

33. William Harper, "Memoir on Slavery," in *The Pro-Slavery Argument*, 47, 67.

34. "Hammond's Letters on Slavery," in *The Pro-Slavery Argument*, 121. Sounding like none other than Benjamin Franklin, Hammond then listed the various expenses of slave labor: "besides the first cost of the slave, he must be fed and clothed, well fed and well clothed, if not for humanity's sake, that they may do good work, retain health and life, and rear a family to supply his place. When old or sick, he is a clear expense, and so is the helpless portion of his family. No poor law provides for him when unable to work, or brings up his children for our service when we need them."

35. Harper, "Memoir on Slavery," in *The Pro-Slavery Argument*, 67, 89. Emphasis added.

36. Samuel A. Cartwright, "Slavery in the Light of Ethnology," in Elliot, ed., *Cotton is King*, 699.

37. Ibid. 109–10.

38. Quoted in Shore, *Southern Capitalists*, 19.

39. Ibid.

Notes to "COMMENTARY"
by Walter Johnson

1. Other important considerations of the racialized character of discussions about the capacity of emancipated slaves to function in a "free" labor economy include Amy Dru Stanley, *From Bondage to Contract: Wage Labor, Marriage, and the Market Revolution in the Age of Slave Emancipation* (Cambridge, Eng., 1998), and Thomas Holt, "An Empire Over the Mind: Emancipation, Race, and Ideology in the British West Indies and the American South" and Barbara Jeanne Fields, "Ideology and Race in American

History," both of which are in J. Morgan Kousser and James M. McPherson, eds., *Race, Region, and Reconstruction: Essays in Honor of C. Vann Woodward* (New York, 1982).

2. The opposition between the capitalist North and the culturalist South has been a persistent feature of the literature on antebellum slavery. Much of this seems to me to emerge out of the insistence of American historians on trying to figure out what it was that Marx said about slavery (damn little) rather than turning the question around and asking what slavery says about Marx. Why, for instance, writing the first volume of *Capital*, would he choose a bolt of linen as the object out of which to generate his (magnificent) critique of the "commodity fetishism" rather than a bolt of cotton? Thinking from the standpoint of slavery, it seems an astonishing evasion, one which allowed for the generation of an account of "capitalism" which reduced relations of exploitation to those experienced by industrial workers in Europe, and, in the same motion, reduced the history of mercantile (and financial) capital in which slavery played such an important world-historical role. Oakes' earlier work, particularly *The Ruling Race: A History of American Slaveholders* (New York, 1982), but also *Slavery and Freedom: An Interpretation of the Old South* (New York, 1992), seemed to me to play into this polarity (capitalism v. slavery) by simply reversing it—arguing that the South was, in some way, at bottom, capitalist. The move here is much more interesting. By focusing on the historical process by which a set of ideas about work, motivation, and history were spread and then applied to the North, Oakes is treating capitalist ideology as being itself a cultural formation—a set of ideas about the nature of right and reality that were related but not reducible to underlying economic structures and exploitative social relations. Thinking this way, the idea of "capitalism" itself can be seen as an ideology of domination.

3. See Thomas C. Holt, "Marking Race: Race-making, and the Writing of History," *American Historical Review* 50 (1995): 1–20.

4. See Thomas C. Holt, *The Problem of Freedom: Race, Labor, and Politics in Jamaica and Britain, 1832–1938* (Baltimore, 1992).

5. See Benedict Anderson, *Imagined Communities: Reflections on the Origins and Spread of Nationalism* (London, 1983).

6. See Daniel T. Rodgers, *The Work Ethic in Industrial America, 1850–1920* (Chicago, 1978) and Stanley, *From Bondage to Contract*.

7. Michel–Rolph Trouillot, *Silencing the Past: Power and the Production of History* (Boston, 1995).

Notes to "REFLECTIONS ON LAW, CULTURE, AND SLAVERY"
by Ariela Gross

1. For examples of this scholarship, see generally Lois G. Carr and Lorena S. Walsh, "The Planter's Wife: The Experience of White Women in Seventeenth-Century

Maryland," *William and Mary Quarterly*, 3d ser., 34 (1977): 542; Darrett Rutman and Anita Rutman, *A Place In Time: Middlesex County, Virginia, 1650–1750* (New York, 1984); Russell R. Menard, "From Servant to Freeholder: Status Mobility and Property Accumulation in Seventeenth-Century Maryland," *William and Mary Quarterly*, 3d ser., 30 (1973): 37; Suzanne Lebsock, *The Free Women of Petersburg: Status and Culture in a Southern Town, 1784–1860* (New York, 1984); Linda K. Kerber, *Women of the Republic: Intellect and Ideology in Revolutionary America* (Chapel Hill, 1980); Norma Basch, *In the Eyes of the Law: Women, Marriage, and Property in Nineteenth-Century New York* (Ithaca, 1982).

2. See, e.g., Edward L. Ayers, *Vengeance and Justice: Crime and Punishment in the 19th-Century American South* (New York, 1984), 18, 32 (only a "circumscribed . . . segment of life . . . was controlled by law"; "honor and legalism . . . are incompatible"); Bertram Wyatt-Brown, *Southern Honor: Ethics and Behavior in the Old South* (New York, 1982); Christopher Waldrep, "Substituting Law for the Lash: Emancipation and Legal Formalism in a Mississippi County Court," *Journal of American History* 82 (1996): 1425–51 ("The state only reluctantly intervened in master–slave relations, regarding law as too burdened with procedure effectively to control human chattel. Owners realized law must be kept from their slaves," 1428); Winthrop D. Jordan, *Tumult and Silence at Second Creek: An Inquiry into a Civil War Slave Conspiracy* (Baton Rouge, 1993) (important conflicts remain outside the formal legal system); Michael Wayne, *Reshaping Plantation Society: The Natchez District, 1860–1880* (Baton Rouge, 1983), 16 (plantation its own law); Michael Wayne, "An Old South Morality Play: Reconsidering the Social Underpinnings of the Proslavery Ideology," *Journal of American History* 77 (1990): 838–63 (important conflicts remain outside the formal legal system); Peter Kolchin, *American Slavery, 1619–1877* (New York, 1993), 127–32 (looking only at legislation, and noting that most slave discipline took place on the plantation).

3. Kenneth M. Stampp, *The Peculiar Institution: Slavery in the Ante-bellum South* (New York, 1975), 141–236; Eugene D. Genovese, *Roll, Jordan, Roll: The World The Slaves Made* (New York, 1976), 25–49; James Oakes, *Slavery And Freedom: An Interpretation of the Old South* (New York, 1990); Charles S. Sydnor, "The Southerner and the Law," *Journal of Southern History* 6 (1940): 3–23.

4. Stanley N. Katz, "Opening Address; Bondage, Freedom & The Constitution: The New Slavery Scholarship and Its Impact on Law and Legal Historiography," *Cardozo Law Review* 17 (1996): 1689–93, 1690.

5. *State v. Mann*, 13 N.C. (1 Dev.) 263, 266 (1829).

6. See, e.g., Robert M. Cover, *Justice Accused: Antislavery and the Judicial Process* (New Haven, 1975); Mark V. Tushnet, *The American Law of Slavery, 1810–1860: Considerations of Humanity and Interest* (Princeton, 1981), 11–27.

7. Oakes, *Slavery and Freedom*, 137–39, 160–63.

8. For the most forceful statement of this position, see Genovese, *Roll, Jordan, Roll*, 25–49. But many scholars who do not endorse his theoretical statement of the

"hegemonic function of law" still discuss Southern law in instrumentalist, functionalist terms. Legal doctrines were developed *in order to* further the interests of slaveholders, or *in order to* facilitate economic goals. For more citations, see Laura F. Edwards, "Law, Domestic Violence, and the Limits of Patriarchal Authority in the Antebellum South," *Journal of Southern History* 65 (1999): 733–70, 734–35.

9. See, e.g., A. Leon Higginbotham, Jr., *In The Matter of Color: Race and the American Legal Process* (New York, 1978) (emphasizing the harshness of slave law); A. E. Keir Nash, "Fairness and Formalism in the Trials of Blacks in the State Supreme Courts of the Old South," *Virginia Law Review* 56 (1970): 64–100 (arguing that slaves received surprisingly fair trials); Nash, "A More Equitable Past? Southern Supreme Courts and the Protection of the Antebellum Negro," *North Carolina Law Review* 48 (1970): 197–241 (surprising fairness); Arthur F. Howington, "Not in the Condition of a Horse or an Ox," *Tennessee Historical Quarterly* 34 (1975) 249–63 (surprising fairness).

10. For early women's histories emphasizing women's agency, even in creating domestic ideology, see Kerber, *Women of the Republic*; Gerda Lerner, *The Woman in American History* (Menlo Park, Calif., 1971); Nancy F. Cott, *The Bonds of Womanhood: "Woman's Sphere" in New England, 1780–1835* (New Haven, 1977); Mary P. Ryan, *Cradle of the Middle Class: The Family in Oneida County, New York, 1790–1865* (Cambridge, Eng., 1981); for histories of immigrants and white workers, see Herbert G. Gutman, *Work, Culture, and Society in Industrializing America: Essays in American Working-Class and Social History* (New York, 1975); David Montgomery, *Workers' Control in America: Studies in the History of Work, Technology, and Labor Struggles* (Cambridge, Eng., 1979).

11. The works they reacted against were Stanley K. Elkins, *Slavery: A Problem in American Intellectual and Institutional Life* (Chicago, 1976), and Robert W. Fogel and Stanley L. Engerman, *Time On The Cross: The Economics of American Negro Slavery*, 2 vols. (Boston, 1974). See especially Lawrence W. Levine, *Black Culture and Black Consciousness: Afro-American Thought from Slavery to Freedom* (New York, 1977) (studying slave stories, songs, jokes, and religious practices); John Blassingame, *The Slave Community: Plantation Life in the Antebellum South* (New York, 1979) (discussing community-building, family, and resistance); Herbert G. Gutman, *The Black Family in Slavery and Freedom, 1750–1925* (New York, 1977) (on naming practices, marrying abroad and other family and community-building practices); Albert J. Raboteau, *Slave Religion: The "Invisible Institution" in the Antebellum South* (New York, 1978) (on religion); Peter H. Wood, *Black Majority: Negroes in Colonial South Carolina from 1670 through the Stono Rebellion* (New York, 1974) (revealing African survivals in slave culture); Sterling Stuckey, *Slave Culture: Nationalist Theory and the Foundations of Black America* (New York, 1987) (discussing African survivals).

12. See, e.g., Wood, *Black Majority*, 138–34, 208–10; Genovese, *Roll, Jordan, Roll*, 535–40; Raboteau, *Invisible Institution*, 222–23.

13. See, e.g., Norrece T. Jones, Jr., *Born a Child of Freedom, yet a Slave: Mechanisms of Control and Strategies of Resistance in Antebellum South Carolina* (Middletown, Conn., 1990) (emphasizing separation of families under slavery); Peter Kolchin, *Unfree Labor: American Slavery and Russian Serfdom* (Cambridge, Mass., 1989) (comparing U.S. South to Russian society); Anthony Kaye, "The Personality of Power: The Ideology of Slaves in the Natchez District and the Delta of Mississippi, 1830–1865," (Ph.D. diss., Columbia University, 1999) (arguing against the concept of a unified "slave community").

14. Oakes, *Slavery and Freedom*, 183–94.

15. Kathleen M. Brown, *Good Wives, Nasty Wenches, and Anxious Patriarchs: Gender, Race, and Power in Colonial Virginia* (Chapel Hill, 1996), 100.

16. On women's gossip networks, see Mary Beth Norton, "Gender and Defamation in Seventeenth-Century Maryland," *William and Mary Quarterly*, 3d ser., 44 (1987): 3–39. Women participated as litigants or witnesses in 54.5 percent of defamation suits in seventeenth-century Maryland, although they were only one-fourth to one-third of the population. Norton, "Gender and Defamation," 5. For the nineteenth century, see Andrew J. King, "Constructing Gender: Sexual Slander in Nineteenth Century America," *Law and History Review* 13 (1995): 63–110.

17. Brown, *Good Wives*, 306–12.

18. Edwards, "Law, Domestic Violence, and the Limits of Patriarchal Authority," 740.

19. Frederick Douglass, *An Account of American Slavery*, in John W. Blassingame, ed., *The Frederick Douglass Papers*, Vol. 1 (New Haven, 1979), 141. Italics added.

20. See, e.g., Henry Bibb, in *Puttin' on Ole Massa: The Slave Narratives of Henry Bibb, William Wells Brown, and Solomon Northup*, Gilbert Osofsky ed. (New York, 1969), 76–77; William and Ellen Craft, *Running a Thousand Miles for Freedom* (1860; reprint, New York, 1969), 13–15. Of course, the quotations from statute books may suggest coaching or editing by white abolitionists; however, the overall theme of the importance of law in maintaining slavery pervades all of the narratives.

21. Jon-Christian Suggs, *Whispered Consolations: Law and Narrative in African American Life* (Ann Arbor, 2000), 28.

22. James Lucas Autobiography in George P. Rawick, *The American Slave: A Composite Autobiography* (Westport, Conn., 1977), Supp. Ser. 1, vol. 8: Mississippi Narratives, Part. 3, p. 1339.

23. Richard Mack Autobiography, in Rawick, *American Slave*, Vol. 2: South Carolina Narratives, Parts 1 and 2, p. 151. See also Jim Allen Autobiography, in Rawick, *American Slave*, Supp. Series 1, Vol. 6: Mississippi Narratives Part 1, p. 54 ("Mars John Bussey drunk my Mudder up. I means by dat, Lee King took her and my brudder George for a whiskey debt"); Sam McAllum Autobiography, in Rawick, *American Slave*, Supp. Series 1, Vol. 9: Mississippi Narratives Part 4, p. 1352 ("Mr. Stephenson were a surveyor an' he fell out wid Mr. McAllum an' had a lawsuit an' had to pay it in darkies.

An' Mr. McAllum had de privilege of takin' me an' my mother, or another woman an' her two; an' he took us"); Ephraim Robinson Autobiography, Ibid., 1852 (". . . the Marster knew if he hurt you or killed you it was his loss. Once when a slave hand ran away and they were trying to catch him, another plantation owner shot his Marster's slave in the hip and magots [sic] got in the place. The slave died, and not only did the slave owner sue the other man but never spoke to him again"); Adline Thomas Autobiography, in Rawick, *American Slave*, Supp. Series 1, Vol. 10: Mississippi Narratives Part 5, p. 2094 ("She, her mother, sister, and a brother were put on the block and sold to settle the debt at Ripley, Mississippi").

24. Northup Narrative, in *Puttin On Ole Massa*, Osofsky ed., 285.

25. Walter Johnson, *Soul By Soul: Life Inside the Antebellum Slave Market* (Cambridge, Mass., 1999), 176–88.

26. Charles Ball, *Fifty Years in Chains; or, The Life of an American Slave* (1859; reprint, Detroit, 1969), 10–11, 70.

27. Ibid., 70–71.

28. Ibid., 70.

29. Interview with Rose Russell, in Rawick, *American Slave*, Supp. Ser. 1, Vol. 9: Mississippi Narratives, Part 4, p. 1903. According to the interviewer, Rose "laugh[ed] as she t[old] how they fooled her away from the old plantation."

30. See, e.g., Adam Singleton Autobiography, in Rawick, *American Slave*, Supp. Ser. 1, Vol. 10: Mississippi Narratives, Part 5, p. 1946; Lewis Adams Autobiography, in Rawick, *American Slave*, Supp. Ser. 1, Vol. 6: Mississippi Narratives, Part 1, pp. 5–6; Ariela J. Gross, *Double Character: Slavery and Mastery in the Antebellum Southern Courtroom* (Princeton, 2000), 44.

31. *Johnson v. Wideman*, 1 Rice 325, 327–40 (S.C. 1839).

32. Ibid., 334, 338, 340.

33. Ibid., 342–43.

34. *Smith v. McCall*, 12 S.C. (1 McCord) 220, 224 (1821). See Ariela Gross, "Pandora's Box: Slave Character on Trial in the Antebellum Deep South," *Yale Journal of Law and the Humanities* 7 (1995): 267, 271.

35. On courts as sites of performance, see, generally, Mindie Lazarus-Black and Susan F. Hirsch, eds., *Contested States: Law, Hegemony and Resistance* (New York, 1994). On performativity, see Judith Butler, *Gender Trouble: Feminism and The Subversion of Identity* (New York, 1990) and *Bodies That Matter: On The Discursive Limits of "Sex"* (New York, 1993). See also Elin Diamond, ed., *Performance and Cultural Politics* (New York,1996); Sue-Ellen Case, ed., *Performing Feminisms* (New York, 1990); Eve Kosofsky Sedgwick & Andrew Parker, eds., *Performativity and Performance* (New York, 1995).

36. Walter Johnson, "The Slave Trader, the White Slave, and the Politics of Racial Determination in the 1850s," *Journal of American History* 87 (2000): 13–38.

37. Transcript of Trial, Miller v. Belmonti, No. 5623 (La. New Orleans Dist. Ct. May 1845) (collection of Earl K. Long Library, Special Collections and Archives,

University of New Orleans, New Orleans, La., Supreme Court Records), rev'd, 11 Rob. 339 (La. 1845); Ariela J. Gross, "Litigating Whiteness: Trials of Racial Determination in the Nineteenth-Century South," *Yale Law Journal* 108 (1998): 109–88, 168.

38. Sedgwick, "Queer Performativity," 15; Gross, "Litigating Whiteness," 181–85.

39. Stephanie McCurry, *Masters of Small Worlds: Yeoman Households, Gender Relations, and the Political Culture of the Antebellum South Carolina Low Country* (New York, 1995); Elizabeth Fox-Genovese, *Within The Plantation Household: Black and White Women of the Old South* (Chapel Hill, 1988); Nancy Dunlap Bercaw, "The Politics of the Household during the Transition from Slavery to Freedom in the Yazoo-Mississippi Delta, 1861–1876" (Ph.D. diss., University of Pennsylvania, 1996); Christine Daniels & Michael V. Kennedy, eds., *Over The Threshold: Intimate Violence in Early America* (New York, 1999).

40. Peter W. Bardaglio, *Reconstructing The Household: Families, Sex, and the Law in the Nineteenth-Century South* (Chapel Hill, 1995); Laura F. Edwards, *Gendered Strife and Confusion: The Political Culture of Reconstruction* (Urbana, 1997); Edwards, "Law, Domestic Violence, and the Limits of Patriarchal Authority."

41. Victoria E. Bynum, *Unruly Women: The Politics of Social and Sexual Control in the Old South* (Chapel Hill, 1992).

42. Edwards, "Law, Domestic Violence, and the Limits of Patriarchal Authority," 754.

43. Diane Miller Sommerville, "The Rape Myth in the Old South Reconsidered," *Journal of Southern History* 61 (1995): 481; Peter W. Bardaglio, "Rape and Law in the Old South: 'Calculated to Excite Indignation in Every Heart,'" *Journal of Southern History* 60 (1994): 749; Sharon Block, "Lines of Color, Sex, and Service: Comparative Sexual Coercion in Early America," in *Sex, Love, Race: Crossing Boundaries in North American History*, Martha Hodes, ed. (New York, 1999), 141–63.

44. Block, "Lines of Color."

45. Oscar and Mary F. Handlin, "Origins of the Southern Labor System," reprinted in *Colonial America: Essays in Politics and Social Development*, Stanley N. Katz and John M. Murrin, eds. (New York, 1983), 230; Carl N. Degler, "Slavery and the Genesis of American Race Prejudice," *Comparative Studies in Society and History* 2 (1959): 49.

46. Winthrop D. Jordan, *White Over Black: American Attitudes Toward the Negro, 1550–1812* (Chapel Hill, 1968).

47. Johnson, *Soul By Soul*, 136.

48. Brown, *Good Wives*, 116.

49. Ibid., 116.

50. Ibid., 122.

51. Ibid., 125.

52. Ibid., 131.

53. Ibid., 132.

54. Ibid., 198.

55. Ibid., 187.
56. Ibid., 198.
57. Ibid., 209.
58. Kirsten Fischer, "'False, Feigned, and Scandalous Words,' Sexual Slander and Racial Ideology Among Whites in Colonial North Carolina," in *The Devil's Lane: Sex and Race in the Early South*, Catherine Clinton and Michelle Gillespie, eds. (New York, 1997), 139–53.
59. Brown, *Good Wives*, 211.
60. Ibid., 76.
61. Ibid.
62. Ibid., 77.
63. George M. Fredrickson, *The Black Image in the White Mind: The Debate on Afro-American Character and Destiny, 1817–1914* (New York, 1981); Reginald Horsman, *Race and Manifest Destiny: The Origins of American Racial Anglo-Saxonism* (Cambridge, Mass., 1981).
64. Gross, "Litigating Whiteness," 151–76.
65. Amy Dru Stanley, *From Bondage to Contract: Wage Labor, Marriage, and the Market in the Age of Slave Emancipation* (Cambridge, Eng., 1998).
66. Tushnet, *The American Law of Slavery*.
67. See Paul Finkelman, "Slaves as Fellow Servants: Ideology, Law, and Industrialization," *American Journal of Legal History* 31 (1987): 269–305; Andrew Fede, "Legal Protection for Slave Buyers in the U.S. South: A Caveat Concerning *Caveat Emptor*," *American Journal of Legal History* 31 (1987): 322–58; James L. Hunt, "Note: Private Law and Public Policy: Negligence Law and Political Change in Nineteenth-Century North Carolina," *North Carolina Law Review* 66 (1988): 421–42; Thomas D. Morris, "'As If the Injury Was Effected by the Natural Elements of Air or Fire': Slave Wrongs and the Liability of Masters," *Law and Society Review* 16 (1981–82): 569–99.
68. Thomas D. Morris, *Southern Slavery and the Law, 1619–1860* (Chapel Hill, 1996).
69. Jenny Bourne Wahl, *The Bondsman's Burden: An Economic and Historical Analysis of the Common Law of Slavery in the United States* (Cambridge, Eng., 1998).
70. Walter Johnson, "Inconsistency, Contradiction, and Complete Confusion: The Everyday Life of the Law of Slavery," *Law and Social Inquiry* 22 (1997): 405–33, at 413. "Humanity" and "interest" refer to the dichotomy set up by Mark Tushnet, in which "humanity" represents the total social relations of master and slave, and "interest" refers to the commercial economy. Tushnet, *American Law of Slavery*. "Humanity" and "interest" were also terms used frequently by Southern planters, who often remarked on the compatibility of humanity to slaves with economic self-interest, or "interest." I have argued that this compatibility stemmed from the slave's identity as a form of capital. See Gross, *Double Character*, 102.

71. Shearer Davis Bowman, *Masters and Lords: Mid-Nineteenth-Century U.S. Planters and Prussian Junkers* (New York, 1993), 162–83.

72. Johnson, *Soul By Soul*, 111.

73. Johnson, "Inconsistency, Contradiction, and Complete Confusion," at 430.

74. Ibid., 422.

75. For works emphasizing national leaders and organizations, see generally Harvard Sitkoff, *The Struggle for Black Equality, 1954–1980* (New York, 1981); Hugh Davis Graham, *The Civil Rights Era: Origins and Development of National Policy, 1960–1972* (New York, 1990); David J. Garrow, *Bearing The Cross: Martin Luther King, Jr. and the Southern Christian Leadership Conference* (New York, 1986). For local studies with new periodizations of civil rights history, see John Dittmer, *Local People: The Struggle for Civil Rights in Mississippi* (Urbana, 1994); Adam Fairclough, *Race and Democracy: The Civil Rights Struggle in Louisiana, 1915–1972* (Athens, 1995); Charles M. Payne, *I've Got The Light of Freedom: The Organizing Tradition and The Mississippi Freedom Struggle* (Berkeley, 1995); Robert J. Norrell, *Reaping the Whirlwind: The Civil Rights Movement in Tuskegee* (New York, 1985).

76. Hendrik Hartog, *Man and Wife in America: A History* (Cambridge, Mass., 2000), 3.

77. Christopher Waldrep, *Roots of Disorder: Race and Criminal Justice in the American South, 1817–1880* (Urbana, 1998).

78. Gross, *Double Character*, 35–41.

79. Many thanks to Laura Edwards for her insightful commentary on this essay, and to the participants at the Porter L. Fortune Symposium on Slavery at the University of Mississippi. It was a special honor for me to participate in this event at the invitation of Winthrop Jordan. At crucial moments in my studies, when other senior scholars were skeptical, Winthrop Jordan gave me the encouragement I needed to believe that this was an enterprise worth attempting. I am deeply grateful for his generosity and his example.

Notes to "RAPE IN BLACK AND WHITE: SEXUAL VIOLENCE IN THE TESTIMONY OF ENSLAVED AND FREE AMERICANS"
by Norrece T. Jones, Jr.

1. In the 1998 publication, *A Historical Guide to World Slavery*, edited by Seymour Drescher and Stanley L. Engerman, there is no entry for "rape." In fact, of the more than one hundred entries in this encyclopedic work, the only indexed reference to rape is to my own discussion of it in the "Psychology" entry that I wrote. One does find, however, an index citation for the "Sexual Use of slaves." What is said of rape in the two entries under that heading follows. In his "Family" entry, historian Larry E. Hudson, Jr. writes that the focus of slavery historiography in the 1980s warrants

their being called the "gender years." Referring to this time period, he asserts: "Some scholars, morally troubled by arguments that economic benefits could accrue to planters who succeeded in encouraging stable and productive slave families, maintain that slaveholders frequently intruded into the more intimate lives of their slaves. Indeed, a good deal of the literature of the 'gender years' dealt with the sexual coercion and rape of black females by white males, . . ." In her entry, "Gender and Slavery," historian Ruth Mazo Karras claims: "Sexual use of slaves could be violent or coercive but was not considered rape: the slave was the master's property to be used as he wished." And, without any explanation of how the escapes she cites could—or did—lead to rape, Karras writes that slave women "escaped some of the disadvantages of femininity—they did not have to be weak and submissive within the family, or deny an interest in sexuality—but this escape was not an advantage to them. Rather, it subjected them to forcible dissolution of their families and to rape." Seymour Drescher and Stanley L. Engerman, eds., *A Historical Guide to World Slavery* (New York, 1998), 202–03, 217.

2. James Hugo Johnston, *Race Relations in Virginia and Miscegenation in the South, 1776–1860*, with a foreword by Winthrop Jordan (Amherst, Mass., 1970), v, 257.

3. Martha Hodes, *White Women, Black Men: Illicit Sex in the Nineteenth-Century South* (New Haven, 1997), 21–22, 24.

4. For an excellent analysis of the idea of race and its history, see Audrey Smedley, *Race in North America: Origin and Evolution of a Worldview* (Boulder, 1999), 13–30, 90–113. Note also the observation of historian Darlene Clark Hine that, "One of the most remarked upon but least analyzed themes in the history of southern black women deals with black women's sexual vulnerability and powerlessness as victims of rape and domestic violence. . . . Virtually every known nineteenth-century female slave narrative contains a reference to, at some juncture, the ever-present threat and reality of rape." Darlene Clark Hine, "Rape and the Inner Lives of Southern Black Women: Thoughts on the Culture of Dissemblance," in Virginia Bernhard et al., eds., *Southern Women: Histories and Identities* (Columbia, Missouri, 1992), 177, 179.

5. Jean Fagan Yellin, introduction to *Incidents in the Life of a Slave Girl, Written By Herself* [Harriet A. Jacobs] (Cambridge, Mass., 2000), vii–viii, xv–xli.

6. According to historian Donald Wright, "There was never enough antipathy to keep black and whites entirely apart in sexual relations, however, and the considerable number of persons of mixed black and white parentage is mute evidence of such activity." Donald Wright, *African Americans in the Colonial Era: From African Origins through the American Revolution* (Wheeling, Ill., 2000), 146.

7. Norrece T. Jones, Jr., *Born a Child of Freedom, Yet a Slave: Mechanisms of Control and Strategies of Resistance in Antebellum South Carolina* (Hanover, N. H., 1990), 3–36.

8. William Hand Browne, ed., *Archives of Maryland: Proceedings and Acts of the General Assembly of Maryland, January, 1637/8-September, 1664* (Baltimore, 1883),

Notes 193

533–34, in Willie Lee Rose, ed., *A Documentary History of Slavery in North America* (New York, 1976), 24.

9. Rose, *A Documentary History*, 24.

10. J. Douglas Deal, *Race and Class in Colonial Virginia: Indians, Englishmen, and Africans on the Eastern Shore During the Seventeenth Century* (New York, 1993), 127–28, 179–81; Sharon Block, "Coerced Sex in British North America, 1700–1820" (Ph.D. diss., Princeton University, 1995), 6–8, 73. The nineteenth century presented even fewer avenues of recourse for enslaved victims of rape. See Gloria Shepherd, "The Rape of Black Women During Slavery" (A.D. diss., State University of New York at Albany, 1987), 3–4; Thelma Jennings, "'Us Colored Women Had to Go Though a Plenty': Sexual Exploitation of African-American Slave Women," *Journal of Women's History* 1 (Winter 1990): 45–47, 54, 64–66.

11. James Oakes, *The Ruling Race: A History of American Slaveholders* (New York, 1998), ix–xiii.

12. Block, "Coerced Sex," 123–25.

13. Rev. T. T. Brown to John Kemp, Albany, 21 July 1762, quoted in Block, "Coerced Sex," 59.

14. John Graham to James Grant, July 19, 1765, bundle 401, Papers of Governor James Grant of Ballindalloch, sometime Governor of East Florida, in ownership of Sir Evan Macpherson-Grant, Bart, Ballindalloch Castle Muniments, Scotland, quoted in Philip D. Morgan, *Slave Counterpoint: Black Culture in the Eighteenth-Century Chesapeake and Lowcountry* (Chapel Hill, 1998), 77, 221, 407, 563.

15. Kenneth Baillie, Sr., Georgia *Gazette* (Savannah), Sept. 26, 1765, quoted in Morgan, *Slave Counterpoint*, 406.

16. For a detailed history of two overseers, their rapes, and the children stemming from them during their respective reigns over the slave families and enslaved individuals whom they managed, see William Dusinberre, *Them Dark Days: Slavery in the American Rice Swamps* (New York, 1996), 216, 225–27, 247–50.

17. Wilma King, *Stolen Childhood: Slave Youth in Nineteenth-Century America* (Bloomington, Ind., 1995), 108.

18. Written By Himself, *The Interesting Narrative of the Life of Olaudah Equiano or Gustavus Vassa, The African*, in Henry Louis Gates, Jr., ed. *The Classic Slave Narratives* (New York, 1987), 80.

19. Ibid., 74.

20. Drescher, *A Historical Guide*, 217.

21. Alfred, a slave v. State of Mississippi, 37 Mississippi Reports, p. 296 (1859), quoted in Johnston, *Race Relations*, 306–07.

22. Joel Williamson, *New People: Miscegenation and Mulattoes in the United States* (New York, 1984), 56.

23. Bertram Wyatt-Brown, *Southern Honor: Ethics and Behavior in the Old South* (New York, 1982), 296.

24. King, *Stolen Childhood*, 108.

25. Melton A. McLaurin, *Celia: A Slave* (Athens, 1991), ix, 6–9, 17–19, 114–15.

26. William Forbes to George Carter, 20 May 1805, Carter Family Papers, Virginia Historical Society, Richmond, Virginia, quoted in Brenda E. Stevenson, *Life in Black and White: Family and Community in the Slave South* (New York, 1996), 239.

27. George Fitzhugh, *Cannibals All! or, Slaves Without Masters* (1857; reprint, Cambridge, Mass., 1960), 205.

28. Ibid., 18.

29. Philip Morgan sketched this vista of slavery early on in *Slave Counterpoint: Black Culture in the Eighteenth-Century Chesapeake and Lowcountry*. Like a revealing number of some of the twentieth- (and now twenty-first) century's most highly-regarded historians, his initial strokes were in harsh colors that captured "the varied complex encounters" that one would expect among individuals of vastly different status and power. To lighten their severity and to frame carefully our first look, he provided this classic splash of humanity: "Patriarchalism," he writes, was "the dominant social ethos of eighteenth-century British America" and it "encouraged the development of close personal relations between masters and slaves, whites and blacks" (xxi). With this beginning—and reams of planter testimony—readers were well prepared for the epigraph three-hundred and eighty-two pages later taken from a white Methodist minister who bemoaned, "I know not which to pity the most—the master or the slave." Thus he opens his chapter, "Social Transactions between Whites and Blacks" (377). There and elsewhere, he fleshes out a canvas that has entranced generations. Earlier we learn, "Patriarchalism was reformulated over the course of the eighteenth century. . . . It was a reflection in the realm of ideas of broad-gauged changes affecting Revolutionary America. Austere patriarchalism slowly gave way to mellow paternalism" (259). Morgan, unlike others, was not so blinded by either that he was unable to see, and therefore to make, this ultimate judgment: "The capacity of slavery to poison the relations of otherwise decent men and women was nowhere more evident than in the realm of sex. Some sexual encounters were marked by tenderness, esteem, and a sense of responsibility, but most were exploitative and unspeakably cruel—nothing more than rapes by white men of black women—a testament to the ugliness of human relations when people are treated as objects. . . . Love and cruelty, affection and callousness, composure and frenzy—such were the contradictory strands in the twisted emotional knot that bound whites and blacks in the sexual arena" (411–12). Morgan, *Slave Counterpoint*, xxi, 259, 377, 411–33. For a sentient view of patriarchalism and its impact on nonblacks and the unfree, see Jan Lewis, *The Pursuit of Happiness: Family and Values in Jefferson's Virginia* (Cambridge, Eng., 1983), 4–5, 21, 35–36, 136, 140–43, 147, 221–22, 269–70.

30. Kenneth S. Greenberg, ed., *The Confessions of Nat Turner and Related Documents* (Boston, 1996), 1–3; [Harriet Jacobs, writing as Linda Brent], *Incidents in the Life of a Slave Girl*, in Gates, *The Classic Slave Narratives*, 383–97; Johnston, *Race Relations*, 307.

31. Executive Papers, Letters Received, September 10, 1830, The Archives of Virginia, Richmond, Virginia, quoted in Johnston, *Race Relations*, 307.

32. Winthrop D. Jordan, *White Over Black: American Attitudes Toward the Negro, 1550–1812* (Chapel Hill, 1968), 158–63.

33. Historian Sharon Block found that patriots during the American Revolution charged loyalists and the Hessian soldiers in their service with rape as propaganda to increase their forces and to fuel hostility against their enemy. Block, "Sexual Coercion," 121, 214–44. For sexual fears and suspicions of blacks during insurrectionary scares, see: Jordan, *White Over Black*, 150–54; Douglas R. Egerton, *Gabriel's Rebellion: The Virginia Slave Conspiracies of 1800 and 1802* (Chapel Hill, 1993), 38, 78; Winthrop D. Jordan, *Tumult and Silence at Second Creek: An Inquiry Into a Civil War Slave Conspiracy* (Baton Rouge, 1993), 14–15, 73, 151–56.

34. Deborah Gray White, "Female Slaves in the Plantation South," in Edward D. C. Campbell, Jr., with Kym S. Rice, eds., *Before Freedom Came: African-American Life in the Antebellum South* (Richmond, Va., 1991), 103; Charles L. Perdue et al., eds., *Weevils in the Wheat: Interviews with Virginia Ex-Slaves* (Bloomington, Ind., 1976), 117.

35. R. J. M. Blackett, *Building an Antislavery Wall: Black Americans in the Atlantic Abolitionist Movement, 1830–1860* (Ithaca, N. Y., 1983), 4; Moses Roper, *A Narrative of the Adventures and Escape of Moses Roper, From American Slavery* (1838; reprint, New York, 1970), 9.

36. William and Ellen Craft, *Running A Thousand Miles for Freedom* (1860; reprint, New York, 1969), 2, 7–8.

37. The sexual exploitation and rape of slave boys has been a well-documented feature of slave societies elsewhere. Despite the finding of one student of slave testimony in America that there was absolutely no mention of homosexual assaults, the arguments of Orlando Patterson on this absence should inform any conclusions. Patterson concludes: "I have two reasons for speculating that homosexual assaults took place. First, in every known human society, a small minority of men are homosexuals—between 3 and 6 percent—and in the highly probable event that homosexual Euro-Americans found themselves with total power, and no risk of arrest, over fine-looking slave boys, it is a reasonable assumption that they would have exploited them in some cases. . . . My second reason is the fact that Southern culture was highly honorific, with a considerable degree of male bonding and homoerotic male play. We know from the literature on honorific societies that they tend to have a higher than normal proportion of homosexuals." Orlando Patterson, *Rituals of Blood: Consequences of Slavery in Two American Centuries* (New York, 1998), 289.

38. Jordan, *White Over Black*, 157; White, "Female Slaves," 110.

39. George P. Rawick, ed., *The American Slave: A Composite Autobiography*, Series One, 19 vols. (Westport, Conn., 1972), 17: 126, 131.

40. Ibid., 126, 131.

41. Ibid., 128.

42. Brent, *Incidents*, 375.

43. Elliot J. Gorn, "Professing History: Distinguishing Between Memory and the Past," *The Chronicle of Higher Education* 46 (April 28, 2000), B4–B5.

44. What scholars almost never—but should—consider when trying to comprehend the nature of and one of the keys to black survival in America is love. Historian Steven Brown briefly touched on this when he wrote, "Perhaps the most telling observation that may be noted is that slaves continued to develop love for one another despite the circumscribed conditions imposed by slavery." Steven E. Brown, "Sexuality and the Slave Community," *Phylon* 42 (1981), 10. See also, Barbara Omolade, "Hearts of Darkness," in Ann Snitow et al., eds., *Powers of Desire: The Politics of Sexuality* (New York, 1983), 361.

45. Dusinberre, *Them Dark Days*, 213–18, 224–26.

46. Ibid., 225–28, 247–51.

47. George P. Rawick, ed., *The American Slave: A Composite Autobiography*, Supplement, Series 1, I, *Alabama Narratives* (Westport, Conn., 1977), 149–51.

Notes to "COMMENTARY"
by Jan Lewis

1. Eugene D. Genovese, *Roll, Jordan, Roll: The World the Slaves Made* (New York, 1974), 424–25.

2. See Susan Brownmiller, *Against Our Will: Men, Women, and Rape* (New York, 1975).

3. "Rose Describes Being Forced to Live with Rufus," in Willie Lee Rose, ed., *A Documentary History of Slavery in North America* (New York, 1976), 434–37.

4. Rose, *Documentary History*, 434.

5. Norrece T. Jones, Jr., *Born a Child of Freedom, Yet a Slave: Mechanisms of Control and Strategies of Resistance in Antebellum South Carolina* (Middletown, Conn., 1990).

6. Walter Johnson, *Soul By Soul: Life Inside the Antebellum Slave Market* (Cambridge, Mass., 1999), 22–23.

7. Quoted in David Brion Davis, *The Problem of Slavery in the Age of Revolution, 1770–1823* (Ithaca, 1975), 196.

8. For Sambo, see Stanley M. Elkins, *Slavery: A Problem in American Institutional and Intellectual Life* (Chicago, 1959). Deborah Gray White, *Ar'n't I a Woman? Female Slaves in the Plantation South* (New York, 1985).

9. Martha Hodes, *White Women, Black Men: Illicit Sex in the 19th Century South* (New Haven, 1997); Diane Miller Sommerville, "The Rape Myth Reconsidered: The Intersection of Race, Class and Gender in the American South, 1800–1877" (Ph.D. diss., Rutgers, The State University of New Jersey, 1995); and "The Rape Myth in the Old South Reconsidered," *Journal of Southern History* 61 (1995): 481–518.

10. For explorations of this theme, see the essays in Jan Ellen Lewis and Peter S. Onuf, eds., *Sally Hemings and Thomas Jefferson: History, Memory, and Civic Culture* (Charlottesville, 1999).

Notes to "THE LONG HISTORY OF A LOW PLACE: SLAVERY ON THE SOUTH CAROLINA COAST, 1670–1870"
by Robert Olwell

1. Winthrop D. Jordan, *White Over Black: American Attitudes toward the Negro, 1550–1812* (Chapel Hill, 1968); Betty Wood, *Slavery in Colonial Georgia, 1730–1775* (Athens, 1984).

2. Peter H. Wood, *Black Majority: Negroes in Colonial South Carolina, from 1670 to the Stono Rebellion* (Chapel Hill, 1974), 18–21.

3. See for example, Ira Berlin, *Many Thousands Gone: The First Two Centuries of Slavery in North America* (Cambridge, Mass., 1998), 8–9.

4. Wood, *Black Majority*, 25.

5. Philip D. Morgan, *Slave Counterpoint: Black Culture in the Eighteenth-Century Chesapeake and Lowcountry* (Chapel Hill, 1998), 95.

6. Lowcountry population statistics are taken from, Peter A. Coclanis, *Shadow of a Dream: Economic Life and Death in the South Carolina Low Country, 1670–1920* (New York, 1989), 64, 112, 115.

7. See for example, William W. Freehling, *Prelude to Civil War: The Nullification Controversy in South Carolina, 1816–1836* (New York, 1966); Steven A. Channing, *Crisis of Fear: Secession in South Carolina* (New York, 1970); Lacy Ford, *Origins of Southern Radicalism: The South Carolina Upcountry, 1800–1860* (New York, 1988); and Stephanie McCurry, *Masters of Small Worlds: Yeoman Households, Gender Relations, and the Political Culture of the Antebellum South Carolina Low Country* (New York, 1995).

8. Edward Ball, *Slaves in the Family* (New York, 1998).

9. See Ira Berlin, "Time, Space, and the Evolution of Afro-American Society on British Mainland North America," *American Historical Review* 85 (1980): 44–78.

10. Morgan, *Slave Counterpoint*; Robert Olwell, *Masters, Slaves, and Subjects: The Culture of Power in the South Carolina Low Country, 1740–1790* (Ithaca, 1998).

11. Berlin, *Many Thousands Gone*; Morgan, *Slave Counterpoint*.

12. See for example, Margaret Washington Creel, *A Peculiar People: Slave Religion and Community Culture Among the Gullahs* (New York, 1988); Sylvia Frey and Betty Wood, *Come Shouting to Zion: African American Protestantism in the American South and British Caribbean to 1830* (Chapel Hill, 1998).

13. Wood, *Black Majority*, xvii.

14. Eugene D. Genovese, *Roll, Jordan, Roll: The World the Slaves Made* (New York, 1974); Robert Fogel and Stanley Engerman, *Time On the Cross: The Economics of American Negro Slavery* (Boston, 1974).

15. The four works were John Demos, *A Little Commonwealth: Family Life in Plymouth Colony* (New York, 1970); Philip J. Greven, Jr., *Four Generations: Population, Land, and Family in Colonial Andover, Massachusetts* (Ithaca, 1970); Kenneth A. Lockridge, *A New England Town: The First Hundred Years* (New York, 1970); Michael Zuckerman, *Peaceable Kingdoms: New England Towns in the 18th-century* (New York, 1970).

16. According to Richard Dunn, their simultaneous appearance "caused a considerable stir within the historical fraternity," Richard S. Dunn, "The Social History of Early New England," *American Quarterly* 24 (1972): 661; see also, John M. Murrin, "Review Essay," *History and Theory* 11 (1972): 226–75.

17. See Jack P. Greene, *Pursuits of Happiness: The Social Development of Early Modern British Colonies and the Formation of American Culture* (Chapel Hill, 1988), 55–56.

18. For an explication of how the concept of modernization influenced early American historians in this period see Joyce Appleby, "Values and Society," in Jack P. Greene and J.R. Pole, eds., *Colonial British America: Essays in the New History of the Early Modern Era* (Baltimore, 1984), 290–316.

19. Wood, *Black Majority*, 96, 97.

20. Ibid., 229.

21. Ibid., 325.

22. A recent essay for example, concludes that "the isolation and loneliness of the turpentine forests, combined with heavy work demands, poor housing, inadequate clothing and food, and unhealthful and dangerous labor conditions, made the slaves already difficult work and manner of life unbearable," Robert B. Outland III, "Slaves, Work, and the Geography of the North Carolina Naval Stores Industry, 1835–1860," *Journal of Southern History* 62 (1996): 27–56.

23. For Africans exported, see Morgan, *Slave Counterpoint*, 59–61; for an estimate of the number of Indian slaves exported see Timothy Silver, *A New Face on the Countryside: Indians, Colonists, and Slaves in the South Atlantic Forests, 1500–1800* (Cambridge, Eng., 1990), 74.

24. Wood, *Black Majority*, 323.

25. Ibid., 320.

26. Joyce B. Chaplin, *An Anxious Pursuit: Agricultural Innovation and Modernity in the Lower South, 1730–1815* (Chapel Hill, 1993).

27. Daniel Littlefield, *Rice and Slaves: Ethnicity and the Slave Trade in South Carolina* (Baton Rouge, 1981).

28. Creel, *A Peculiar People*.

29. John Thornton, "African Dimensions of the Stono Rebellion," *American Historical Review* 96 (1991): 1101–13.

30. Frey and Wood, *Come Shouting to Zion*, xi.

31. Charles Joyner, *Down By the Riverside: A South Carolina Slave Community* (Urbana, 1984).

32. Fernand Braudel, *The Mediterranean and the Mediterranean World in the Age of Philip II*, trans. Sian Reynolds, 2 vols., (New York, 1972–1975), 20, 1244, cited in Joyner, *Down By the Riverside*, xviii and 245 n. 6.

33. Sidney Mintz and Richard Price, *An Anthropological Approach to the Afro-American Past: A Caribbean Perspective*, (Philadelphia, 1976), cited in Joyner, *Down by the Riverside*, 246–47 n. 12; and in Morgan, *Slave Counterpoint*, xxii n. 11.

34. William Dusinberre, *Them Dark Days: Slavery in the American Rice Swamps* (New York, 1996).

35. For the American Revolution see Sylvia Frey, *Water From the Rock: Black Resistance in a Revolutionary Age* (Princeton, 1991); and Olwell, *Masters, Slaves, and Subjects*; for the American Civil War, see Willie Lee Rose, *Rehearsal for Reconstruction: The Port Royal Experiment* (Oxford, 1964); Eric Foner, *Nothing But Freedom: Emancipation and its Legacy* (Baton Rouge, 1983); and Julie Saville, *The Work of Reconstruction: From Slavery to Wage Labor in South Carolina, 1860–1870* (New York, 1994).

36. Sidney Mintz, "Slavery and the Rise of Peasantries," in *Historical Reflections* 6 (1979): 213–42.

37. Quoted in Perry Anderson, *Arguments within English Marxism* (London, 1980), 17.

Notes to "COMMENTARY"
by William Dusinberre

1. Philip Morgan, *Slave Counterpoint: Black Culture in the Eighteenth-Century Chesapeake and Lowcountry* (Chapel Hill, 1998), and his articles cited below. Ira Berlin, *Many Thousands Gone: The First Two Centuries of Slavery in North America* (Cambridge, Mass., 1998).

2. The following discussion focuses on rice plantations, which dominated the lowcountry until the 1850s. During that decade about one-sixth of the rice slaves were transferred to sea-island cotton planting, and—although rice production continued to grow—for the first time a small majority of lowcountry slaves now raised cotton. In most respects sea-island cotton plantations resembled rice plantations: they tended to be huge; black majorities were almost as great in sea-island parishes as in rice parishes; the task system spread from rice plantations to sea-island cotton plantations; and the sea-island cotton slaves' cultural life surely resembled that of the rice slaves. A fruitful area for further research will be to study how the development of the sea-island cotton industry by 1860 affected the lives of lowcountry slaves.

3. In a twenty-six county sample, nine of the ten richest North American decedents in 1774 resided in Charleston "District," South Carolina. Alice Hanson Jones, *Wealth of a Nation to Be: The American Colonies on the Eve of the Revolution* (New York, 1980), 171, 177.

4. The figure for the 1740s is not quite comparable with that for rice plantations in 1860, because not every South Carolina slave in the 1740s lived on a rice plantation. But so many did that the figures indicate reasonably accurately the trend toward ever larger rice plantations. *"[T]hirty-five slaves"*: interpolated from data in Morgan, *Slave Counterpoint*, 40. *"Just over two hundred slaves"*: The median rice-growing slave lived on a plantation of about two hundred four slaves: interpolated from data in William Dusinberre, *Them Dark Days: Slavery in the American Rice Swamps* (New York, 1996), 389, 391–92, 395, 462.

5. This generalization does not take account of Louisiana sugar plantations, whose size resembled that of the lowcountry's rice plantations. In 1860 the median Southern slave was held by the owner of twenty-two slaves. But as urban slaves were held in much smaller groups than were rural slaves, the median *rural* slave was probably held by the owner of about twenty-four slaves. *"Twenty-two slaves"*: interpolated from U.S. Bureau of the Census, *Census* (1860): *Agriculture*, 224, 247. (In this calculation I have corrected for the Census Bureau's omission [on 247] of 10,329 Arkansas slaveholders [224]. See James Oakes, *The Ruling Race: A History of American Slaveholders* [New York, 1982], 260, n. 6.) On urban slaves, the figures for the District of Columbia are suggestive: *Census* (1860): *Agriculture*, 247.

6. Dusinberre, 415–16, 536–38.

7. In Jamaica, during the second half of the eighteenth century, the slave population had decreased "naturally" (i.e., through excess of deaths over births) at a decennial rate of about 25 percent (the shortfall being made up by importation of slaves from Africa); but by 1817 Jamaica's slave population was almost self-reproducing, declining thereafter at a decennial rate of just 2.7 percent. This was not greatly different from the situation in the American Rice Kingdom where, even in the mid-nineteenth century, the decennial rate of increase was only about 4 percent. Orlando Patterson, *The Sociology of Slavery: An Analysis of the Origins, Development and Structure of Negro Slave Society in Jamaica* (London, 1967), 97, 107. Jamaica's slave population in 1817 was 346,150. In the next fifteen years 128,492 slaves died, while 114,487 were born. *British Parliamentary Papers*, 1833, vol. 26, 474–75. B. W. Higman, *Slave Populations of the British Caribbean, 1807–1834* (Baltimore, 1984), 606.

8. Even if the number of African slaves illegally imported into the United States and Texas after 1810 somewhat exceeded the number of fugitives who permanently escaped from the South, Southern slaves' decennial rate of natural increase, 1810 to 1860, still averaged 27 percent. U.S. Bureau of the Census, *Census* (1860): *Population*, ix.

9. Dusinberre, 410–16.

10. Morgan, *Slave Counterpoint*, 660.

11. Ibid., 264–65. Lowry Ware, "The Burning of Jerry: The Last Slave Execution by Fire in South Carolina?" *South Carolina Historical Magazine* 91 (1990): 102–06.

12. Although Jones considers the whole state of South Carolina, many of his illustrations come from the lowcountry. Norrece T. Jones, Jr., *Born a Child of Freedom, Yet a Slave: Mechanisms of Control and Strategies of Resistance in Antebellum South Carolina* (Hanover, N. H., 1990), 25 (nn. 62–63), 75–78, 85, 88–90, 170, 179, 187, 189. Dusinberre, 161, 303–04, 423–24. Michael S. Hindus, *Prison and Plantation: Crime, Justice, and Authority in Massachusetts and South Carolina, 1767–1878* (Chapel Hill, 1980), chap. 6, esp. 150–61.

13. Morgan's study of fugitive slave advertisements seems to imply that, in the colonial period, a South Carolina slave was up to eleven times as likely to flee as was a Virginia slave. (In colonial South Carolina about fifty-seven hundred fugitives were advertized, while about twelve hundred Virginia fugitives were advertized. As there were about two and one-third times as many slaves in Virginia, 1740–1770, as in South Carolina, a South Carolina slave was eleven times more likely to be advertized as a fugitive than was a Virginia slave. Morgan, *Slave Counterpoint*, 394, n. 61.)

And scattered records suggest that temporary flights from rice plantations remained frequent in the nineteenth century, whereas violent resistance appears to have been far less common (Dusinberre, 142–58 and note 63; 160–68, 251–53, 335–41, 371–73, 421–22, 433). In the late 1850s nearly 80 fugitives were lodged annually in the Savannah jail (Edward Ayers, *Vengeance and Justice: Crime and Punishment in the 19th-Century American South* [New York, 1984], 308, n. 31; 67). If these comprised, say, a fifth of the total number of flights in that region, nearly four hundred slaves there fled annually. True, Norrece Jones has identified about fifteen examples (including three probable insurrectionary conspiracies) of planned or actual violence, by slaves against masters, in the South Carolina lowcountry during a sixty-year period; and he presents strong reasons to suppose there were many others (Jones, *Born a Child of Freedom*, 33–34, 169–70, 173, 177–79, 181–83, 186, 189, 291 [n. 129]). But these cases of violence appear to me to be far outnumbered by the instances of slaves who fled from the plantations; and fugitives usually did not offer violent resistance, even when being captured. They knew they were likely to die if they did resist.

14. Charles Joyner, *Down by the Riverside: A South Carolina Slave Community* (Urbana, 1984); Morgan, *Slave Counterpoint*.

15. Philip Morgan, "Task and Gang Systems: The Organization of Labor on New World Plantations," in Stephen Innes, ed., *Work and Labor in Early America* (Chapel Hill, 1988), 202–06.

16. Morgan, *Slave Counterpoint*, 248–53, 366–68, 370–71, 373–75. Philip Morgan, "Black Life in Eighteenth-Century Charleston," *Perspectives in American History*, New Series, 1(1984), 194–203. Philip Morgan, "The Ownership of Property by Slaves in the Mid-Nineteenth Century Low Country," *Journal of Southern History*

49 (1983): 399–420. Betty Wood, *Women's Work, Men's Work: The Informal Slave Economies of Lowcountry Georgia* (Athens, 1995), 177–87; 80–100. Larry Hudson, Jr., *To Have and to Hold: Slave Work and Family Life in Antebellum South Carolina* (Athens, 1997), 2–5, 11–12, 19–26, 34–47, 82–95, 106–07, 135–38, 142–51, 171–73. Robert Olwell, *Masters, Slaves, and Subjects: The Culture of Power in the South Carolina Low Country, 1740–1790* (Ithaca, 1998), 145–58, 166–80.

17. Morgan, *Slave Counterpoint*, 220–25, 343–46. William Van Deburg's view of the drivers' intermediary role between masters and field hands—though based mainly on evidence from elsewhere in the South—would probably be equally apposite for lowcountry drivers. William Van Deburg, *The Slave Drivers: Black Agricultural Labor Supervisors in the Antebellum South* (Westport, Conn., 1979), esp. 86–91, 109–12.

18. Julie Saville, *The Work of Reconstruction: from Slave to Wage Laborer in South Carolina, 1860–1870* (New York, 1994), 5–11.

19. Creel shows that the "Christian" conversion ritual in the lowcountry bore striking resemblance to the initiation rituals of West Africa; Jesus was seen by lowcountry slaves as a fellow-sufferer, while New Testament doctrines of atonement were ignored; and a plantation's Praise House (with a significant female leadership, and where African beliefs and practices could continue to flourish) developed as a parallel institution to the local church. If the slaves departed some distance from African conceptions of an afterlife—accepting instead a Christian view that ethical conduct would be rewarded or punished after death—the slaves' hearty presumption that most masters would roast in hell bore little resemblance to Protestant ideas about salvation by faith. Margaret Washington Creel, *"A Peculiar People": Slave Religion and Community-Culture among the Gullahs* (New York, 1988), 245–322. Sylvia Frey and Betty Wood, *Come Shouting to Zion: African-American Protestantism in the American South and British Caribbean to 1830* (Chapel Hill, 1998), esp. chap. 7. Joyner, chap. 5.

20. Joyner, chaps. 6–7.

21. Robert Olwell has shown that those lowcountry slaves who became Anglicans could sometimes thereby gain literacy and Bibles, both of which they might then use for the benefit of other slaves. (And this was also true for enslaved Methodists and Baptists.) Furthermore, Olwell suggests that those lowcountry slaves who took communion in an Anglican church—when most of the masters in that same church declined communion—surely gained a sense of moral superiority in doing so. Philip Morgan, too, argues that those slaves who acquired substantial elements of the masters' culture may sometimes have profited by doing so. Olwell, 116–39. Morgan, *Slave Counterpoint*, e.g., 344–46, 353–58 (though Morgan here stresses the pressures imposed on slaves accorded special privilege). Morgan, "Black Life in Eighteenth-Century Charleston," 224–25.

22. Not counting miscarriages and stillbirths, the average slave woman in the mid-nineteenth-century Rice Kingdom had 6.6 live births; of these children some 4.36 died before reaching age fifteen. Dusinberre, 402–04, 131, 415 and its notes 78–79.

23. Berlin, 154–61. 10.9 percent of lowcountry slaves lived in Charleston or Savannah in 1810, 14.0 percent in 1860. U.S. Bureau of the Census, *Aggregate Amount of Persons within the United States in the Year 1810* (Washington, 1811), 79–80; *Census* (1860): *Population*, 65–69, 451–52. ("Lowcountry" = the four South Carolina rice "Districts" and the six coastal Georgia counties.)

24. This resulted from the large size of plantations, which permitted considerable specialization in the labor force; and it also arose from the conditions of rice culture, which involved certain specialized skills such as those of the "trunkminders" (see next note). The masters also needed trained slave engineers to repair the machinery in the rice mills. Specialization also arose from the great wealth of rice planters, who could afford to train skilled butlers, cooks, seamstresses, and housekeepers. Cf. Morgan, *Slave Counterpoint*, chap. 4, esp. 205–08.

25. "Trunkminders" adjusted the sluices ("trunks") through which water flooded, or was drained from, the fields; and some trunkminders became very expert at judging the timing of these vital operations.

26. "10 percent" is an estimate based on the Charles Manigault, Pierce Butler, and Robert Allston rice plantations.

27. Morgan, *Slave Counterpoint*, 273–96.

28. Clarence Walker, *Deromanticizing Black History: Critical Essays and Reappraisals* (Knoxville, Tenn., 1991).

Notes to "PAUL ROBESON AND RICHARD WRIGHT ON THE ARTS AND SLAVE CULTURE"
by Sterling Stuckey

1. For his enduring example, this essay is dedicated to John Hope Franklin.
2. Paul Robeson, *Here I Stand* (1958; reprint, Boston, 1988), 10.
3. *New York Herald Tribune*, October 17, 1926.
4. Robeson, *Here I Stand*, 16.
5. Ibid., 15; Alan Lomax, *The Land Where the Blues Began* (New York, 1993), 365.
6. Robeson, *Here I Stand*, 7.
7. Ibid., 6–7, 9.
8. *The Seaman's (Union of Australia) Journal*, Special Supplement (November 1960), 371.
9. Ibid., 372.
10. See Sterling Stuckey, "My Father's Son: Paul Robeson's Early Years," in *Arts and Sciences*, magazine of the College of Arts and Sciences, Northwestern University (Fall 1983): 2–6. When his own teammates at Rutgers, after having promised to kill him if he went out for the football team, broke his nose and dislocated his shoulder, he continued to study, reading through swollen eyes. Under circumstances of long hours of

practice and games against opponents, Paul never neglected his studies. He faced racial violence in game after game. In one game, he returned blow for blow—in the words of the West Virginia coach, "giving as good as he's gotten." But the coach added, "Why that colored boy's legs were so gashed and bruised that the skin peeled off when he removed his stockings."

11. W. E. B. Du Bois, "The Talented Tenth," reprinted as "W. E. B. Du Bois Argues for a College-Educated Elite" in August Meier, Elliott Rudwick, and Francis L. Broderick, eds., *Black Protest Thought in the Twentieth Century*, First Edition (Indianapolis, 1971) 47–55.

12. Quoted in Paul Robeson, Jr., "Paul Robeson: Black Warrior," in *Paul Robeson: The Great Forerunner* (New York, 1965), 4–5. In time, still more laudatory appraisals were made of Robeson's singing. Benny Green, the respected English critic, reminded his audience of Robeson's greatness as an artist, remarking: "Running like a thread through the texture of the times is Paul Robeson's incomparable voice. . . . I accept all over again the immutability of Robeson as a great artist. . . . When he sings, I hear the unsullied expression of the human spirit" (Ibid., 5). And some years later, when Robeson was practically under house arrest, Nobel Laureate Pablo Neruda wrote, in "Ode to Paul Robeson":

> *You were a subterranean river,*
> *something*
> *that bore*
> *the merest glimmer of light*
> *in the darkness,*
> *the last sword*
> *of dying honour,*
> *the last wounded fork of lightning,*
> *the inextinguishable thunder.*

(Pablo Neruda, "Ode to Paul Robeson," in *Paul Robeson: The Great Forerunner*, 248).

13. James Weldon Johnson, for example, observed, "as an instrument for poetry the dialect has only two main stops, humor and pathos" (Book of American Negro Poetry [1922; reprint, New York, 1959], 3). Ralph Ellison commented that writers who use dialect, including Paul Laurence Dunbar and Charles Waddell Chestnutt, represent a tradition of "Negro American writing . . . [which] started out by reflecting the styles popular at the time, styles uninterested in the human complexity of Negroes. . . . It helped them get published but it got in the way of their subject matter and their goal of depicting Negro personality" (Ralph Ellison, "A Very Stern Discipline," in *Going to the Territory* [New York, 1986], 280–81).

14. Du Bois's powerful and equally subtle argument for slave culture extending into the Reconstruction period is found in "The Coming of the Lord" chapter of *Black Reconstruction*. For the opposing view, see the chapter entitled "The Meaning of Freedom" in Eric Foner, *Reconstruction: America's Unfinished Revolution, 1863–1877* (New York, 1988). Robeson made the comment about dialect after receiving the Gold Medal of the American Academy of Arts and Sciences for the best diction in the American theater. See "Paul Robeson's Approach to the Study of Languages," an interview with Mrs. Bradly of Greensboro, North Carolina, 1944, 6–7. Paul Robeson Manuscript Collection, Howard University, Moorland–Spingarn Research Center.

15. Paul Robeson, "Songs of My People," Sovietskaia muzyka, July 1949, in Philip Foner, ed., *Paul Robeson Speaks* (New York: Brunner/Mazel Publishers, 1978), 212. Robeson had this to say about the body of slave song: "These songs are striking in the noble beauty of their melodies, in the expressiveness and resourcefulness of their intonations, in the startling variety of their rhythms, in the sonority of their harmonies, and in the unusual distinctiveness and poetical nature of their forms" (Ibid.).

16. "A Home in Dat Rock," quoted in Sterling A. Brown, Arthur P. Davis, and Ulysses Lee, *The Negro Caravan* (1941; reprint, New York, 1970), 436 stanzas 2, 3 and 4.

17. Carl Sandburg, quoted in Jon Michael Spencer, *The New Negroes and Their Music* (Knoxville, Tenn., 1997), 14. Meanwhile, Eugene O'Neill, the year before, inscribed a book of his plays to Robeson, who had acted in O'Neill's *The Emperor Jones*: "In gratitude to Paul Robeson in whose interpretation of 'Brutus Jones' I have found the most complete satisfaction an author can get—that of seeing his creation born into flesh and blood!" (Paul Robeson Jr., *Paul Robeson: Great Forerunner*, 6–7). It should be mentioned that Robeson was an admirer of Hayes. Before having begun his career as a singer, he remarked, "So today Roland Hayes is infinitely more a racial asset than many who 'talk' at great length. Thousands of people hear him, see him, are moved by him, and are brought to a clearer understanding of human values. If I can do something of a like character, I shall be happy. . . ." When Robeson began singing, however, what he did was in some ways very different from what Hayes was doing, for he was closer, as Sandburg said, to the original voicings of the music. In this regard, Hayes had been a member of the Fisk Jubilee Singers, who helped popularize the spirituals shortly after the Civil War, and who, under the direction of George L. White, sang spirituals largely bereft of the influences of slave dialect. While the Jubilee Singers and other singing troupes from Negro colleges helped bring the spirituals to the attention of the world, Robeson was the first great artist to take slave music to the concert stage for entire concerts, and without apologies. See "An Actor's Wanderings and Hopes" in Foner, *Robeson Speaks*, 69. See also J. B. Marsh, *The Story of the Jubilee Singers*, 7th ed. (London, [1875] 1877).

18. See G. W. Bishop, "Robeson Acclaimed in Othello Role," *New York Times* (Tuesday, May 20, 1930). Reading the review, prominently displayed in the New York Times, one thinks of Paul's African ancestry since he adopted the strategy,

in studying the role, of equating the plight of Othello, whom he considered African, with that of his people. The racial dimension is interpreted by the critic, who refers to Othello as Ethiopian, in much the way that Robeson, who considered Othello a Moor, has spoken of him: "In this *Othello* there was tragedy of a race.... Until Iago let drop the first hint of suspicion, Othello was a deep, mighty river, flowing serenely. After the calm was ruffled, Robeson expressed with extraordinary power the storm that rose and fell until the final tragedy was reached. Here the actor gave the impression of a priest performing a holy rite.... It was ... a tragedy of honor rather than of jealousy" (Ibid.).

19. *The Daily Herald* (London), January 26, 1935.

20. Ibid.

21. Paul Robeson, "Songs of My People," 212, 213. This position, incidentally, accords with that of David Dalby, who provides this comment on the music of Mali: "The civilization of Mali included a rich musical culture, based on an elaborate range of string, wind and percussion instruments and on a long professional training for its musicians. This musical culture has survived in West Africa for at least a thousand years and, by its influence on American music, has enabled the United States to achieve an independence from European musical traditions and to pioneer new forms" ("Jazz, Jitter and Jam," *New York Times*, Nov. 10, 1970, op-ed page).

22. See Sterling Stuckey, "Paul Robeson in the Caribbean," forthcoming. The remarks about opera and Jackson are found in Paul Robeson, "The Negro Artist Looks Ahead," in Foner, *Robeson Speaks*, 305.

23. Martin Bauml Duberman, *Paul Robeson* (New York, 1988), 245.

24. Ralph Ellison, *Shadow and Act* (1953; reprint, New York, 1964), 87.

25. Paul Robeson, "We Must Come South," reprinted in *Paul Robeson: Tributes: Selected Writings* (New York, 1976), 65.

26. Robeson, *Here I Stand*, 15. Italics added.

27. Robeson did not think Africans alone appreciated the close relationship between speech and song, merely that it was a marked quality of slave art and of the art of the descendants of slaves. In an interview, he remarked that "there is the tradition of speech extending into song. You can find this in the Negro preacher's chant, in flamenco, and in Mussorgsky's *Boris Godunov*. Mussorgsky's music is based on the music of the old Russian church, which in turn utilized ancient folk songs. Mahalia Jackson is another beautiful example of speech into song." In the same interview, Paul's wife Eslanda said: "The reason he still has his natural voice is that he sings the way he talks. He has rejected the formal vocal instructions—placement and that sort of thing—because he's always believed singing originated from the spoken language. Philology, you know, has been his main interest for years" (Nat Hentoff, "Paul Robeson Makes a New Album," *The Recorder* 18 [April 17, 1958], 34–35).

28. See Melville Herskovits Collection, Africana Library, Northwestern University, Evanston, Illinois. Concerning African languages, Robeson commented: "They created their own language, distinguished—like Chinese—by the great precision and subtlety of intonational structure" (Robeson, "Songs of My People," 213). Deep into the study of African languages, music, and folklore in the thirties, Robeson for awhile took the view that jazz was, as he states in an undated, handwritten note, a retrogression from African standards of music. In the following decade he acknowledged that he was mistaken. In fact, he became one of jazz's foremost defenders. See Paul Robeson, "Thoughts on Music," 1959, reprinted in *Tributes*, 72–73.

29. David Dalby, *Black Through White: Patterns of Communication* (Bloomington, Ind., 1970).

30. Paul Robeson, from handwritten notes, 1936, reprinted in *Tributes*, 54.

31. Paul Robeson, "I Want to Be African," in E. G. Cousins, ed., *What I Want From Life* (London, 1934), 75. This view is supported almost precisely by the findings of Lydia Parrish and Jean and Marshall Stearns. Parrish notes that she saw a dance called "Ball the Jack" on St. Simon's Island off the coast of Georgia: "A few years ago I saw it demonstrated by an old resident of Eleuthera, in the Bahamas, and its portrayal in the film *Sanders of the River*—for which 'background shots' were made in villages along the Congo—indicates the region from which it originally came" (*Slave Songs of the Georgia Sea Islands* [New York, 1942], 13–14). The Stearnses also observed other similarities between African American dance and African dance: "A few years ago, watching films of West African dancing taken by Professor Lorenzo Turner of Roosevelt University, the present writers saw the Ibibio of Nigeria performing a shimmy to end all shimmies, the Sherbro of Sierra Leone executing an unreasonably fine facsimile of the Snake Hips, and a group of Hausa girls near Kano moving in a fashion closely resembling the Lindy, or Jitterbug" (*Jazz Dance* [New York, 1964], 13).

32. Robeson, "I Want to Be African," 75. The belief that certain African dances had not changed over long stretches of time is not surprising given the power of the subconscious in initiating and sustaining dance. Improvisation, the essence of change in African dance, need not always take place in performing a particular dance, which means the dancer can return, without appreciable change occurring, to the more standard form of a particular dance, to what appears to be identical in the dance as first conceived and practiced. For the role of the subconscious in dance, see Sterling Stuckey, "Christian Conversion and the Challenge of Dance," in Susan Foster, ed., *Choreographing History* (Bloomington, Ind., 1995), 55–56. Robeson elaborated upon his insights into African American music in 1949: "Rhythm, the most intricate polyrhythmic constructions on the invariable and uniform pulsation of a basic, clear-cut meter—this is the basis of the musical speech of African Negroes. This basis has been fully preserved in the music of their American descendants. This characteristic syncopation, with all its rhythmic freedom and infinite variety, not only underwent its own development in Negro musical folklore, but also had a quite

noticeable effect on the music of those peoples of North and South America among whom the Negroes lived" (Robeson, "Songs of My People," 213).

33. Robeson, "I Want to Be African," 71; Paul Robeson, "The Culture of the Negro," *Spectator* (London), June 15, 1934, 916.

34. Quoted in Sterling Stuckey, *Slave Culture: Nationalist Theory and the Foundations of Black America* (New York, 1987), 350.

35. Richard Wright, "Blueprint for Negro Writing," in John A. Williams and Charles F. Harris, eds., *Amistad 2: Writing on Black History and Culture* (New York, 1971), 8.

36. Ibid., 6. Despite his lack of knowledge of African influences in slave religion, however, Wright, unlike the great majority of scholars, did not claim that slaves on the whole embraced Christianity.

37. Stuckey, *Slave Culture*, chapters 1, 2, and 3, passim.

38. Richard Wright, "I Bite the Hand that Feeds Me," *Atlantic Monthly* 165, no. 6 (June 1940): 827–28.

39. Ibid., 827.

40. Sidney W. Mintz and Richard Price, *The Birth of African-American Culture: An Anthropological Perspective* (Boston, 1992), 95 n. 16. More questionable still is that their study, originally entitled *An Anthropological Approach to the Afro-American Past: A Caribbean Perspective* and meant to cover mainly the Caribbean now presumably covers the entire Americas, though they admit that the 1992 version, *The Birth of African-American Culture*, is the "original essay largely unchanged" (*Birth*, x). The change in titles is meant to justify the far broader application of their theories, presumably. Furthermore, Mintz and Price ask us to take them largely at their word, failing to provide evidence for the sweeping claims in their book. They are dangerously open, however, about the rationale for their study: "If we seem to underemphasize the African past to stress the motile nature of Afro-America," they write, "it is in part because the usual emphasis seems to have been the reverse." Any claim on their part to objectivity seems questionable, therefore.

In fact, conditions were exactly the opposite of what Mintz and Price would have us believe. There were, beyond Herskovits himself, virtually no proponents of African cultural influence in North America in academic circles in the thirties, or in conventional disciplines such as literature and history as late as the seventies. What Du Bois wrote in 1939 was largely true when the Mintz and Price book first appeared: "The Negro is the clown of history, the football of anthropology and the slave of industry" (W. E. B. Du Bois, *Black Folk Then and Now* [New York, 1975], 144). Following this line of thought, Harvard's Daniel Moynihan and Nathan Glazer, in *Beyond the Melting Pot*, wrote that "It is not possible for the Negroes to view themselves as other ethnic groups viewed themselves because—and this is the key to much in the Negro World—the Negro is only an American, and nothing else. He has no values and culture to guard and protect" (Cambridge, Mass., 1963), 53. Judging from work being done at the time in history, anthropology, literature, and other disciplines, the

Moynihan/Glazer thesis was supported almost universally. With so few major universities in the nation offering courses in African history and with none offering courses in Afro-American history, it was not long before there was a call for Black Studies.

41. According to Ellison, pluralism brought slave art into view beside other, unnamed, artistic forms in antebellum America. Slave music, dance, and folklore were products of democracy, he asserts, without a shred of supporting documentation apart from the excessive claim that slaves borrowed "ruthlessly" from the larger society because they lacked investment in "articulate cultural styles." In a rare nod to Africa, he admits that the African cultural past gave slaves an artistic "edge" that he takes away, in his discussion of pluralism, by failing to give attention to the dangerous conditions under which African creativity occurred, preferring instead to emphasize, inexplicably, democracy. His basic argument is that "Negro life is a by-product of Western civilization;" it is "of America and the West. . . ." (Ellison, *Going to the Territory*, 142). See page 94–95, footnote 10, of Mintz and Price, and Ellison, *Shadow and Act*, pages 93 and 172.

42. Richard Wright, *Black Boy* (1937; reprint, New York, 1966), 45, 43.

43. Wright, "Blueprint for Negro Writing," 7.

44. Wright, *Black Boy*, 43. It would follow that Ellison's opposition to dialect argues that he would favor the singing of the spirituals in standard English. See footnote 13 above.

45. See Carla Capetti, "Sociology of an Existence: Wright and the Chicago School," in Henry Louis Gates and K. A. Appiah, eds., *Richard Wright: Critical Perspectives Past and Present* (New York, 1993), 255–71. The impact of this school of thought on Wright appears vividly in *Black Boy* when he describes his father: "From far beyond the horizons that bound this bleak plantation there had come to me through my living the knowledge that my father was a black peasant who had gone to the city seeking life, but who had failed in the city; a black peasant whose life had been hopelessly snarled in the city, and who had at last fled the city—that same city which had lifted me in its burning arms and borne me toward alien and undreamed-of shores of knowing" (43). Regarding those shores, Wright did not exaggerate; due to the harsh circumstances of his environment, his three years in elementary school was the extent of his formal training.

46. Richard Wright, "Red Clay Blues," in Jerry W. Ward, Jr., ed., *Trouble the Water: 250 Years of African-American Poetry* (New York, 1997), 145–46.

47. Richard Wright, "King Joe," reprinted in Appendix B of Michel Fabre, *The World of Richard Wright* (Jackson, Miss., 1985), 249.

48. Richard Wright, "Ah Feels It in Mah Bones," reprinted in Fabre, 236.

49. He had claimed in 1940, however, in response to a critic of his fiction, that before being wrenched from their moorings and forcibly brought to America, blacks had known "a rich and complex culture," a notion not implied in "Blueprint," and certainly not in *Black Boy* (Wright, "I Bite the Hand That Feeds Me," 827).

50. Fabre, 155, 193.

51. Ibid., 199–200. No doubt politics entered profoundly in Wright's suggestions, not so much because of the names he recommended but because of his omission of two preeminent authorities on the African diaspora, Paul Robeson and W. E. B. Du Bois, both of whom were pro-Soviet while Wright was passionately anti-Soviet.

52. Richard Wright, *Black Power: A Record of Reactions in a Land of Pathos* (New York, 1954), 56–57.

53. James Rawley writes that 25 percent of the Africans brought into slavery in North America were from Congo-Angola and almost as many from Nigeria-Dahomey-Togo-Ghana: "Scrutiny of the African origins of American slaves in general reveals that about one-quarter of the whole came from Angola [Congo-Angola] and a lesser portion from the Bight of Biafra. Of the remainder, in descending order, the Gold Coast, Senegambia, the Windward Coast, and Sierra Leone, the Bight of Benin, and Mozambique-Madagascar supplied the rest" (*The Transatlantic Slave Trade* [New York, 1981] 335).

54. Wright, *Black Power*, 57. Indeed, in his later years, Wright even differed with those who believed that slave converts, however strong or meek, were genuinely Christian: "There is a degree of suppression for which there is no sublimation. It is so immediately and insistently painful that it is impossible to assume an attitude of spiritual contemplation, to regard the situation as an example of human tragedy. The Negro, despite his formal profession of the Christian virtues of meekness and altruism, is by nature not a Christian. . . . Such altruism and benevolence as he may exhibit are the results of need, a part of the imposed technique of survival" ("An Interview with Richard Wright, 1946," in Keneth Kinnamon and Michel Fabre, eds., *Conversations with Richard Wright* [Jackson, Miss., 1993], 108).

Furthermore, the reader will recall that Robeson used precisely the language of Wright in comparing African dance to black dance in America, Wright saying that the former was an "exact duplicate" of the latter, Robeson that the dances were "identical." Their findings are particularly deserving of notice in light of Alan Lomax's remark that "dance is the very heart of African creativity" (*The Land Where the Blues Began*, 365).

55. Ibid., 58.

56. The writer visited the United House of Prayer for All People, Washington D.C., on a number of occasions in 1984, finding a large area, in front of the pulpit, for dance and possession. It was not until years later, on rereading *Black Power*, that I came to realize that what I had witnessed was sacred dance.

57. Wright, *Black Power*, 66.

58. Nina Siegal, "Awash in Baptismal Waters on an East Harlem Street," *New York Times*, August 7, 2000, A18.

59. Richard Wright, "Foreword," in Paul Oliver, *The Meaning of the Blues* (1960; reprint, New York, 1966), 8.

60. Ibid., 7.

61. Ibid., 8.

62. Ibid., 9–10. For a discussion of the blues and Frederick Douglass and James Baldwin, see Sterling Stuckey, "'Ironic Tenacity': Frederick Douglass's Seizure of the Dialectic," in Eric J. Sundquist, *Frederick Douglass: New Literary and Historical Essays* (New York, 1990), 32–33.

63. Wright, "Foreword," in Oliver, 8.

64. Ibid., 8–9.

65. Marshall W. Stearns's observations support this argument. He states that "The continued existence of the ring-shout is of critical importance to jazz, because it means that an assortment of West African musical characteristics are preserved, more or less intact, in the United States—from rhythms and blue tonality, through the falsetto break and the call-and-response pattern, to the songs of allusion and even the motions of the African dance. And an entire way of life has survived with it. Many jazzmen, even among the ultramoderns, are familiar with all or part of it because they lived with or near one of the Sanctified Churches during childhood. . . . The ring-shout is a reservoir of West African qualities that are continually giving new life to jazz" (*The Story of Jazz* [1956; reprint, New York, 1982], 13–14).

Notes to "COMMENTARY"
by Roger Abrahams

1. William Francis Allen, Charles Pickard Ware and Lucy McKim Garrison, *Slave Songs of the the United States* (New York, 1867).

2. Thomas Wentworth Higginson, "Negro Spirituals," *Atlantic Monthly*, June 1867: 684–97.

3. *The Complete Civil War Journal and Selected Letters of Thomas Wentworth Higginson*, ed. and with an introduction by Christopher Looby (Chicago, 2000), 58.

4. Ibid., 59.

5. Cf. my *Singing the Master* (New York, 1992).

6. Gustavus D. Pike, *The Jubilee Singers and Their Campaign for Twenty Thousand Dollars* (Boston, 1873). See also, J. B. T. Marsh, *The Story of the Jubilee Singers* (Cleveland, 1892); Louis D. Silveri, "The Singing tours of the Fisk Jubilee Singer: 1871–1874," in *Feel the Spirit: Studies in Nineteenth-Century Afro-American Music*, ed. George R. Keck and Serrill V. Marten (Westwood, Conn., 1988).

7. Donald J. Waters, ed., *Strange Ways and Sweet Dreams: Afro-American Folklore from the Hampton Institute* (Boston, 1983). Waters includes these speeches and all of the papers presented at these meetings and printed in *The Southern Workman and Hampton School Record*.

Contributors

ROGER D. ABRAHAMS
University of Pennsylvania
Author of *Singing the Master: The Emergence of African American Culture in the Plantation South*

WILLIAM DUSINBERRE
University of Warwick
Author of *Them Dark Days: Slavery in the American Rice Swamps*

LAURA F. EDWARDS
Duke University
Author of *Scarlett Doesn't Live Here Anymore: Southern Women in the Civil War Era*

ANNETTE GORDON-REED
New York Law School
Author of *Thomas Jefferson and Sally Hemings: An American Controversy*

ARIELA GROSS
University of Southern California Law School
Author of *Double Character: Slavery and Mastery in the Antebellum Courtroom*

WALTER JOHNSON
New York University
Author of *Soul by Soul: Life inside the Antebellum Slave Market*

NORRECE T. JONES, JR.
Virginia Commonwealth University
Author of *Born a Child of Freedom, Yet a Slave: Mechanisms of Control and Strategies of Resistance in Antebellum South Carolina*

Jan Lewis
Rutgers University, Newark
Author of *The Pursuit of Happiness: Family and Values in Jefferson's Virginia*

James Oakes
CUNY Graduate Center
Author of *Slavery and Freedom: An Interpretation of the Old South*

Robert Olwell
University of Texas at Austin
Author of *Masters, Slaves, and Subjects: The Culture of Power in the South Carolina Low Country, 1740–1790*

Peter S. Onuf
University of Virginia
Author of *Jefferson's Empire: The Language of American Nationhood*

Sterling Stuckey
University of California, Riverside
Author of *Slave Culture: Nationalist Theory and the Foundations of Black America*

Index

Abolitionists, x, xvii, 36, 43, 44, 67, 74, 99, 100, 103, 115, 137, 172, 173, 183 n, 187 n
Accra, 163
Adams County, Miss., 63, 80
Africa and Africans, x, xi, 25, 35, 41, 42, 45, 46, 49, 62, 71, 72, 94, 95, 98, 107, 109, 118, 126, 130, 131, 132, 134, 143, 150, 153, 154, 156, 157, 158, 159, 160, 162, 163, 164, 165, 166, 167, 169, 170, 171, 174, 202 n, 207 n, 208 n, 209 n, 210 n, 211 n. *See also specific locales and ethnic groups*
African Methodist Episcopal church, 132
Agency: of slaves, 5–66, 85–87, 89, 136, 138–39, 141, 186 n; of white women, 81
Akan, 163, 164
Alabama, 107, 148
Alfred (slave), 100
Allen, Richard, 158
Allen, William, 172, 173
American Folklore Society, 174
American Historical Association, xi
American Revolution, xi, 3, 4, 21, 24, 25, 30, 34, 35, 69, 113, 116, 118, 120, 124, 125, 133, 136–37, 138, 195 n
Anderson, Marian, 154
Angelou, Maya, 169
Anglicans, 126, 202 n
Angola, 210 n
Animals. *See individual species*
Annales, 134
Anthropology, 134, 159, 208 n

Antislavery, 6, 13, 14, 15, 16, 49, 76, 113, 181 n. *See also* Abolitionists; Colonization; Emancipation; Manumission
Aptheker, Herbert, xiii–xiv, xv
Arator (Taylor), 35
Asante, 164
Association for the Study of Negro Life and History, xii
Atkins, John, 73
Autonomy. *See* Agency

Bacon's Rebellion, 71
Bahamas, 207 n
Baker, Josephine, 172
Baldwin, James, 167, 169, 176
Ball, Charles, 64
Ball, Edward, 121
"Ballad for Americans," 171
Bancroft, George, xi
Baptism, 72
Baptists, 202 n
Bardaglio, Peter, 68
Basie, Count, 154, 161
Bass, Nathaniel, 73
Bechet, Sidney, 172
Benin, Bight of, 210 n
Bercaw, Nancy, 68
Berkeley (Univ. of Calif.), 177 n
Berlin, Ira, 123–24, 139, 145, 167
Berry, Henry, 38, 39
Betty (slave), 107
Bible, 126, 152, 158, 169, 202 n
Bishop, G. W., 153
Black Majority (P. Wood), 127, 128, 129, 130, 131

215

Blackface, 169, 170, 171, 174
Blacks, free, 34. *See also* Fugitive slaves
Bland, Bobby "Blue," 175
Block, Sharon, 69–70
Blues. *See* Songs
Bolling, Philip, 37
Boris Godunov (Mussorgsky), 206 n
Braudel, Fernand, 134
Brent, Linda, 69, 94
British. *See* American Revolution; England; English
Brown decision (1954), xvi
Brown, Kathleen, 62, 71–73, 74
Brown, Sterling, 176
Brown, Rev. T. T., 97
Buenos Aires, 167
Burgesses, House of (Va.), 12
Burning alive, xvii, 141
Burns, Robert, 153
Bussey, John, 187 n
Butler, Judith, 66
Butler, Pierce, 107
Bynum, Victoria, 68

Callaway County, Mo., 101
Calvin, John, 148
Cambridge, Mass., 127
Camp, Walter, 150
Cannibals All! (Fitzhugh), 102, 112
Capitalism, 75–77, 81, 89, 91, 92, 128, 148, 182–83 n, 184 n, 190 n
Caribbean. *See* West Indies
Carnegie Corporation, xv
Carpenters, 144
Carter, "Ol' Man" (slaveowner), 108
Cartwright, Samuel, 45, 50
Cavanaugh, Inez, 172
Celia (slave), 101
Chain of Being, 74
Chambers, L. G., 63

Chapin (overseer of Northrup), 63–64
Chaplin, Joyce, 131
Charles (slave), 65–66
Charleston, S.C., xiv, 117, 119, 120, 125, 132, 137, 142, 144
Charlotte (slave), 100
Charlottesville, Va., 17, 20
Chesapeake (region), 71, 122, 140
Chestnutt, Charles Waddell, 204 n
Chicago School of Sociology, 160
Chickens, 60, 142
Chicora Wood plantation, 135
Child mortality, 140, 144
Children, 7, 8, 9, 31, 62, 64, 68, 71, 96, 97, 99, 101, 102, 104, 106, 107, 108, 111, 183 n, 195 n. *See also* Hemings children
Chinese, 207 n
Christianity, 126, 132, 143, 158, 166, 170, 202 n, 210 n
Christie, David, 43–44
Churches, 7, 8, 9, 50, 71, 149, 151, 155, 158, 163, 166, 169, 173, 211 n. *See also* Baptists
Civil rights, ix, xv, 78, 168
Civil War (U.S.), 5, 7, 8, 9, 26, 50, 61, 71, 76, 80, 107, 118, 120, 125, 126, 134, 136, 137, 138, 168, 172, 176
Climate. *See* Political economy
Clothing, slave, 104, 133, 142
Colleges, Negro, 205 n. *See also* Universities; *individual institutions*
Colonization, of blacks, 6, 25, 26, 35, 36, 37, 40. *See also* Manumission
Columbia, S.C., 117
Columbia University, 150
Community: slave, xvii, xviii, xix, 61, 130, 133–34, 186 n; studies, 128
Concert Parties, 170
Congo: region, 210 n; river, 207 n

Index

Congress of Negro Writers, 162
Constitution (U.S.), 35
Cooks, 144
Cooper, Anna J., 174
Cooper River, 117
Copenhagen, 167
Corn, 33
Cotton, 39, 43, 44, 120, 125; sea island, 199 n
Cotton Is King, 43–44
Council on African Affairs, 157
Courts. *See* Law(yers)
Cover, Robert, 58
Cows, 142
Craft, Ellen, 105
Craft, William, 104–05
Crafts, 142, 144
Creel, Margaret Washington, 126, 132, 143
Crummell, Alexander, 174

Dalby, David, 156, 206 n
Dance, 157, 160, 163, 165, 166, 167, 168, 169, 170, 175, 176, 207 n, 209 n, 210 n
Davis, Jefferson, xvi
Davis, Rachel, 69
Debates. *See* Virginia slavery debates
Debow's Review, 53
Declaration of Independence, 5, 15, 16
Degler-Handlin debate, 70–71
Delegates, House of (Va.), 12, 13. *See also* Virginia slavery debates
Descent, law of slave, 95, 96
Dew, Thomas Roderick, 40, 45, 49, 52, 183 n
Diop, Alioune, 162
DNA, 115
Doctors. *See* Physicians
Domestic servants, 144–45
Douglass, Frederick, xii, 158, 167

Dred Scott case, 59
Drivers, 107, 142–43, 144, 145, 202 n
Duberman, Martin, 154
DuBois, W. E. B., xi, 150, 169, 205 n, 210 n
Dueling, xiii
Dunbar, Paul Laurence, 204 n
Dusinberre, William, 107, 135

Economy: development and study of, 34, 47, 49–55, 60, 76, 126, 128, 131, 134, 137, 142, 181 n; slave, 29–36. *See also* Political Economy
Education, public, 27, 148, 173. *See also* Universities
Edwards, Laura F., 62, 68, 69
Elkins, Stanley, xvii–xviii
Ellington, Duke, 154
Ellison, Ralph, 151, 154–55, 159, 160, 163, 169, 176, 204 n, 209 n
Emancipation, 14, 15, 17, 19, 25, 34, 53, 94, 111, 121, 125, 126, 136, 176, 183 n. *See also* Manumission
Engerman, Stanley, 127
England, 15, 17, 31, 32, 44, 73, 101, 139, 157, 162. *See also* Great Britain
English, 93, 94, 109, 115. *See also* American Revolution
Enlightenment, 3, 30, 181 n
Equiano, Olaudah, 98–99
Europe, 33, 41, 46, 154, 170, 172, 173, 176, 184 n
Europeans, 93, 94, 109, 115, 153, 154
Evangelicals, 34, 126, 143
Evanston, Ill., 156
Everett, Louisa, 105–06
Everett, Sam, 105–06
Executions, 97, 102, 138. *See also* Burning alive
Ex-slaves. *See* Former slaves

Family, 71, 79, 108, 112, 114, 116, 129, 130, 133, 142, 144, 147, 186 n, 187–88 n, 191 n, 196 n. *See also* Households
Faulkner, Charles, 38, 182 n
Faulkner, William, 117
Federal Writers' Project, 105. *See also* WPA
Federalism, 26–27
Federalists (party), 3, 26
Feminists, 68
Fishing, 142
Fisk Jubilee Singers, 173, 205 n
Fiske, John, xi
Fitzhugh, George, 52, 102, 112, 113
Flag, Confederate, 117
Florida, 105; east, 98
Fogel, Robert, 127
Folklore, 57, 141, 143, 154, 155, 160, 174, 176, 186 n, 208 n, 209 n
Football, 150, 203–04 n
Ford, William, 63
Former slaves, 63, 151, 175
Fornication, 72
Fort Sumter, 125, 172
Fox-Genovese, Elizabeth, 68
France, 4, 101, 162, 175
Frank (slave), 107
Franklin, Benjamin, xix, 30–33, 45, 46, 52, 183 n
Franklin, John Hope, xiii
Frazier, E. Franklin, 163
Fredrickson, George, 74
Free blacks, 96, 97. *See also* Emancipation; Manumission
Freedman's Bureau, 137
Frey, Sylvia, 126, 132
Fugitive slaves, 61, 63, 64, 69, 86, 94, 136, 137, 147, 149, 172, 200 n
Fundamental Constitutions of Carolina, 119

Gabriel's Rebellion, 180 n
Gambling, 65, 66
Gang labor system, 125, 142, 181 n
Garland, Samuel, 37
Garnet, Henry Highland, 158
Garrison, Lucy McKim, 172, 173
Gaston, Judge, 58, 59
Geertz, Clifford, 134
Gender, 59, 62, 66, 70, 71–74, 81, 95, 153
Genovese, Eugene, 58, 75, 76, 87, 88, 110, 127
George III, 25, 69, 137, 138
Georgia, xii, xix, 98, 104, 107, 119, 163, 164, 207 n
Georgia Gazette, 98
Germany, 67
Ghana, 164, 165, 166
Gholson, James, 38, 182 n
Gibson, Mel, 118
Glazer, Nathan, 208–09 n
God, 166
Goode, William, 38
Gordon-Reed, Annette, 109
Gorn, Eliot, 106
Gowrie plantation, 135
Grace, Daddy, 165
Graham, John, 98
Gray, Francis C., 18
Great Awakening, 126. *See also* Revivals
Great Britain, 34, 99. *See also* England
Great Depression, xv
Greek, 147
Greeley, Horace, 29
Green, Benny, 204 n
Grossberg, Michael, 68, 84, 85
Guitars, 175
Gullah, 132, 143
Guns, 60

Hall, Thomas(ine), 73–74
Hamman, Mr. & Mrs. (slaveowners), 104

Index

Hammond, James Henry, 44, 45, 47, 52, 183 n
Hampton Folklore Society, 174
Hampton Institute, 173
Hampton Park (Charleston, S.C.), 117
Harper, William, 43, 44, 45–47, 50, 53
Hartog, Hendrick, 79
Harvard University, xi, xii, xvi, 208 n
Hausa, 207 n
Hawkins, Mr. & Mrs. (slaveowners), 111, 113
Hayes, Roland, 152, 205 n
Health, slaves, 140, 145, 169, 170, 183 n. *See also* Child mortality
Hegemony, 60–61, 78
Hemings, Beverley, 19, 20
Hemings children, 115
Hemings, Eston, 19, 20
Hemings family, 17–20
Hemings, Harriet, 19, 20
Hemings, John, 20
Hemings, Madison, 16, 17, 19, 20
Hemings, Sally, xviii, 16–23, 27, 115
Henry, Patrick, 24, 113
Herskovits, 169, 208 n
Higginson, Thomas Wentworth, 172, 173, 174
Hiring, of slaves, 60
History, practice of, xi, xiv, xvi, xvii, 83, 85, 99, 100, 109, 112, 115, 121, 128, 134–35, 151, 167, 208 n, 209 n
Hodes, Martha, 115
Holidays, for slaves, 60
Homosexual, 105, 195 n
Horses, 142
Horsman, Reginald, 74
House servants, 203 n
Household, 68–69, 70, 97
Housing, 160
Howell, Samuel, 5, 6, 7, 8, 9, 10, 17, 21, 23, 27

Howell v. Netherland, 7, 10, 14, 15, 23
Hunting, 142
Hurt, Mississippi John, 175

"I Got a Home in Dat Rock," 152
Immigrants, from Europe, 60, 67, 154
Incest, 103
Incidents in the Life of a Slave Girl (Jacobs), 94
Indian Ocean, x
Indians. *See* Native Americans
Indigo, 125
Irish, 154
Israelites, 126

Jackson, Eslanda, 206 n
Jackson, Mahalia, 154, 155, 206 n
Jacobs, Harriet, 69, 94–95, 103, 106
Jamaica, 140, 142, 200 n
Jamestown, Va., 119
Jazz. *See* Music
Jefferson, Thomas, xviii, 3–27, 35, 43, 52, 115, 179 n, 180 n
Jesus, 202 n
Jews, 153, 171
Joe Louis Blues (Company), 161
Johnson, James Weldon, 151, 204 n
Johnson (owner of Charles), 66
Johnson, Walter, 64, 66, 71, 76–77, 78, 91, 108, 109, 112, 114, 115
Johnson v. Wideman, 65–66
Johnston, James Hugo, 93, 94
Jones, Norrece T., 141
Jordan, Winthrop D., 71, 103
Journal of Negro History, xii, xiii
Joyce, James, 176
Joyner, Charles, 132–33, 134, 135, 141, 143

Kansas-Nebraska Act, 48
Karras, Ruth Mazo, 100

Katz, Stanley, 58
Kemble, Frances, 107, 173
King, B. B., 175
"King Joe" (song), 161
King, Lee, 187 n
King, Rodney, 59
King, Roswell, Jr., 107
King, Roswell, Sr., 107
King, Wilma, 98, 101

Latin, 147
Law(yers), xviii, 3–27, 57–92, 96, 137, 142, 147, 150, 186 n. *See also* Natural law
Lee, Arthur, 33–34
Legislation. *See* Statutes
Lincoln, Abraham, xii, 48
Lipscomb, Mance, 175
Liquor, 60, 65, 66, 108, 187 n
Literacy, 80, 147
Littlefield, Daniel, 132
Lloyd, Marie, 153
Locke, John, 119
Lomax, Alan, 210 n
London, 153, 156, 162, 167
London School of Oriental Languages, 150, 156
Louisiana, 61, 107, 200 n
Lowcountry, xix, 117–46, 172, 199 n, 201 n, 202 n
Lucas, James, 63
Lydia (slave), 58
Lynching (post–Civil War), 69

Mack, Richard, 63
Madison, James, 13, 36
Malone, Dumas, 7
Malthus, 40, 45, 182 n
Mammy (slave mother), 108
Manigault estate, 135
Mann, John, 58

Manumission, 13, 34, 62, 145. *See also* Emancipation
Marshall, Alfred, 47
Marshall, Thomas, 37
Marx, Karl, 47, 184 n
Mary (slave), 62
Maryland, 95–96
Massachusetts, 38, 128
Masters, Subjects, and Slaves (Orwell), 136
McAllum, Mr. (slaveowner), 187–88 n
McClain, "Big Jim," 106
McCurry, Stephanie, 68
M'Dowell, James, 39
Meat, 145
Memoir on Slavery (Harper), 43
Memory, historical, 118, 133
Memphis, Tenn., 161
Methodists, 126, 170, 194 n, 202 n
Michigan, University of, xii
Middle class, 29, 31, 37, 149, 160
Midwives, 62
Mill, John Stuart, 40
Miller, Diane, 115
Miller, Sally, 67
Ministers (religious). *See* Preachers
Mintz, Sidney, 134, 137, 159, 208 n
Miscegenation, 8–11, 15–27, 67, 72–75, 93–110, 112, 114, 115, 192 n, 193 n. *See also* Rape
Missionaries, 126, 158, 170
Mississippi, ix, xv, xvi, 100, 147, 161, 162
Mississippi, University of, ix, x
Mississippi Valley State College, ix
Montgomery, Ala., 155
Monticello, 3, 18, 19
Moore, Samuel, 37
Morgan, Philip, 122–24, 131, 132–33, 134, 136, 139, 141, 142, 145
Morison, Samuel Eliot, xii-xiii, xvi-xvii

Index

Morris, Thomas, 76
Morris, William, 139
Morrison, Alexina, 66, 75
Morrison, Tony, 169
Moton, M. M., 174
Moynihan, Daniel, 208 n
Mulattoes, 96, 97, 100, 101, 104
Mules, 142
Murder, 4, 100, 101, 103
Murray, Albert, 169, 176
Music, 149, 150, 154, 155, 161, 167, 168, 169, 170, 171, 172, 173–74, 175, 176, 206 n, 207–08 n, 209 n, 211 n
Myrdal, Gunnar, xv

NAACP, 162
Narrative history, 90, 91, 92
Native Americans, 42, 62, 75, 98, 109, 130
Natural law, 7–8, 10
Natural rights, 24, 25
Negro History Week, xii
Neruda, Pablo, 204 n
New England towns, 127, 128, 129
New Jersey, 149
New Orleans, La., 103, 155
New York, 97
New York Times, xiv, xv, 150, 153
New York World, 150
Newell, William Wells, 174
Newsome, Robert, 101
Newspapers, 53, 57, 149
Nigeria, 98, 207 n
Norcom, Dr. James, 95
Norfolk, Va., 106
North Carolina, 58, 69, 94, 147
North (U.S.), 30, 34, 38, 39, 45, 46, 49, 51, 52, 61, 76, 92, 114, 137, 148, 165, 183 n, 184 n. *See also* New England towns; *individual cities*
Northwest Ordinance(s), 13–14

Northrup, Solomon, 63–64
Notes on the State of Virginia (Jefferson), 13, 25, 26
Nott, Abraham, 66

Oakes, James, 58, 61, 77, 86, 97
Observations . . . Increase of Mankind (Franklin), 30
Oliver, Paul, 166
O'Neill, Eugene, 205 n
Othello, 153, 171
Othello, 206 n
Overseers, 35, 63–64, 98, 100, 107, 108, 141, 142, 145, 193 n
Oxford, Miss., ix

Paris, 162, 166, 167, 211 n
Parks, Rosa, xvi
Parrish, Lydia, 207 n
Paternalism and Patriarchalism, 60, 68, 70, 72, 75–77, 87–88, 89, 95, 97, 100, 102, 104, 109, 112, 113, 115, 145, 194 n
Patrick (slave), 103
Patriot, The (film), 117–18, 137
Patrols, slave, 27
Payne, Daniel, 158
Peggy (slave), 103
Pentacostal churches, 166
Phi Beta Kappa, 150
Phillips, Ulrich Bonnell, xii, xv, xvii
Physicians, 75, 95
Pigs, 142
Planters, 15, 22, 24, 27, 33, 38, 39, 80, 87–88, 97, 101, 106, 107, 136, 140–41, 142, 145, 166, 191 n
Political economy, 29–30, 39, 40, 44–46, 47–48, 49–55, 78, 181 n
Population, 40, 45, 80, 118, 119, 120, 125, 128, 131, 135, 140, 144, 145, 187 n, 200 n, 202–03 n
Powhatan, Va., 107, 108

Preachers, 143, 148, 149, 150, 151, 155, 194 n, 206 n
Price, Richard, 134, 159, 208 n
Prince George County, Va., 34
Princeton, N.J., 147, 148, 149
Princeton University, 147–48
Proslavery, 30, 41–44, 47, 49–55, 74, 112
Provision grounds, 142

Quantitative analysis, 47, 80

Race-mixing. *See* Miscegenation; Hemings family
Racial attitudes and ideology, 21, 26, 42, 45–46, 49–55, 59–60, 62, 70–75, 77, 81–82, 89, 93–94, 103, 116, 128, 129, 148, 164, 166, 183 n; white supremacy, 4, 5, 6, 23, 41–42
Randolph, John, 36–37
Randolph, Pearl, 106
Randolph family. *See* Jefferson, Thomas
Rape, xix, 65, 68, 69, 72, 81, 93–116, 144, 191 n, 192 n, 193 n, 194 n, 195 n
Rawley, James, 210 n
Rebellions, slave. *See* Revolts and conspiracies; *individual revolts and conspiracies*
Reconstruction, xv, 76, 137–38, 143, 205 n
Religion, 126, 129, 143, 151, 152, 157, 158, 160, 163, 165, 166–67, 169, 173, 186 n, 208 n. *See also* Christianity; Churches; Evangelicals; Missionaries; Revivalism; *individual churches*
Republican ideology, 25–26, 35
Republican party, 29, 30, 34, 48
Resistance, by slaves, xiii, 54, 59, 60, 61, 65, 67, 86, 87, 104, 110, 129, 137, 138, 139, 141, 145, 155, 168, 201 n. *See also* Revolts and conspiracies; Running away; *individual plots*

Review of the Debates (Dew), 40–42
Revivalism, 151
Revolts and conspiracies, xiii–xv, 138. *See also individual revolts and conspiracies*
Revolution. *See* American Revolution; French Revolution
Rice, 120, 124, 125, 128, 130, 131, 140, 141, 142, 144, 199 n, 200 n, 201 n, 203 n
Richmond, Va., 108, 183 n
Ripley, Miss., 188 n
Robeson family, 147–50
Robeson, Paul, xx, 147–58, 160, 161, 162, 167, 168, 169, 171, 172, 176, 203–08 n, 210 n
Robeson, Sabra, 148, 149
Robeson, William Drew (Paul's father), 147–48, 149, 151, 155, 157
Rome, 167
Roosevelt University, 207 n
Roper, Moses, 104
Rose (former slave), 111, 112, 113
Rose, Willie Lee, 96, 111, 112
Rothman, Joshua, 17
Ruffin, Edmund, 46
Ruffin, Thomas, 58, 59
Rufus (slave), 111
Running away, 19, 55, 58, 60, 61, 64, 65, 86, 108, 141, 144, 201 n. *See also* Fugitive slaves
Rutgers University, 150, 203 n

Sambo (concept), xiii, xv, xvi–xviii, 114
Sandburg, Carl, 152, 205 n
Sanders of the River (film), 207 n
Sartre, Jean Paul, 162
Savannah, Ga., 142, 144
Savannah River, 135
Saville, Julie, 143
Schwarz, Philip, 15
Scots, 154

Index

Scottsboro Boys, 172
Sea-islands, 125. *See also* Lowcountry
Secession, xiii, 118, 120
Sedgwick, Eve, 67
Senate (U.S.), 44
Serfs, 61
Seward, William, 29, 31, 48
Sexual violence. *See* Rape
Sexuality, 59
Shaftesbury, Lord, 119
Shakespeare, William, 153
Sharecroppers, 148, 149
Shell, John, 38
Shendandoah Valley, 29
Sherman, William T., 137
Shore, Lawrence, 52, 181 n
Short, William, 4
Silk Hope plantation, 135
Simpson, O. J., 59
Slave economy. *See* Economy, slave
Slave trade: Atlantic, x, 13, 33–34, 98, 99, 107–08, 120, 125, 130, 164, 171, 200 n, 210 n; domestic, 51, 64, 65, 66–67, 71, 77, 98, 101, 104, 107–08, 114, 144, 187–88 n; Indian, 130, 198 n; Roman, 168
Smith, Adam, xix, 31–33, 36, 38, 43, 45, 46, 49, 50, 52, 54
Smith, Bessie, 175
Smith, Mamie, 175
Songs (slave), 57, 60, 149, 150, 151, 152–53, 154, 155, 156, 157, 160, 164, 166, 167–68, 169, 170, 171, 172–76, 186 n, 204 n, 205 n, 206 n
South Africa, 157
South Carolina, xix, 44, 65, 66, 68, 104, 117–46, 172, 201 n. *See also* Charleston, S.C.
Southampton County, Va., 36
Southern Agriculturalist, 53
Spanish people, 154

Species, 9, 24
Spirituals. *See* Songs
St. Domingo, 180 n
Stampp, Kenneth M., xvi, 58
Stanley, Amy Dru, 76
Stanton, Lucia, 18–19
State v. Mann, 58–59
State v. Will, 58
Statutes, 63, 68, 71, 72, 86, 89, 95, 100. *See also* Law(yers)
Stearns, Jean, 207 n
Stearns, Marshall, 207 n
Stephenson, Mr. (slaveowner), 187 n
Stockholm, 167
Stono Rebellion, 123, 124, 128, 129, 131, 132
Strayhorn, Billy, 172
Sugar, 32–33, 50, 140, 142, 200 n
Suggs, Jon-Christian, 63
Summary View (Jefferson), 13
Swahili, 156
Sweetinham (colonial Fla. man), 98
Sydnor, Charles, 58

Tar, 130
Task system, 125, 141–43, 145, 199 n
Taylor, John, 35–36, 43
Tea Meetings, 170
Territories (U.S.), 14, 94
Testimony, slave, 94–95, 99, 105, 110, 112
Textbooks, history, xii, xiii, xvi-xvii
Theory of Moral Sentiments (Smith), 31, 33
Thomas Jefferson and Sally Hemings (Gordon-Reed), 21
Thornton, John, 132
Thorpe, Rosetta, 154
Tibeats (owner of Northrup), 63
Tobacco, 32–33, 39, 50, 71
Tories, 26
Towns, 183 n; in South Carolina, 146. *See also* New England towns

Trombones, 165
Truillot, Michel-Rolphe, 55
Trunkminders, 144, 203 n
Tucker, St. George, 14
Turner, Lorenzo, 207 n
Turner, Nat, revolt, xiv–xv, 36, 54, 103
Turpentine, 130, 198 n
Tushnet, Mark, 76
Tuskegee Institute, 173
Twi, 156, 164

United House of Prayer for All People, 165, 166, 210 n
Universities, ix–xi, 162, 209 n. *See also individual colleges and universities*

Vesey Plot, xiv, 125, 132
Vietnam War, 58
Virginia slavery debates, xix, 36–40, 43, 47–48, 54
Virginia, ix, xiv, 3, 11–20, 24, 25, 33, 34, 35, 37, 38, 62, 71–74, 98, 102, 103, 119, 166, 183 n, 201 n. *See also* Jefferson, Thomas

Waccamaw Neck, S.C., 133
Waldrep, Christopher, 80
Walker, Clarence, 145
Walker, David, 158
Wall Street, 148
War, 26, 109; slavery as a state of, 95, 98, 101. *See also individual wars*
Ware, Charles Pickard, 172, 173
Warraskoyack, Va., 73
Warren County, 80
Washington, D.C., 165, 210 n
Wealth of Nations (Smith), 31–32
Weld, Theodore Dwight, xvii
West Indies, 33, 53, 99, 130, 141, 170, 208 n

West (U.S.), 14, 38, 39
Western Reserve University, xiii
Whipping, xvi, xvii, 104, 105, 106, 108, 111, 112, 113
White, Bukka, 175
White, Deborah, 114
White, George L., 205 n
Whiteness. *See* Miscegenation
Wilkins, Roy, 162
William and Mary, College of, 40
William & Mary Quarterly, xiv
William (slave), 108
Williams, George Washington, x, xi
Williamson, Joel, 100–01
Windward Coast, 210 n
Wish, Harvey, xiii, xv
Witherspoon Street (Princeton), 149
Wolfe, Hans, 156
Women: African, 163; black, 7, 58, 144, 145; white, 6, 9, 15, 60, 61, 62, 64, 68, 69–70, 71–74, 79, 81, 86, 95, 97, 102, 104, 110, 115, 187 n. *See also* Rape
Women's history, 57, 60, 70
Wood, Betty, 126, 132
Wood, Peter, 123, 124, 127, 128, 129, 130, 131, 132
Woodson, Carter G., xi, xii, xiii
World War II, xv
WPA interviews, 63, 111. *See also* Testimony, slave
Wright, Frances, 36
Wright, Richard, xx, 147, 158–68, 169, 172, 176, 208 n, 209 n, 210 n
Wyatt-Brown, Bertram, 101, 110
Wythe, George, 7, 14, 179 n

Yale University, 177 n
Yamasee war, 124, 130
Yergan, Max, 157
Yoruba, 156

www.ingramcontent.com/pod-product-compliance
Lightning Source LLC
Chambersburg PA
CBHW022057160426
43198CB00008B/256